D1406820

Voices of Change

Sixth Custom Edition for Orange Coast College

Taken from:
A Concise Public Speaking Handbook, Fifth Edition
by Steven A. Beebe and Susan J. Beebe

Contributors:
Kat Carroll, Felicia Coco, Norm Fricker and Georgie Monahan

Special thanks for all the great example outlines:
Ian Cone, Jodi Della Marna, Norm Fricker, John Kelley

Pearson Education, Inc., 330 Hudson Street, New York, New York 10013
A Pearson Education Company
www.pearsoned.com

Printed in the United States of America

7   18

000200010272095013

NH

ISBN 10: 1-323-62659-X
ISBN 13: 978-1-323-62659-7

Contents

Preface

This fifth edition of *A Concise Public Speaking Handbook* integrates the steps in preparing and delivering a speech with the ongoing process of considering the audience. Although developed and delivered by the speaker, a good speech is centered on the needs, values, and hopes of the audience. Therefore, the audience should be kept in mind during every step of the speech crafting and delivery process. Being "audience-centered" means that, as a speaker, you are constantly aware of and striving to adapt to the cultural, gender, and experiential diversity of the people to whom you are speaking. Adapting to diverse audiences is incorporated into every step of the audience-centered approach.

A Concise Public Speaking Handbook, Fifth Edition, also emphasizes that an effective speaker is an ethical speaker. Ethical speakers articulate truthful messages, formulated so as to give the audience free choice in responding to the message, while also using effective means of ensuring message clarity and credibility. In addition to emphasizing ethics throughout the book and in Chapter 4, "Ethics and Free Speech," we provide an Ethics Assessment question at the end of each chapter to spark thought and discussion on ethical issues in public speaking.

Revel™

Educational technology designed for the way today's students read, think, and learn

When students are engaged deeply, they learn more effectively and perform better in their courses. This simple fact inspired the creation of Revel: an immersive learning experience designed for the way today's students read, think, and learn. Built in collaboration with educators and students nationwide, Revel is the newest, fully digital way to deliver respected Pearson content.

Revel enlivens course content with media interactives and assessments—integrated directly within the authors' narrative—that provide opportunities for students to read about and practice course material in tandem. This immersive educational technology boosts student engagement, which leads to better understanding of concepts and improved performance throughout the course.

Learn more about Revel

http://www.pearsonhighered.com/revel/

SPECIAL FEATURES FOR PUBLIC SPEAKING STUDENTS Revel is a dynamic learning experience that offers students a way to study the content and topics relevant to communication in a whole new way. Rather than simply offering opportunities to read about and study public speaking, Revel facilitates deep, engaging interactions with the concepts that matter most. For example, in Chapter 3, students are presented with the authors' hallmark audience-centered model as an interactive figure diagramming the various tasks involved in the speechmaking process. In addition, students are presented with video examples throughout the book on topics such as improving listening skills, audience analysis, primary sources, speech delivery, using presentation aids, and the fear of public speaking. As part of our commitment to boosting students' communication confidence, our first discussion of improving your confidence in Chapter 2 features the Personal Report of Public Speaking Anxiety in Revel. Students can take this assessment in the context of our chapter, get their score, and continue reading about how to improve their own level of confidence. By providing opportunities to read about and practice public speaking in tandem, Revel engages students directly and immediately, which leads to a better understanding of course material. A wealth of student and instructor resources and interactive materials can be found within Revel. Some of our favorites include the following:

- **Videos and Video Self-Checks**
  Video clips appear throughout the narrative to boost mastery, and many videos have correlating self-checks, enabling students to test their knowledge.
- **Interactive Figures**
  Interactive figures help students understand hard-to-grasp concepts through visualizations.
- **Audio Excerpts**
  Throughout the text, audio excerpts highlight effective speech examples. Students can listen to audio clips while they read, bringing examples to life in a way that a printed text cannot. These audio examples reinforce learning and add dimension to the printed text.
- **Integrated Writing Opportunities**
  To help students connect chapter content with personal meaning, each chapter offers two varieties of writing exercises: the Journal prompt, which elicits free-form, topic-specific responses addressing content at the module level, and the Shared Writing prompt, which encourages students to share and respond to each other's brief responses to high-interest topics in the chapter.

For more information about all the tools and resources in Revel and access to your own Revel account for *A Concise Public Speaking Handbook*, Fifth Edition, go to www.pearsonhighered.com/revel.

New to the Fifth Edition

- New and **expanded examples** throughout the text ensure that the examples are contemporary and useful for students.
- To increase visual interest, the fifth edition is now in full-color.
- Updated **How To** boxes provide clear instructions for applying textbook concepts to real-life public speaking.
- Chapter 3 provides an overview of the audience-centered speaking process, jump-starting the speechmaking process for students who are assigned to present speeches early in the term. A new example on developing your central idea has been added to this chapter. The section on gathering supporting material has also been updated.
- We have included new research on the consequences of plagiarism in Chapter 4.
- Chapter 5 has been streamlined by removing topics already covered in other chapters. The section on becoming an active listener has also been revised.

- The discussion of culture, ethnicity, and race in Chapter 6 has been updated based on new research.

- An updated section on evaluating Internet resources in Chapter 9 includes a new discussion of *Wikipedia*, guiding students to think critically about information they find on the Internet. The section on interviewing has also been streamlined and revised.

- The revised discussion of primacy, recency, and complexity in Chapter 11 helps students understand how to organize their main points based on one of these three principles.

- Chapter 12, which covers outlining and revising your speech, has been moved before the chapters on developing an introduction and conclusion.

- A new example on reemphasizing the central idea in a memorable way has been added to Chapter 14.

- Chapter 17 offers new tips for using gestures effectively and monitoring your facial expressions.

- In Chapter 19, selected content on adapting your delivery to a diverse audience has been distributed throughout the chapter where appropriate. This content was previously presented in a separate section.

- Chapters 20 and 21 now have a greater focus on computer-generated presentation aids.

- The final section in Chapter 22, Developing an Audience-Centered Informative Speech, has been revised.

- Additional content has been added about changing or reinforcing audience values in Chapter 23.

- In Chapter 24, the section on establishing your credibility has been revised. New research has also been added throughout the chapter.

Every chapter contains a number of effective, pedagogical features, including:

- **Learning Objectives** at the beginning of every chapter provide a preview of chapter content and help students focus their study. Objectives are also repeated at the start of every section.

- **Quick Checks** list items that can be checked off as each step in the process of preparing a speech is completed.

- **How To** boxes provide clear instructions for applying textbook concepts to real-life public speaking.

- **Study Guides** at the end of each chapter summarize chapter content that reinforces the learning objectives listed at the beginning of the chapter. Each end-of-chapter Study Guide also includes (1) Self-Assessment questions to help readers evaluate how prepared they are to apply the chapter material in their own speeches; (2) Ethics Assessment questions to encourage consideration of ethical issues; and (3) Critical Assessment questions that provide a variety of speechmaking scenarios to help students think critically and further apply chapter concepts.

Strategies to Improve Speaker Confidence

To help students manage the anxiety they may experience when they think about speaking to an audience, an entire chapter (Chapter 2) is devoted to improving speaker confidence. Techniques for managing speaker apprehension, such as how to look for positive listener support when delivering a message, are also included throughout the book.

Critical Listening Skills

Besides learning how to speak in public, one of the most valued benefits of studying public speaking is becoming a more discriminating listener. A section on listening, critical thinking, and analyzing and evaluating speeches helps students better understand their roles as speakers and listeners, and Critical Assessment questions at the ends of chapters offer further critical thinking, listening, and analysis opportunities.

MediaShare
A one-stop media-sharing tool that facilitates interactive learning

MediaShare is a learning application for sharing, discussing, and assessing multimedia. Instructors easily can assign instructional videos to students, create quiz questions, and ask students to comment and reflect on the videos to facilitate collaborative discussion. MediaShare also allows students to record or upload their own videos and other multimedia projects, which they can submit to an instructor and peers for both evaluation via rubrics and review via comments at time-stamped intervals. Additionally, MediaShare allows students working in a group to submit a single artifact for evaluation on behalf of the group.

MediaShare offers a robust library of pre-created assignments, all of which can be customized, to give instructors flexibility.

 Pearson

- Assess students using customizable, Pearson-provided rubrics or create your own around classroom goals, learning outcomes, or department initiatives.
- Grade in real time during in-class presentations or review recordings and assess later.
- Set up learning objectives tied to specific assignments, rubrics, or quiz questions to track student progress.
- Sync slides to media submissions for more robust presentation options.
- Set up assignments for students with options for full-class viewing and commenting, private comments between you and the student, peer groups for reviewing, or as collaborative group assignments.
- Use MediaShare to assign or view speeches, outlines, presentation aids, video-based assignments, role plays, group projects, and more in a variety of formats including video, Word, PowerPoint, and Excel.

Record video directly from a tablet, phone, or other webcam (including a batch upload option for instructors) and tag submissions to a specific student or assignment.

Time-stamped comments provide contextualized feedback that is easy to consume and learn from.

- Embed video from YouTube via assignments to incorporate current events into the classroom experience.
- Ensure a secure learning environment for instructors and students through robust privacy settings.
- Upload videos, comment on submissions, and grade directly from our MediaShare app, available free from the iTunes store and GooglePlay. To download, search for "Pearson MediaShare."

Create quiz questions for video assignments to ensure students master concepts and interact and engage with the media.

Instructor and Student Resources

Key instructor resources include an Instructor's Manual (ISBN 0-13-440179-4), Test Bank (ISBN 0-13-440182-4), and PowerPoint™ Presentation Package (ISBN 0-13-440180-8) available at www.pearsonhighered.com (instructor login required). MyTest online test-generating software (ISBN 0-13-440184-0) is available at www.pearsonmytest.com (instructor login required). For a complete list of the instructor and student resources available with the text, please visit the Pearson Communication catalog, at www.pearsonhighered.com/communication.

Acknowledgments

Thanks to Ellen Keohane, our skilled development editor, for spearheading this revision and working so closely with us. We are extremely grateful to all of the instructors who provided us with invaluable feedback that helped shape the features and content within this new edition. We'd like to extend our sincere appreciation to the following instructors who shared their expertise and insight: Kristin M. Barton, Dalton State College; Hope E. Bennin, Big Sandy Community and Technical College; Jennifer Fairchild, Eastern Kentucky University; Diane Ferrero-Paluzzi, Iona College; Amanda Houdashell, Mesa Community College; and Mark May, Clayton State University.

STEVEN A. BEEBE
SUSAN J. BEEBE

PART 1
Introduction
SPEAKING IN PUBLIC

OBJECTIVES

1.1 Explain why it is important to study public speaking.

1.2 Discuss in brief the history of public speaking.

1.3 Sketch and explain a model that illustrates the components and the process of communication.

WHY STUDY PUBLIC SPEAKING?

1.1 Explain why it is important to study public speaking.

As you study **public speaking**, you will learn and practice strategies for effective delivery and critical listening. You will discover new applications for skills you may already have, such as focusing and organizing ideas and gathering information from print and electronic sources. In addition to learning and applying these fundamental skills, you will gain long-term advantages related to *empowerment* and *employment*.

The ability to speak with competence and confidence will provide **empowerment**. It will give you an edge that less-skilled communicators lack—even those who may have superior ideas, training, or experience.

Perhaps an even more compelling reason to study public speaking is that the skills you develop may someday help you get a job. In a nationwide survey, prospective employers of college graduates said they seek candidates with "public speaking and presentation ability."[1] Surveys of personnel managers, both in the United States and internationally, have confirmed that they consider communication skills the top factor in helping college graduates obtain employment.[2]

THE RICH HERITAGE OF PUBLIC SPEAKING

1.2 Discuss in brief the history of public speaking.

When you study public speaking, you are also joining a long history with many traditions, including the following:

- **Fourth to first centuries BCE.** During this golden age of public speaking, the Greek philosopher Aristotle formulated, and Roman orators refined, guidelines for speakers that we still follow today.

- **Nineteenth century.**   Students of public speaking practiced the arts of **declamation**—the delivery of an already famous address—and **elocution**—the expression of emotion through posture, movement, gestures, facial expression, and voice.
- **Twentieth and twenty-first centuries.**   Audio, video, computer, and mobile technologies let speakers reach worldwide audiences and expand the parameters of public speaking, as they draw on age-old public-speaking traditions to address some of the most difficult challenges in history.

THE COMMUNICATION PROCESS

1.3   Sketch and explain a model that illustrates the components and the process of communication.

Even the earliest communication theorists recognized that communication is a process. The models they formulated were linear, suggesting a simple transfer of meaning from sender to receiver. More recently, theorists have created models that better demonstrate the complexity of the communication process.

Communication as Action

- A public speaker is a **source** of information and ideas for an audience.
- The job of the source or speaker is to **encode**, or translate, the ideas and images in his or her mind into a **code**, made up of verbal or nonverbal symbols, that an audience can recognize. The speaker may encode into words (for example, "The fabric should be two inches square") or into gestures (showing the size with his or her hands).
- The **message** in public speaking is the speech itself—both what is said and how it is said.
- If a speaker has trouble finding words to convey his or her ideas or sends contradictory nonverbal symbols, listeners may not be able to **decode** the speaker's verbal and nonverbal symbols back into a message.
- A message is usually transmitted from sender to receiver via two **channels**: *visual* and *auditory*. Audience members see the speaker and decode his or her nonverbal symbols—eye contact (or lack of it), facial expressions, posture, gestures, and dress. If the speaker uses any visual aids, such as PowerPoint™ slides or models, these too are transmitted along the visual channel. The auditory channel opens as the speaker speaks. Then the audience members hear words and such vocal cues as inflection, rate, and voice quality.
- The **receiver** of the message is the individual audience member, whose decoding of the message will depend on his or her own particular blend of past experiences, attitudes, beliefs, and values. An effective public speaker should be receiver- or audience-centered.
- Anything that interferes with the communication of a message is called *noise*. A noisy air conditioner or incessant coughing is an example of **external noise**. **Internal noise** may stem from either *physiological* or *psychological* causes and may directly affect either the source or the receiver. A bad cold (physiological noise) may cloud a speaker's memory or subdue his or her delivery. An audience member who is worried about an upcoming exam (psychological noise) is unlikely to remember much of what the speaker says. Noise interferes with the transmission of a message.

Communication as Interaction

One way that public speaking differs from casual conversation is that the public speaker does most or all of the talking. But public speaking is still interactive. See Figure 1.1 for an interactive model of communication. Without an audience to hear and provide **feedback**, public speaking serves little purpose.

The **context** of a public-speaking experience is the environment or situation in which the speech occurs. It includes such elements as the time, the place, and both the speaker's and the audience's cultural traditions and expectations. For example, if the room is hot, crowded, or poorly lit, these conditions affect both speaker and audience. A speaker who fought rush-hour traffic for 90 minutes to arrive at his or her destination may find it difficult to muster much enthusiasm for delivering the speech.

Communication as Transaction

The most recent communication models focus on communication as a simultaneous process. For example, in a two-person communication transaction, both individuals are sending and receiving *at the same time*. In public speaking, listeners nonverbally express their thoughts and feelings at the same time the speaker is talking.

Public Speaking and Conversation

Models of communication suggest that public speaking has much in common with conversation. Public speaking also differs from conversation in the following key ways.

PUBLIC SPEAKING REQUIRES MORE PREPARATION   Public speaking is more planned than conversation. A public speaker might spend hours or even days planning and practicing his or her speech.

PUBLIC SPEAKING IS MORE FORMAL   A public speaker's delivery is more formal than the way most people engage in ordinary conversation. The slang or casual language we often use in conversation is usually not appropriate for most public speaking. Audiences expect speakers to use standard English grammar and vocabulary.

Figure 1.1   An interactive model of communication.

PUBLIC SPEAKING INVOLVES MORE CLEARLY DEFINED ROLES FOR SPEAKER AND AUDIENCE   Public speaking is more structured and less interactive than conversation. People in conversation may alternately talk and listen and perhaps even interrupt one another, but in public speaking, the roles of speaker and audience are more clearly defined and remain stable. Rarely do audience members interrupt or talk back to speakers.

Respond to Audience Messages

When you have a conversation, you have to make decisions "on your feet." For example, if your friends look puzzled or interrupt with questions, you may need to explain your idea a second time. You can use the same audience-centered skills to help you become an effective and confident speaker. Pay attention to the nods, facial expressions, and murmurings of the audience. Respond to those messages by adjusting your rate of speaking, volume, vocabulary, or other variables. As a bonus, focusing on the needs of your audience can keep you from focusing on any nervousness you might be feeling.

QUICK CHECK

Become an Effective Public Speaker

- Plan your speech.
- Focus and vocalize your thoughts.
- Adapt your speaking to your listeners.
- Use standard English vocabulary and grammar.
- Use more formal nonverbal communication.

STUDY GUIDE

MEET YOUR OBJECTIVES

1.1   Explain why it is important to study public speaking.

Public speaking can empower you and help you secure employment or advance your career.

1.2   Discuss in brief the history of public speaking.

Speakers today use many technologies to deliver speeches, but rely on guidelines formulated more than 2,000 years ago in ancient Greece and Rome.

1.3   Sketch and explain a model that illustrates the components and the process of communication. Public speaking is an example of the communication process, by which a source transmits a message through a channel to a receiver within a particular context. Senders and receivers simultaneously exchange messages and feedback to build a shared meaning. Public speaking is more formal and planned, with clearly defined roles, than conversation.

THINK ABOUT THESE QUESTIONS

1. **Self Assessment** As you begin a course in public speaking, take stock of your general skill and experience as a speaker. Write a summary of your current perception of yourself as a speaker, including strengths and areas for development. At the end of the course, revise what you have written to assess how you have improved.

2. **Ethics Assessment** *Declamation* is defined as "the delivery of an already famous address." Is it ethical to deliver a speech that was written or already delivered by someone else? Explain your answer.

3. **Critical Assessment** Reflect on the most recent public-speaking situation in which you were an audience member. Identify the specific elements in the communication model presented in Figure 1.1. Which elements of the model explain the speaker's effectiveness? (For example, the message was interesting and there was little noise.) If the speaker was ineffective, which elements in the model explain why the speaker was ineffective?

IMPROVING YOUR CONFIDENCE

OBJECTIVES

2.1 Explain the reasons for and processes involved in nervousness about public speaking.

2.2 Describe effective strategies for building public-speaking confidence.

UNDERSTAND YOUR NERVOUSNESS

2.1 Explain the reasons for and processes involved in nervousness about public speaking.

It's normal to be nervous about giving a speech. Research continues to confirm that most people are apprehensive about giving a speech.[1] More than 80 percent of people report feeling anxious about public speaking,[2] and one in five college students feels "highly apprehensive" about speaking in front of others.[3] In one classic survey, respondents said that they were more afraid of public speaking than of death![4]

Even if your anxiety is not overwhelming, you can benefit from learning some positive approaches that allow your nervousness to work *for you*.[5]

Know Your Reasons for Anxiety

Understanding why you and many others may experience apprehension can give you insights into how to better address your anxiety.[6] As you read the following list, you'll probably find a reason that resonates with you.

- One study found several reasons people feel anxious about public speaking: fear of humiliation, concern about not being prepared, worry about their appearance, pressure to perform, personal insecurity, concern that the audience won't be interested in them or the speech, lack of experience, fear of making mistakes, and an overall fear of failure.[7]
- Another study found that men are likely to experience more anxiety than women when speaking to people from a culture different from their own.[8]
- There is also evidence that being a perfectionist may be linked to increased apprehension.[9]

In addition, some people may have inherited a trait, or genetic tendency, to feel more anxiety than others would in any speechmaking situation.[10] Even if you have a biological tendency to feel nervous, you can use strategies to help manage your apprehension.[11]

Use Your Anxiety

Begin by realizing that you are going to feel more nervous than you look. Your audience cannot see evidence of everything you feel. If you worry that you are going to appear nervous to others, you may, in fact, increase your own internal symptoms of anxiety. Some of these internal symptoms are:

- extra adrenaline
- increased blood flow
- pupil dilation
- increased endorphins to block pain
- increased heart rate

REALIZE YOUR BODY IS HELPING YOU Your heightened state of readiness can actually help you speak better, especially if you view the public-speaking event positively instead of negatively. Speakers who label their increased feelings of physiological arousal as "nervousness" are more likely to feel anxious and fearful, but the same physiological feelings could also be labeled as "enthusiasm" or "excitement." You are more likely to benefit from the extra help your brain is trying to give you if you think positively rather than negatively about speaking in public. Don't let your initial anxiety convince you that you cannot speak effectively.

HOW TO BUILD YOUR CONFIDENCE

2.2 Describe effective strategies for building public-speaking confidence.

There are several additional things you can do to help manage your nervousness and anxiety.

Know Your Audience

Learn as much about your audience as you can. The more you can anticipate the kind of reaction your listeners will have to your speech, the more comfortable you will be in delivering your message.[12]

Don't Procrastinate

Fear of speaking often leads speakers to delay preparing their speeches until the last minute. The lack of thorough preparation often results in a poorer speech performance, which reinforces a speaker's perception that public speaking is difficult. Don't let fear freeze you into inaction. Take charge by preparing early.

Select an Appropriate Topic

You will feel less nervous if you talk about something with which you are familiar or in which you have a lot of interest. Your focus on the subject of your speech will be reflected in your delivery.

Be Prepared

Being prepared means that you have researched your topic, developed a logically coherent outline, and practiced your speech several times before you deliver it.

Be Organized

For most North American listeners, speeches should follow a logical outline pattern and have a clear beginning, middle, and end. Anxiety about a speech assignment decreases and confidence increases when you closely follow the directions and rules for developing a speech.

Know Your Introduction and Conclusion

You are likely to feel the most anxious during the opening moments of your speech. Being familiar with your introduction will help you feel more comfortable about the entire speech.

If you know how you will end your speech, you will have a safe harbor in case you lose your place. If you need to end your speech prematurely, a well-delivered conclusion can permit you to make a graceful exit.

Make Practice Real

Practice aloud. Stand up. Vividly imagine the room where you will give your speech, or consider rehearsing in the actual room. Picture what you will be wearing and what the audience will look like.

Breathe

Nervous speakers tend to take short, shallow breaths. Break that pattern: Take a few slow, deep breaths before you rise to speak. Besides breathing deeply, try to relax your entire body.

Channel Your Nervous Energy

An adrenaline boost before speaking can make you jittery. Channel the energy, using tips from the How To box.

Visualize Your Success

Imagine yourself giving your speech. Picture yourself walking confidently to the front and delivering your well-prepared opening remarks. Visualize yourself as a controlled, confident speaker. Imagine yourself calm and in command.

HOW TO

Dissipate Nervous Energy

- Take a slow, relaxing walk before you arrive at your speech location.
- While seated and waiting to speak, keep both feet on the floor and wiggle your toes.
- Gently (and without calling attention to yourself) grab the edge of your chair and squeeze it.
- Unobtrusively, lightly tense and release the muscles in your legs and arms.
- As you wait to be introduced, focus on remaining calm.
- Walk to the front of the room in a calm and collected manner.
- Take a moment to look for a friendly, supportive face before you begin.

Give Yourself a Mental Pep Talk

Replace any negative, anxious thoughts with positive messages, such as the following:

Negative Thought	Positive Self-Talk
I'm going to forget what I'm supposed to say.	I've practiced this speech many times. I've got notes to prompt me. If I forget or lose my place, no one will know I'm not following my outline.
So many people are looking at me.	I can do this! My listeners want me to do a good job. I'll seek out friendly faces when I feel nervous.

Focus on Your Message, Not on Your Fear

The more you think about being anxious about speaking, the more you will increase your level of anxiety. Instead, in the few minutes before you speak, mentally review your major ideas, introduction, and conclusion. Focus on your ideas rather than on your fear.

Look for Positive Listener Support

When you are aware of positive audience support, you will feel more confident and less nervous. Although some audience members may not respond positively to you or your message, the overwhelming majority of listeners will be positive. One study found that speakers experienced less apprehension if they had a support group or a small "learning community" that provided positive feedback and reinforcement.[13] And when you are listening, be sure to support other speakers with your full attention.

QUICK CHECK

Build Your Confidence

- Prepare your speech early.
- Know your audience and select an appropriate topic.
- Be prepared and well organized. Know your introduction and conclusion.
- Recreate the speech environment when you practice.
- Use deep-breathing techniques.
- Channel your nervous energy.
- Visualize your success.
- Give yourself a mental pep talk.
- Focus on your message, not on your fear.
- Look for positive listener support.
- Seek additional speaking opportunities.
- After your speech, focus on your accomplishment, not on your anxiety.

Seek Speaking Opportunities

The more experience you gain as a public speaker, the less nervous you will feel.[14] Consider joining organizations and clubs that provide opportunities for you to participate in public presentations, such as Toastmasters, an organization dedicated to improving public-speaking skills.

Focus on What You Have Accomplished, Not on Your Fear

When you finish your speech, celebrate your accomplishment. Say to yourself, "I did it! I spoke and people listened." Don't replay your mental image of yourself as nervous and fearful. Instead, mentally replay your success in communicating with your listeners.

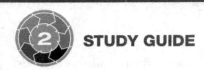

STUDY GUIDE

MEET YOUR OBJECTIVES

2.1 Explain the reasons for and processes involved in nervousness about public speaking.
Genetic traits, as well as several specific reasons, can cause anxiety. Physical symptoms, such as a racing heart, are signs your body is trying to support you. Speakers can also experience different types of anxiety.

2.2 Describe effective strategies for building public-speaking confidence.
Manage your apprehension by being prepared and knowing your audience, imagining the speech environment when you rehearse, and using relaxation techniques, such as visualization, deep breathing, and focusing thoughts away from your fears.

THINK ABOUT THESE QUESTIONS

1. **Self Assessment** Take a quiz, available at www.jamescmccroskey.com/measures/prca24.htm, to assess your level of communication apprehension. At the end of your public-speaking class, reassess your level of communication apprehension to see if the course has had an effect on your overall level of communication apprehension.
2. **Ethics Assessment** Should a speaker reveal to the audience that he or she is nervous?
3. **Critical Assessment** Mike Roberts, president of his fraternity, is nervous about his first report to the university academic council. What advice would you give him?

PRESENTING YOUR FIRST SPEECH

OBJECTIVES

3.1 Explain why it is important to be audience-centered during each step of the speechmaking process.

3.2 Select and narrow an appropriate topic for a speech.

3.3 Differentiate between a general speech purpose and a specific speech purpose.

3.4 Develop a sentence that captures the central idea of a speech.

3.5 Identify three strategies for generating the main ideas for a speech.

3.6 Describe several types of supporting material that could be used to support speech ideas.

3.7 Develop a speech with three main organizational parts—an introduction, a body, and a conclusion.

3.8 Identify successful strategies for rehearsing a speech.

3.9 Describe the essential elements of effective speech delivery.

CONSIDER YOUR AUDIENCE

3.1 Explain why it is important to be audience-centered during each step of the speechmaking process.

Although you have heard countless speeches, you may still have questions about how a speaker prepares and presents a speech. To help you begin, this chapter gives a step-by-step overview of the steps and skills you need for your first speech. Those steps are diagrammed in Figure 3.1.

Considering your audience is at the center of the model because your audience influences the topic you choose and every step of the speechmaking process. Considering the audience is a continuous process rather than a step in preparing a speech.

Being audience-centered involves making decisions about the content and style of your speech *before* you speak, based on knowledge of your audience's interests, needs, and values. If you learn new information about your audience at any point during the process of preparing your speech, you may need to revise your thinking or your material. It also means being sensitive to your audience's responses *during* the speech so that you can make appropriate adjustments.

To be effective, an audience-centered speaker also needs to understand, affirm, and adapt to diverse audiences. Being sensitive to your audience and adapting your message accordingly will serve you well not only when addressing listeners with cultural backgrounds different from your own, but also in all types of situations. Depending on who your audience members are and what

Figure 3.1 This model of the speechmaking process emphasizes the importance of considering your audience as you work on each task in the process of designing and presenting a speech.

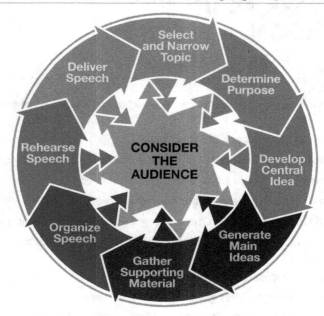

topics they are interested in, you will want to adjust your delivery style and possibly your topic, pattern of organization, and the examples you select.

SELECT AND NARROW YOUR TOPIC

3.2 Select and narrow an appropriate topic for a speech.

While keeping your audience foremost in mind, determine what you will talk about and how to limit your topic to fit the constraints of your speaking assignment.

You might be asked to speak about a specific subject. Often, though, the task of selecting and narrowing a topic will be yours. You may discover a topic by asking three standard questions:

1. Who is the audience?
2. What are my interests, talents, and experiences?
3. What is the occasion?

Give yourself plenty of time to select and narrow your topic. Don't wait until the last minute to ponder what you might talk about. *The amount of time you spend preparing for your speech is one of the best predictors of a good grade on your speech.*[1]

DETERMINE YOUR PURPOSE

3.3 Differentiate between a general speech purpose and a specific speech purpose.

Decide on both a general purpose and a specific purpose before you start the research process. There are three **general purposes** for giving speeches:

1. **To inform.**   When you inform, you teach, define, illustrate, clarify, or elaborate on a topic. The primary objective of class lectures, seminars, and workshops is to inform.

2. **To persuade.**   A speech to persuade seeks to change or reinforce listeners' attitudes, beliefs, values, or behavior. Ads on the TV, radio, and Internet; sermons; political speeches; and sales presentations are designed to persuade.

3. **To entertain.**   After-dinner speeches and comic monologues are intended mainly as entertainment. The key to an effective, entertaining speech lies in your choice of stories, examples, and illustrations, as well as in your delivery.

After you are sure you understand your general purpose, formulate a **specific purpose**: a concise statement indicating what you want your listeners to be able to do when you finish your speech. For example, "At the end of my speech, the class will be able to identify three counseling facilities on campus and describe the best way to get help at each one."

Create and Use a Specific-Purpose Statement

- Always consider your audience.
- Start with the phrase *At the end of my speech the audience will [be able to]...*
- Add your audience-centered goal. State the response you desire, in precise, measurable terms.
- Write down your specific purpose, and keep it before you as you read and gather ideas for your talk.
- Use your specific purpose to guide your research and help you choose supporting materials.
- Modify your purpose, if necessary, as you continue to work on your speech.

DEVELOP YOUR CENTRAL IDEA

3.4 Develop a sentence that captures the central idea of a speech.

You should now be able to write the **central idea** of your speech, sometimes called your *thesis statement*. Your central idea identifies the essence of your message. Think of it as a one-sentence summary of your speech. If you met someone in the elevator after your speech, and this person asked you to summarize the speech as you traveled between floors, you would be stating your central idea. Here is an example:

Topic:	British TV shows that inspired American TV shows
General Purpose:	To inform
Specific Purpose:	At the end of my speech the audience will be able to identify three classic British TV shows that inspired American versions.
Central Idea:	*The Office, Antiques Roadshow*, and *House of Cards* began as British TV programs that have become successful American TV shows.

GENERATE THE MAIN IDEAS

3.5 Identify three strategies for generating the main ideas for a speech.

Effective speakers are good thinkers; they know how to play with words and thoughts to develop their **main ideas**. The ancient Romans called this skill **invention**—the ability to develop or discover ideas that result in new insights or new approaches to old problems.

Once you have an appropriate topic, a specific purpose, and a well-worded central idea, identify the major divisions of your speech, or key points you wish to develop. To determine how to subdivide your central idea into key points, ask these three questions:

1. *Does the central idea have logical divisions?* For example, if the central idea is "There are three ways to interpret the stock market page of your local newspaper or financial website," your speech can be organized into three parts. You will simply identify the three ways to interpret stock market information and use each as a major point. Looking for logical divisions in your speech topic is the simplest way to determine key points.

2. *Are there several reasons the central idea is true?* If, for example, your central idea is "New legislation is needed to ensure that U.S. citizens' privacy is protected," each major point of your speech could be a reason why you think new privacy laws are needed.

3. *Can the central idea be supported with a series of steps?* Suppose your central idea is "Running for a campus office is easy to do." Your speech could be developed around a series of steps, telling your listeners what to do first, second, and third to get elected.

Your time limit, topic, and information gleaned from your research will determine how many major ideas will be in your speech. A three- to five-minute speech might have only two major ideas. In a very short speech, you might develop only one major idea with examples, illustrations, and other forms of support. Don't spend time trying to divide a topic that does not need dividing.

GATHER SUPPORTING MATERIAL

3.6 Describe several types of supporting material that could be used to support speech ideas.

With your main idea or ideas in mind, gather material to support them—facts, examples, definitions, and quotations from others that illustrate, amplify, clarify, provide evidence, or tell a story. As you gather and prepare your supporting material, think about how you can connect stories, descriptions, facts, or statistics to the lives of your audience:

- Tell stories based on your own experiences, and help the audience see how the stories relate to them.
- Supporting material should be personal, concrete, and appeal to your listeners' senses. The more senses you trigger with words, the more interesting your talk will be.
- Relate abstract statistics to something tangible. It is easier for an audience to understand that a company sells 2.6 billion pounds of snack food each year if you also tell them that 2.6 billion pounds is triple the weight of the Empire State Building.[2]

You can find interesting and relevant supporting material by developing good research skills. Although it is important to have good ideas, it is equally important to know how to build on existing knowledge. To speak intelligently about a topic to an audience, you will probably need to do some research.

- Learn to use the various electronic databases your library subscribes to, your library's computerized card catalog, an e-version of *Bartlett's Familiar Quotations*, and a wide assortment of Internet indexes such as Google Scholar.
- Be on the lookout as you read, watch TV or YouTube, receive tweets, and search the Internet for examples, illustrations, and quotations that you can use in a speech.

QUICK CHECK

Gather Effective Supporting Material

- Learn to research Internet and library resources.
- Look for materials throughout your daily life.
- Relate materials to your audience.
- Tell stories and give vivid descriptions.
- Make statistics understandable.

ORGANIZE YOUR SPEECH

3.7 Develop a speech with three main organizational parts—an introduction, a body, and a conclusion.

A clearly and logically structured speech helps your audience remember what you say. A logical structure also helps you feel more in control of your speech, and greater control helps you feel more comfortable while delivering your message.

Divide Your Speech

Every well-prepared speech has three major divisions:

1. The introduction helps capture attention, serves as an overview of the speech, and provides the audience with reasons to listen to you.

2. The body presents the main content of your speech.

3. The conclusion summarizes your key ideas.

Because your introduction previews the body of your speech and your conclusion summarizes it, prepare your introduction and conclusion *after* you have carefully organized the body of your talk.

Outline Your Speech

If you have already generated your major ideas on the basis of logical divisions, reasons, or steps, you are well on your way to developing an outline.

Use Roman numerals to indicate your major ideas. Use capital letters for your supporting points. Use Arabic numerals if you need to subdivide your ideas further.

Do not write your speech word for word. If you do, you will sound mechanical and less appealing to your audience. It may be useful, however, to use brief notes—written cues on note cards—instead of a complete manuscript. Increasingly, many speakers use handheld computer tablets such as iPads to display their speaking notes during their presentations.

REHEARSE YOUR SPEECH

3.8 Identify successful strategies for rehearsing a speech.

The best way to practice is to rehearse your speech aloud, standing just as you will when you deliver it to your audience. As you rehearse, try to find a comfortable way to phrase your ideas, but don't try to memorize your talk. In fact, if you have rehearsed your speech so many times that you are using exactly the same words every time, you have rehearsed long enough. Rehearse just enough so that you can discuss your ideas and supporting material without leaving out major parts of your speech. It is all right to use notes, but limit the number of notes you use.

Here are a few points to remember as you rehearse:

- Practice making eye contact with your imaginary audience as often as you can. For video, do not use overly animated gestures or facial expressions.
- Speak loudly enough for all in the room to hear.
- If you are not sure what to do with your hands when you rehearse, just keep them at your side. Focus on your message, rather than worrying about how to gesture.

The words you choose and your arrangement of those words make up the style of your speech. To be a good speaker, you must become familiar with the language your listeners are used to hearing, and you must know how to select the right word or phrase to communicate an idea.

DELIVER YOUR SPEECH

3.9 Describe the essential elements of effective speech delivery.

Delivery is the final step in the preparation process. Before you walk to the front of the room, look at your listeners to see whether the audience assembled is what you expected. Are the people of the age, race, and gender that you had predicted? Or do you need to make last-minute changes in your message to adjust to a different mix of audience members?

- When you are introduced, walk calmly and confidently to the front of the room.
- Establish eye contact with your audience.
- Smile naturally.
- Deliver your attention-catching opening sentence.
- Concentrate on your message and your audience.
- Deliver your speech in a conversational style.
- Deliver your speech just as you rehearsed it before your imaginary audience:

  Maintain eye contact.

  Speak loudly enough to be heard.

  Use some natural variation in pitch.
- Remember the advice of columnist Ann Landers: "Be sincere, be brief, and be seated."

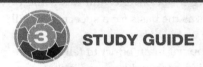

STUDY GUIDE

MEET YOUR OBJECTIVES

3.1 Explain why it is important to be audience-centered during each step of the speechmaking process.

Your audience influences your topic selection and every aspect of presenting a speech.

3.2 Select and narrow an appropriate topic for a speech.

Answers to three questions can help you select and narrow your speech topic: Who is the audience? What are my interests, talents, and experiences? And what is the occasion?

3.3 Differentiate between a general speech purpose and a specific speech purpose.

Your general purpose is the overarching goal of your speech (to inform, persuade, entertain, or some combination of these purposes). Your specific purpose is a concise statement of what you want your listeners to be able to do when you finish your speech.

3.4 Develop a sentence that captures the central idea of a speech.

A central idea states the essence of your speech in a one-sentence summary.

3.5 Identify three strategies for generating the main ideas for a speech.

Virtually any speech can be organized by answering the following three questions: Does the central idea have logical divisions? Are there several reasons the central idea is true? Can you support the central idea with a series of steps?

3.6 Describe several types of supporting material that can be used to support speech ideas.

Supporting material consists of facts, examples, definitions, and quotations from others that illustrate, amplify, clarify, provide evidence, or tell a story. You can find supporting material through the Internet, library resources, other people, or your daily life.

3.7 Develop a speech with three main organizational parts—an introduction, a body, and a conclusion.

Your introduction provides an overview of your main points, the body of your speech presents the key points, and the conclusion summarizes what you have said.

3.8 Identify successful strategies for rehearsing a speech.

Rehearse your speech several times in a way that recreates the actual speech presentation experience.

3.9 Describe the essential elements of effective speech delivery.

The essential aspects of effective delivery include good eye contact with your listeners, a voice that can be heard by all, and appropriate gestures and posture that seem natural.

THINK ABOUT THESE QUESTIONS

1. **Self Assessment** Explain how you think your culture influences your expectations of a public speaker.
2. **Ethics Assessment** One of your friends took public speaking last year and still has a file of speech outlines. Is it ethical to use one of your friend's outlines as the basis for a speech you will deliver? Explain your answer.
3. **Critical Assessment** Shara is preparing to address the city council in an effort to tell its members about the Food for Friendship program she has organized in her neighborhood. What steps should she follow to prepare and deliver an effective speech?

ETHICS AND FREE SPEECH

4

ETHICS

4.1 Describe the relationships among ethics, free speech, and credibility.

Ethics are the beliefs, values, and moral principles by which people determine what is right or wrong. Ethics serve as criteria for many of the decisions we make in our personal and professional lives and also for our judgments of others' behavior.

Ethics and Free Speech

Although you are undoubtedly familiar with ethical issues, you may have given less thought to those that arise in public speaking. In a country where **free speech** is protected by law, the right to speak freely must be balanced by the responsibility to speak ethically.

Ethical considerations should guide every step of the public-speaking process. The National Communication Association Credo for Communication Ethics emphasizes the essential role of ethics: "Ethical communication is fundamental to responsible thinking, decision making, and the development of relationships and communities."[1]

Ethics and Speaker Credibility

Aristotle used the term *ethos*—the root word of *ethics* and *ethical*—to refer to a speaker's **credibility**, or believability. A credible speaker is one whom an audience perceives to be competent, knowledgeable, dynamic, and trustworthy. The last of those four factors—trustworthiness—is dependent in large part on the speaker's known consistent adherence to ethical principles.

THE HISTORY OF FREE AND ETHICAL SPEECH

4.2 Explain how free speech has been both challenged and defended throughout U.S. history.

The history of the United States reflects our evolving thought on the ethical limitations to free speech:

1791   **First Amendment** to the U.S. Constitution guaranteed that "Congress shall make no law...abridging the freedom of speech."

1919   Supreme Court ruled that it was lawful to restrict speech that presented "a clear and present danger" to the nation. This led to the founding of the American Civil Liberties Union, the first organization formed to protect free speech.

1940   Congress declared it illegal to urge the violent overthrow of the federal government. However, for most of the last half of the twentieth century, the Supreme Court continued to protect rather than to limit free speech, upholding it as "the core aspect of democracy."[2]

1964   Supreme Court narrowed the definition of slander and ruled that before a public official can recover damages for slander, he or she must prove that the slanderous statement was made with "actual malice."[3]

1989   Supreme Court defended the burning of the U.S. flag as a "**speech act**" protected by the First Amendment.

1997   Supreme Court struck down the federal Communications Decency Act of 1996 and ruled that "the interest in encouraging freedom of expression in a democratic society outweighs any theoretical but unproven benefit of censorship."[4]

2001   The September 11 terrorist attacks sparked passage of the Patriot Act and new debate over the balance between national security and free speech.[5]

2010s   In a digital era, free speech, especially via the Internet and cell phones, has become a global issue.[6]

SPEAKING ETHICALLY

4.3   List and explain five criteria for ethical public speaking.

Each person's ethical decisions reflect his or her individual values and beliefs, as well as cultural norms. Any discussion of **ethical speech** is complicated by the fact that ethics are not hard-and-fast objective rules. However, many agree that ethical speakers have a clear, responsible goal; use sound evidence and reasoning; are sensitive to, and tolerant of, differences; are honest; and avoid plagiarism.

Have a Clear, Responsible Goal

The goal of a public speech should be clear to the audience. A socially responsible goal conveys respect and offers the listener choices, whereas an irresponsible, unethical goal is demeaning or psychologically coercive or oppressive.

   If your overall objective is to inform or persuade, it is probably ethical; if your goal is to demean, coerce, or manipulate, it is unethical.

Use Sound Evidence and Reasoning

Ethical speakers use critical-thinking skills such as analysis and evaluation to formulate arguments and draw conclusions. Unethical speakers substitute false claims and emotional manipulation for evidence and logical arguments. It may sometimes be tempting to resort to false claims to gain power over others, but it is always unethical to do so.

   One important requirement for the ethical use of evidence and reasoning is to share with an audience all information that might help them reach a sound decision, including information that may be potentially damaging to your case. Even if you proceed to refute the opposing evidence and arguments, you have fulfilled your ethical responsibility by presenting the perspective of the other side.

Be Sensitive to, and Tolerant of, Differences

Being audience centered requires that you become as aware as possible of others' feelings, needs, interests, and backgrounds. Sometimes called **accommodation**, sensitivity to differences does not mean that you must abandon your own convictions. It does mean that you should demonstrate a willingness to listen to opposing viewpoints and learn about different beliefs and values. Such willingness not only communicates respect but can also help you to select a topic, formulate a purpose, and design strategies to motivate an audience.

A speaker who is sensitive to differences also avoids language that might be interpreted as biased or offensive. Learn more about avoiding biased language in Chapter 15.

Be Honest

Knowingly offering false or misleading information to an audience is an ethical violation. However, many speakers rely on hypothetical illustrations—stories that never actually occurred, but that *might* happen. To use hypothetical illustrations ethically, make it clear to the audience that the story is indeed hypothetical. For example, begin with a phrase such as, "Imagine that…."

Don't Plagiarize

Honesty also requires that speakers give credit for ideas and information that are not your own. Presenting the words and ideas of others without crediting them is called **plagiarism**.

Even those who would never think of stealing money or shoplifting may be tempted to plagiarize. Perhaps you can remember copying a grade-school report directly from an online or printed encyclopedia, or maybe you've even purchased or "borrowed" a paper to submit for an assignment. These are obvious forms of plagiarism. A less obvious, but still serious, form is **patchwriting**—lacing a speech with compelling phrases that you find in a source but do not credit.[7] A speaker whose sentences were very similar to those used in a news article would be patchwriting if he or she did not acknowledge that the phrasing came from the article.

DO YOUR OWN WORK   You will be doing yourself a disservice if you do not learn how to compose a speech on your own. The most flagrant cases of plagiarism result from speakers not doing their work. Another way speakers may attempt to shortcut the speech preparation process is to ask another person to edit their speech so extensively that it becomes more that other person's work than their own. This is another form of plagiarism and another way of cheating themselves out of the skills they need to develop.

ACKNOWLEDGE YOUR SOURCES   An ethical speaker is responsible for doing his or her own research and then sharing the results of that research with audience members. Some information is so widely known that you do not have to acknowledge a source for it. For example, you need not credit a source if you say that a person must be infected with HIV to develop AIDS. This information is widely available in a variety of reference sources. However, if you decide to use any of the following in your speech, then you must give credit to the source:

- direct quotations, even if they are only brief phrases
- opinions, assertions, or ideas of others, even if you paraphrase them rather than quote them verbatim
- statistics
- any unoriginal visual materials, including graphs, tables, and pictures

TAKE CAREFUL NOTES   To be able to acknowledge your sources, you must first practice careful and systematic note-taking. Indicate with quotation marks any phrases or sentences that you photocopy, copy by hand, or electronically cut and paste verbatim from a source. Be sure to record the author, title, publisher or Web site, publication date, and page numbers for all sources from which you take quotations, ideas, statistics, or visual materials.

CITE SOURCES CORRECTLY   In addition to keeping careful records of your sources, you must also know how to cite your sources for your audience, both orally and in writing. The How To box offers advice for integrating an **oral citation** smoothly into a speech.

You can also provide a **written citation** for a source. Style guides, such as those published by the Modern Language Association (MLA) or the American Psychological Association (APA), are now available online as well as in print format.

HOW TO

Present an Oral Citation

- **Name the source.** For example, "On its 2013 Web page 'Bed Bugs,' the Centers for Disease Control and Prevention outlines three problems caused by bed bug infestations."
- **Pause briefly.** The pause signals listeners that you are about to begin quoting.
- **State the quote.** "Property loss, expense, and inconvenience."[8]
- **Provide enough information.** Tell listeners the author, the title, the year, and the fact that the information is available online.

What about those times when you are not certain whether information or ideas are common knowledge? A good rule is this: When in doubt, document. You would never be guilty of plagiarism if you documented something you didn't need to, but you could be committing plagiarism if you did not document something you really should have.

QUICK CHECK

Deliver an Ethical Speech

- Have a clear, responsible goal.
- Provide your listeners with choices, and use sound evidence and reasoning.
- Share all evidence that will help your audience reach a sound decision.
- Be sensitive to, and tolerant of, differences, and avoid language that is biased or offensive.
- Be honest and do your own work.
- Avoid plagiarism, and give credit for any ideas and information that are not your own.
- Acknowledge your sources accurately and completely.

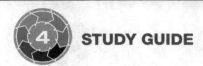 **STUDY GUIDE**

MEET YOUR OBJECTIVES

4.1 Describe the relationships among ethics, free speech, and credibility.

In the United States, citizens have the right to speak freely, but that right comes with the responsibility to speak ethically. Speaking ethically allows your audience to trust you. Being trustworthy is an important part of being credible, or believable.

4.2 Explain how free speech has been both challenged and defended throughout U.S. history.

Although the U.S. Congress and courts have occasionally limited the constitutional right to free speech, more often they have protected and broadened its application. Social media offer a new context for twenty-first-century challenges to free speech.

4.3 List and explain five criteria for ethical public speaking.

An ethical public speaker should have a clear, responsible goal; use sound evidence and reasoning; be sensitive to, and tolerant of, differences; be honest; and take appropriate steps to avoid plagiarism. Avoid plagiarizing by doing your own work and acknowledging—orally, in writing, or both—the sources for any quotations, ideas, statistics, or visual materials you use in a speech.

THINK ABOUT THESE QUESTIONS

1. **Self Assessment** You have found the perfect pie chart for your talk in *USA Today*. It shows U.S. Census figures for population trends. If you tell the audience that the source of the visual is *USA Today*, do you also need to cite the U.S. Census Bureau?
2. **Ethics Assessment** Speechwriters have written many of the best speeches made by U.S. presidents. Is such use of speechwriters ethical? Is it ethical for presidents to get the credit for the speeches?
3. **Critical Assessment** As you listen to classmates' speeches, try to identify specific ways in which they try to gain your trust.

LISTENING

5.1 List and describe five barriers to effective listening.

5.2 Identify and implement strategies for becoming a better listener.

5.3 Identify and implement strategies for improving your critical-listening and critical-thinking skills.

5.4 Use criteria to effectively and appropriately evaluate speeches.

OVERCOMING BARRIERS TO EFFECTIVE LISTENING

5.1 List and describe five barriers to effective listening.

You hear more than 1 billion words each year. Yet how much information do you retain? Improving your listening skills will make you not only a better listener but also a better speaker. Listening requires you to do all of the following:

- **Select** or single out a message from several competing messages. Your job as a speaker is to motivate listeners to focus on *your* message.
- **Attend** to, or focus on, the message.
- **Understand**, or assign meaning to the message.
- **Remember** ideas and information.
- **Respond**, or react with behavior that demonstrates you listened to the message.

   Listening barriers are created when you fail to perform any of these activities effectively.

Information Overload

According to the **working memory theory of listening**, as listeners, we find it harder to concentrate on and remember messages when our working memory is full.[1]

   As a public speaker, you can keep your audience from tuning out by:

- delivering a message that is clear and easy to understand.
- using interesting and vivid supporting material to keep your listeners listening.
- building redundancy into your message so that if listeners miss an idea the first time you present it, perhaps they will catch it during your concluding remarks.

Personal Concerns

Are you thinking about the upcoming weekend while your instructor speaks? As a listener, recognize when your own agenda keeps you from listening, and then force yourself to focus on the speaker's message. As a speaker, focus on maintaining your audience's attention and use occasional "wake-up" messages such as "Now listen carefully, because…"

Outside Distractions

As a listener, do your best to control the listening situation.

- Move to another seat.
- Turn off and put away your phone, laptop, and tablet (unless you are using one of these devices to take notes).
- Close the blinds.
- Turn up the heat.
- Turn off the lights.
- Close the door.
- Do whatever is necessary to minimize distractions.

When you are a speaker, use the tips in the How To box.

Prejudice

Are you convinced speakers from another political party have nothing useful to say? As a listener, guard against becoming so critical of a message that you don't listen to it or, doing the opposite, becoming so impressed that you decide too quickly that the speaker is trustworthy.

To counteract **prejudice** when you are the speaker, use your opening statements to grab the audience's attention so they will listen to your message. If you think audience members are likely to disagree with you, ask them to withhold evaluation until they have heard your entire speech. In addition, use detailed arguments and credible evidence rather than strong emotional appeals.

Minimize Listeners' Distractions

- Arrive early at the speaking space so you can assess the physical arrangements before you speak.
- Sit where your audience will be seated.
- Listen and look around you for any possible distractions.
- Reduce or eliminate distractions before listeners need to do it themselves.
- Tactfully discourage whispering in the audience.

Differences between Speech Rate and Thought Rate

Most people talk at a rate of 125 words a minute,[2] but are able to listen to up to 700 words a minute. The difference gives listeners time to ignore a speaker periodically. Eventually, you stop listening. Listen more effectively by mentally summarizing what the speaker is saying from time to time.

As a speaker, be aware of your listeners' tendency to stop paying attention. Build in message redundancy and internal summaries, use clear transitions, be well organized, and make your major ideas clear.

QUICK CHECK

Overcoming Your Listening Barriers

- Decide what is important in a speech and focus on that.
- Force yourself to focus on the speaker's message.
- Try to minimize outside distractions.
- Don't prejudge a message or speaker.
- Use the time lag created by the difference between speech rate and thought rate to summarize what the speaker is saying.

HOW TO BECOME A BETTER LISTENER

5.2 Identify and implement strategies for becoming a better listener.

Good listeners focus on a speaker's message, not on delivery style. Although poor speakers are a challenge to good listening, you also need to be wary of glib, well-polished speakers. An attractive style of delivery does not necessarily mean that a speaker's message is credible.

Listen with Your Eyes as Well as Your Ears

Nonverbal clues play a major role in communicating a speaker's emotions and messages. Interpret the speaker's expressions, posture, and gestures in the context of the speaker's words; look for clusters of cues that occur together; and look for cues that show the speaker's level of power, attitude toward listeners, and responsiveness to listeners.

If you have trouble understanding a speaker's words, get close enough so that you can see the speaker's mouth. A good view can increase your level of attention and improve your understanding.

Listen Mindfully

Good listeners are open-minded. They put their own thoughts aside so they can be present mentally as well as physically. They invest time in listening and make a conscious, mindful effort to listen. If you get off task and find that you're not doing these things, periodically remind yourself why the message can be helpful or important to you.[3]

Monitor Your Emotional Reaction to a Message

If you become angry or emotional in response to something a speaker says, your listening comprehension decreases. Don't let your anger toward a speaker's language get in the way of listening and understanding.

Be a Selfish Listener

If you find your attention waning, ask yourself questions such as, "What's in this for me?" Find ways to benefit from the information you are listening to, and try to connect it with your own experiences and needs.

Listen for Major Ideas

Listen for major ideas and principles. In speeches, facts as well as examples are used primarily to support major ideas. Facts are useful only when you can connect them to a principle or concept. As you listen, try to mentally summarize the major ideas that the specific facts support.

Practice Listening

Listening skills do not develop automatically. Skill develops as you practice listening to speeches, music, and programs with demanding content.

Understand Your Listening Style

There are at least four different **listening styles**. Understanding your listening style can help you become a better and more flexible listener.[4]

- **Relational-oriented listeners** are comfortable listening to others express feelings and emotions.
- **Task-oriented listeners** listen for actions that need to be taken. Task-oriented listeners tend to be skeptical and prefer being given evidence to support recommendations for action.
- **Analytical listeners** prefer to listen to complex information laced with facts and details. They often withhold judgment before reaching a specific conclusion.
- **Critical listeners** spend time evaluating messages. They are likely to catch inconsistencies and errors in the reasoning and evidence used to reach a conclusion.

Become an Active Listener

An active listener is one who remains alert and mentally re-sorts, rephrases, and repeats key information when listening to a speech. To be a more active speaker:

- **Re-sort.** Use your listening time to re-sort disorganized or disjointed ideas.[5] Figure out ways to rearrange them into a new, more logical pattern. Put a series of examples into chronological order, for example.
- **Rephrase.** Mentally summarize the key points or information you want to remember. Listen for the main ideas and then paraphrase them in your own words. Looking for "information handles" in the form of previews, transitions, signposts, and summary statements can also help you remain actively involved as a listener.
- **Repeat.** Periodically *repeat* key points you want to remember. Go back to essential ideas and restate them to yourself.

QUICK CHECK

Become a Better Listener

- Adapt to the speaker's delivery.
- Listen with your eyes as well as your ears.
- Monitor your emotional reaction to a message.
- Stay on task and be a selfish listener.
- Listen for major ideas.
- Understand your listening style, practice listening, and become an active listener.

Listen Ethically

Audience members share responsibility with speakers for ethical communication. The following guidelines for ethical listening incorporate what Harold Barrett calls "attributes of the good audience."[6]

COMMUNICATE YOUR EXPECTATIONS AND FEEDBACK   As an audience member, you have the right—even the responsibility—to enter into a communication situation with expectations about the message and how the speaker will deliver it.

- Know what information and ideas you want to get out of the communication transaction.
- Expect a coherent, organized, and competently delivered presentation.
- Communicate your objectives, and react to the speaker's message and delivery with appropriate nonverbal and verbal feedback.

BE SENSITIVE TO AND TOLERANT OF DIFFERENCES   As a member of an audience, it is important for you to exercise social and cultural awareness and tolerance.

- Be attentive and courteous.
- Remember that different cultures have different styles of speaking. If a speaker uses an approach different from the one you prefer, the speaker's approach is not necessarily wrong, just different.
- Try to understand the needs, goals, and interests of both the speaker and other audience members so that you can judge how to react appropriately and ethically as a listener.

IMPROVE CRITICAL-LISTENING AND CRITICAL-THINKING SKILLS

5.3   Identify and implement strategies for improving your critical-listening and critical-thinking skills.

Critical listening is the process of listening to evaluate the quality, appropriateness, value, and importance of the information you hear. Related to being a critical listener is being a critical thinker. **Critical thinking** is a mental process of making judgments about the conclusions presented in what you see, hear, and read. Your goal as a critical listener and critical thinker is to assess the quality of the information and the validity of the conclusions presented.

Separate Facts from Inferences

Facts are information that has been proven true by direct observation. An **inference** is a conclusion based on partial information or an evaluation that has not been directly observed. The ability to separate facts from inferences is a basic skill in critical thinking and listening.

Evaluate the Quality of Evidence

Evidence consists of the facts, examples, opinions, and statistics that a speaker uses to support a conclusion. Without credible supporting evidence, it would not be wise to agree with a speaker's conclusion.

Some speakers support a conclusion with **examples**. But if the examples aren't representative or typical, or only one or two examples are offered, or other known examples differ from the one the speaker is using, then you should question the conclusion.

An **opinion** is a quoted comment from someone. To be a credible source, the person quoted must have the credentials, experience, and skill to make an observation about the topic at hand.

A **statistic** is a number that summarizes a collection of examples. Are the statistics reliable, unbiased, recent, representative, and valid?

ANALYZE AND EVALUATE SPEECHES

5.4 Use criteria to effectively and appropriately evaluate speeches.

When you evaluate something, you judge its value and appropriateness. In making a judgment about the value of something, such as a speech, it's important to use criteria for what is and is not effective or appropriate. **Rhetorical criticism** is the process of using a method or standards to evaluate the effectiveness and appropriateness of messages.

Give Feedback to Others

When you have an opportunity to critique a speech, follow these guidelines to give feedback.

1. **Be descriptive.** In a neutral way, describe what you saw the speaker doing. For example, say, "You made eye contact during about half of your speech" rather than, "Your eye contact was lousy."

2. **Be specific.** Make sure your descriptions are precise enough. Instead of saying, "I liked your visuals," say, "Dawn, the use of color in your PowerPoint slides helped to keep my attention."

3. **Be positive.** Begin and end your feedback with positive comments. Beginning with negative comments immediately puts the speaker on the defensive and can create so much internal noise that she or he stops listening.

4. **Be constructive.** Give the speaker some suggestions or alternatives for improvement.

5. **Be sensitive.** Use *I-statements* as a way of phrasing your feedback so that your comments reflect your personal point of view ("I found my attention drifting during your speech"). A *you-statement* is less sensitive because it implies that the other person did something wrong ("You didn't summarize very well").

6. **Be realistic.** Provide usable information. Provide feedback about things over which the speaker has control.

Give Feedback to Yourself

Consider the following suggestions for enhancing your own self-critiquing skills.

1. **Look for and reinforce your skills and speaking abilities.** Take mental note of how your audience analysis, organization, and delivery were effective in achieving your objectives.
2. **Evaluate your effectiveness based on your specific speaking situation and audience.** Give yourself permission to adapt principles and practices to specific speech situations.
3. **Identify one or two areas for improvement.** Identify what you did right; then give yourself a suggestion or two for ways to improve. Concentrate on one or two key skills you would like to develop.

 STUDY GUIDE

MEET YOUR OBJECTIVES

5.1 List and describe five barriers to effective listening.

Barriers to listening include information overload, personal concerns, outside distractions, prejudice, and differences in speech rate and listening rate.

5.2 Identify and implement strategies for becoming a better listener.

"Listen" to nonverbal messages with your eyes. Understand your listening style. Listen mindfully, monitoring your emotional reactions to messages, and avoid jumping to conclusions. Listen for major ideas. Re-sort, restate, or repeat key messages. Be an ethical listener.

5.3 Identify and implement strategies for improving your critical-listening and critical-thinking skills.

Evaluate the speaker's use of facts, examples, opinions, and statistics as evidence.

5.4 Use criteria to effectively and appropriately evaluate speeches.

A good speech is understandable to the audience and achieves its intended effect. When offering feedback to yourself or others, be descriptive, specific, positive, constructive, sensitive, and realistic.

THINK ABOUT THESE QUESTIONS

1. **Self Assessment** One of your professors does nothing during lectures but read in a monotone voice from old notes. What are some strategies you can use to increase your listening effectiveness in this challenging situation?

2. **Ethics Assessment** Janice thought her classmate's speech was pretty good, but she gave the speaker low marks because she strongly disagreed with what the speaker was saying. Was this an ethical evaluation?

3. **Critical Assessment** For some reason, when Alberto hears the president speak, he just tunes out. What are some of the barriers that may keep Alberto from focusing on the message he is hearing?

ANALYZING YOUR AUDIENCE

GATHER INFORMATION ABOUT YOUR AUDIENCE

6.1 Describe informal and formal methods of gathering information about your audience.

As an audience-centered speaker, try to find out as much as you can about the audience before planning the speech. There are two approaches you can take: informal and formal.

Gathering Information Informally

Observe your audience informally and ask questions of people who know something about the audience you will be addressing. What is the audience's average age? What are their political affiliations? What are their attitudes toward your topic?

Gathering Information Formally

If time and resources permit, you may want to conduct a more formal survey of your listeners. Your topic and the speaking occasion can help you determine what you want to know about your audience that you don't already know. You may want to ask questions about audience members' age, sex, occupation, and memberships in professional organizations. Whenever possible, you should also ask specific questions about their attitudes. You can ask two basic types of questions:

1. **Open-ended questions** allow for unrestricted answers without limiting responses to specific choices or alternatives. An open-ended question asks, "What do you believe is the best way to lower our district's high-school drop-out rate?" rather than a yes-or-no question, such as, "Do you believe that a longer school year will lower the drop-out rate?" Use open-ended questions when you want more detailed information from your audience.

2. **Closed-ended questions** offer alternatives from which to choose. Multiple-choice, true/false, and agree/disagree questions are examples of closed-ended questions.

After you develop your own questions, test them out on a small group of people to make sure they are clear and will encourage meaningful answers.

ANALYZE AUDIENCE INFORMATION

6.2 Explain how to analyze and use information to adapt to your audience.

Once you have gathered information, you can begin the processes of **audience analysis**, examining information about your listeners, and **audience adaptation**, ethically using your information to customize your speech to the audience.

Use the results of your audience analysis to tailor your message so that listeners will understand it and you will achieve your speaking goal. Ethically adapt your topic, speech goal, content—including organization, information, examples, and visual aids—as well as your delivery.[1] For example, use popular culture references your listeners are likely to know. *Adapting ethically means you do not tell your listeners only what they want to hear or fabricate information simply to please your audience or achieve your goal.*

Analyze Audience Information

As you examine your data, look for these three things:

- **Audience member similarities**, whether in demographics or in beliefs and attitudes, can help you craft a message that resonates in the same way with many of your listeners.
- **Audience member differences** will alert you to the range of people you must reach with your message.
- **Common ground** with your audience refers to the ways you and your listeners are alike. The more you have in common with your audience, the easier it will be to establish a **relationship** with them that helps them understand your message and helps you achieve your purpose.

DEMOGRAPHIC AUDIENCE ANALYSIS

6.3 List important demographic characteristics of audience members.

Demographics are statistics on audience characteristics, such as age, gender, sexual orientation, race and culture, group membership, and socioeconomic status. Demographic information can help you develop a clear and effective message by providing clues about your listeners. Use caution in making inferences based on general information, however, because they may lead to faulty conclusions.

Age

The audience's age can suggest topics, as well as the kinds of examples, humor, illustrations, and other types of supporting material to use in your speech. Be careful, however, about generalizing from only one factor.

Gender and Sexual Orientations

Gender is the culturally constructed and psychologically based perception of one's self as feminine or masculine. Listeners' gender identities can fall anywhere along a continuum from female to male and may or may not reflect their biological **sex**. Your listeners may also have a range of sexual orientations. As an audience-centered speaker, avoid assumptions about gender identity, as well as sexist language or remarks. Take time to educate yourself about what words, phrases, or perspectives are likely to offend or create psychological noise and distract your audience from listening. Make your language, and your message, as inclusive of all gender identities and sexual orientations as possible.

Culture, Ethnicity, and Race

Culture is a learned system of knowledge, behavior, attitudes, beliefs, values, and norms shared by a group of people. **Ethnicity** is that portion of a person's cultural background that includes such factors as nationality, religion, language, and ancestral heritage, which are shared by a group of people who have a common geographic origin. **Race** is a term that has evolved to include a group of people with a common cultural history, nationality, or geographical location, as well as genetically transmitted physical attributes.[2] To be an effective speaker, adapt to differences in culture, race, and ethnicity.

Ethnocentrism is the assumption that your own cultural approaches are superior to those of other cultures. Be sensitive to cultural differences and avoid remarks that disparage the cultural background of the audience.

Group Membership

Know what political, social, service, professional, work, or religious groups your listeners belong to so that you can make inferences about their likes, dislikes, beliefs, and values. Making references to the activities that your audience members may participate in can help you tailor your speech to your specific audience. Use great care, however, when touching on religious beliefs or an audience's values.

Socioeconomic Status

Socioeconomic status is a person's perceived importance and influence based on such factors as income, occupation, and educational level. The amount of disposable income your listeners have

QUICK CHECK

Analyze Audience Demographics

- Know the age of your audience.
- Avoid making sweeping judgments based on gender stereotypes.
- Consider your audience's sexual orientations.
- Avoid an ethnocentric mind-set, and use great care when touching on religious beliefs.
- Learn what groups, clubs, or organizations your audience belongs to. Consider the socioeconomic status of audience members.
- Remember that your audience will be made up of diverse individuals.

can influence your topic and your approach to the topic. Knowing what people do for a living can give you useful information about how to adapt your message to them. Knowing the educational background of your audience can also help you make decisions about your choice of vocabulary, language style, and use of examples and illustrations.

PSYCHOLOGICAL AUDIENCE ANALYSIS

6.4 Discuss audience attitudes that can affect your speech.

A **psychological audience analysis** explores an audience's attitudes toward a topic, purpose, and speaker, while probing the underlying beliefs and values that might affect these attitudes.

- An **attitude** reflects likes or dislikes.
- A **belief** is what you hold to be true or false.
- A **value** is an enduring concept of good and bad, right and wrong. More deeply ingrained than either attitudes or beliefs, values are also more resistant to change.

Analyze Attitudes toward Your Topic

Knowing how members of an audience feel about your topic lets you adjust your message accordingly. Try to categorize your audience and their attitudes according to the following three dimensions.

INTERESTED–UNINTERESTED With an interested audience, your task is simply to hold and amplify interest throughout the speech. If your audience is uninterested, you need to find ways to "hook" the members. Tell listeners why your message relates to their needs and interests. Visual aids may also help you to gain and maintain the attention of apathetic listeners.

FAVORABLE–UNFAVORABLE Even if your general purpose is just to inform, it is useful to know whether your audience is predisposed to respond positively or negatively toward you or your message. Some audiences may be neither; instead, they may be neutral, apathetic, or simply uninformed about your topic. If they are already favorable, use their interest to move them closer to your speaking goal. If not, be realistic. Acknowledge their opposing point of view and consider using facts to refute misperceptions they may hold.

CAPTIVE–VOLUNTARY A captive audience has externally imposed reasons for being there (such as a requirement to attend class). Your goal with a captive audience is to make your speech just as interesting and effective as one designed for a voluntary audience. You still have an obligation to address your listeners' needs and interests and to keep them engaged in what you have to say. If your audience is attending voluntarily, anticipate why they are coming and speak about the issues they want you to address.

Analyze Attitudes toward You, the Speaker

Your **credibility**—the degree to which you are perceived as trustworthy, knowledgeable, and dynamic—is one of the main factors that will shape your audience's attitude toward you. An audience's positive attitude toward you as a speaker can overcome negative or apathetic attitudes they may have toward your topic or purpose.

If you establish your credibility before you begin, your listeners will be more likely to believe what you say and to think that you are knowledgeable, interesting, and dynamic. If you have had personal experience with your topic, be sure to let the audience know. You will gain credibility instantly. If your analysis reveals that your audience does not recognize you as an authority on your subject, you will need to build your credibility into the speech.

SITUATIONAL AUDIENCE ANALYSIS

6.5 Analyze key aspects of the speaking situation.

Situational audience analysis includes an examination of the time and place of your speech, the size of your audience, and the speaking occasion. Table 6.1 summarizes situational audience analysis.

ANALYZE YOUR AUDIENCE AFTER YOU SPEAK

6.6 Identify methods of assessing audience reactions after your speech.

After you have given your speech, evaluate your audience's positive or negative response to your message. Use your evaluation to help you prepare your next speech.

Table 6.1 Analyzing the Situation

Factor	Importance
Time	
• What time of day will you speak? • At what point in the program will you speak? • For how long are you scheduled to talk?	• Listeners may be tired in the afternoon or after listening to several other speakers. • Be sure to end your talk right on time or a little early.
Location	
• Can you visit before you speak? • How will audience seating be arranged? • How close will you be to the audience? • Will you be on a stage or raised platform? • Will you speak from a lectern? • Do you need to use a microphone? • Will you have the appropriate equipment and lighting for your visual aids?	• Visit, if possible. Determine what you can and cannot change about the location. • Adapt your speech and visual aids to factors you cannot change. • Rehearse appropriate movements and gestures for the conditions. • Arrive early to practice with microphones and equipment.
Size of Audience	
• How many people are expected to attend?	• Larger audiences tend to expect a more formal style. • You can take questions during your talk from a group of ten or fewer.
Occasion	
• What is the occasion that brings the audience together?	• Knowing the occasion can help you predict audience demographics and state of mind.

Nonverbal Responses

The most obvious nonverbal response is applause. Is the audience simply clapping politely, or is the applause robust and enthusiastic, indicating pleasure and acceptance? Responsive facial expressions, smiles, and nods are signs that the speech was well received. Remember, however, that listeners from different cultures respond to speeches with different behavior and levels of enthusiasm.[3]

Verbal Responses

If you have the chance, try to ask audience members how they responded to the speech in general, as well as to points you are particularly interested in. Their specific comments can indicate where you succeeded and where you need improvement.

Survey Responses

You can use the same survey techniques discussed previously. Develop survey questions that will help you determine the general reactions to you and your speech, as well as specific responses to your ideas and supporting materials.

Behavioral Responses

Your listeners' actions are the best indicators of your speaking success. If the purpose of your speech was to persuade your listeners to do something, you will want to learn whether they ultimately behave as you intended.

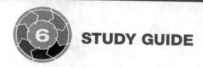

STUDY GUIDE

MEET YOUR OBJECTIVES

6.1 Describe informal and formal methods of gathering information about your audience.
Gather information through informally observing listeners and questioning people who know them. Use open-ended and close-ended questions to formally survey listeners.

6.2 Explain how to analyze and use information to adapt to your audience.
Look for similarities and differences among listeners and common ground between you and the audience. Use information to ethically adapt your topic, content, and delivery to help the audience understand and to achieve your goal.

6.3 List important demographic characteristics of audience members.
Adapt your speech to your listeners' ages, genders, sexual orientations, cultures and ethnicities, group memberships, and socioeconomic status.

6.4 Discuss audience attitudes that can affect your speech.

Learn whether listeners attend your speech voluntarily or as a captive audience. Know their level of interest and support of your topic or position. You must also consider their opinions about your credibility.

6.5 Analyze key aspects of the speaking situation.

Ethically adapt your speech depending on the time and location for it, the size of the audience, and the occasion.

6.6 Identify methods of assessing audience reactions after your speech.

Use nonverbal, verbal, survey, and behavioral responses to assess your effectiveness.

THINK ABOUT THESE QUESTIONS

1. **Self Assessment** After your next speech, describe the extent to which you accomplished your speaking goal, based on assessment techniques described in this chapter.
2. **Ethics Assessment** Tynisha wants to convince her audience to ban alcohol in all city parks. Her survey results suggest that 85 percent of her audience want to continue the current policy of permitting alcohol in city parks. Should she change her purpose to fit the existing attitudes of her audience? Why or why not?
3. **Critical Assessment** Dr. Ruiz thought the audience for her speech on birth control would be women of childbearing age. After writing her speech, however, she found out that all the women to whom she would be speaking were at least 20 years older than she expected. What changes, if any, should she make to her speech?

ADAPTING TO YOUR AUDIENCE AS YOU SPEAK

READ NONVERBAL CUES

7.1 Explain how to read nonverbal cues to understand listeners' reactions to your speech.

Audience analysis and adaptation do not end when you have crafted your speech. They continue as you deliver your speech. Once you begin speaking, you must rely on nonverbal cues from the audience to judge how people are responding to the message. Learn to be aware of the often unspoken clues that your audience is either hanging on your every word or is bored.

Eye Contact

The best way to determine whether your listeners are maintaining interest in your speech is to note the amount of eye contact they have with you. The more contact they have, the more likely it is that they are listening to your message. If you find them repeatedly looking at their phones, checking e-mail, tapping out a text message, looking down at the program or, worse yet, closing their eyes, you can reasonably guess that they have lost interest in what you're talking about.

Facial Expression

Members of an attentive audience not only make direct eye contact but also have attentive facial expressions. Beware of a frozen, unresponsive face; we call this sort of expression the "listener-stupor" look. The classic listener-stupor expression consists of a slightly tilted head, a faint, frozen smile, and often a hand holding up the chin. This expression may give the appearance of interest, but more often it means that the person is daydreaming or thinking of something other than your topic.

Movement and Posture

An attentive audience doesn't move much. Squirming, feet shuffling, and general body movement often indicate that members of the audience have lost interest in your message. A slight forward lean is a good sign your listeners are interested and paying attention.

Nonverbal Responsiveness

Frequent applause and nods of agreement are indicators of interest and support. An interested audience also responds when encouraged or invited to do so by the speaker. If you ask for a show of hands and audience members sheepishly look at one another and eventually raise a finger or two, you can reasonably infer lack of interest and enthusiasm.

RESPOND TO NONVERBAL CUES

7.2   Describe several adaptations you can make to respond to listeners' nonverbal cues.

After learning to "read" your listeners, you can use a repertoire of behaviors to help you connect with them.

If your audience seems inattentive or bored:

- Tell a story.
- Use an example to which the audience can relate, or use a personal example.
- Remind your listeners why your message should be of interest to them.
- Eliminate some abstract facts and statistics.
- Use appropriate humor. If listeners do not respond to your humor, use more stories or personal illustrations.
- Make direct references to the audience.
- Encourage audience participation by asking questions or requesting examples.
- Ask for a direct response, such as a show of hands, to see whether your listeners agree or disagree with you.
- Speed up the pace of your delivery, or pause for dramatic effect.

Adapt Your Speech While You Are Speaking

- iWatch the audience and notice listeners' nonverbal cues.
- If listeners seem interested, supportive, and attentive, continue speaking as you have planned, based on your prespeech analysis.
- If the audience is not interested and responsive, or is disagreeing with you, try one of the ideas listed in this chapter.
- If the audience's responses do not change, try another adaptation.
- If all else fails, you may need to abandon a formal speaker–listener relationship with your audience and open up your topic for discussion.
- Continue to listen and monitor so that you may learn more about the audience.

If your audience seems confused or doesn't seem to understand your point:

- Be more redundant. Repeat key points.
- Phrase your information in another way, or think of a more concrete example to illustrate your point.
- Use a visual aid, such as a chalkboard or flipchart, to clarify your point.
- If you have been speaking rapidly, slow your speaking rate.
- Ask for feedback from audience members to help you discover what may be unclear to them.
- Ask someone in the audience to summarize the key points you are making.

If your audience seems to be disagreeing with your message:

- Provide additional data and evidence to support your point.
- Remind your listeners of your credibility, credentials, or background.
- Rely less on anecdotes and more on facts to present your case. Write facts and data on a chalkboard, overhead transparency, or flipchart if one is available.
- If you don't have the answers and data you need, tell listeners you will provide more information by mail, telephone, or e-mail (and make sure you get back in touch with them).

CUSTOMIZE YOUR MESSAGE TO YOUR AUDIENCE

7.3   List several ways you can customize your message to your audience.

Audiences prefer messages that are adapted just to them. What are some ways to communicate to your listeners that your message is designed specifically for them? Here are a few suggestions.

- Appropriately use audience members' names to relate information to specific people. Before you speak, ask those people for permission to use their names in your talk.
- Make a specific reference to the place where you are speaking.
- Refer to a significant event that happened on the date of your speech. An Internet search for "this day in history" should reveal a number of interesting events. Link the event to the topic and audience. For example, "Today is the anniversary of one of the great battles of the Civil War. Today, I want to tell you about another battle in our country. The outcome will change all of our lives."
- Refer to a recent news event. Visit the Web site or local news source of an institution or group to whom you are speaking for stories that you can connect to the central idea of your talk.
- Refer to a group or organization. If you're speaking to an audience of service, religious, political, or work group members, make specific positive. But be honest—don't offer false praise; audiences can sniff out phony flattery.
- Find ways to apply facts, statistics, and examples to the people in your audience. For example, "Forty percent of women listening to me now are likely to experience gender discrimination. That means of the twenty women in this audience, eight of you are likely to be discriminated against."

ADAPT TO DIVERSE LISTENERS

7.4 Discuss strategies for adapting to diverse groups of listeners.

Audience diversity involves more factors than just ethnic and cultural differences. *Diversity* simply means differences. Audiences are diverse.

Because of your efforts to gather information about your audience, you should know something about the people who will likely be present for your talk. Based on your information, you may want to identify a **target audience**, a specific segment of your audience that you most want to address or influence.

Although you should avoid making generalizations based on cultural background, knowing that many people accept their culture's view on the following variables may help you adapt your message, supporting materials, and delivery.[1] You can use the following suggested strategies to help you adapt to your diverse listeners. Be sure to assess your own cultural background and expectations, too. Avoid developing a message that would be effective with only people like you.

- **Individualistic or collectivistic**—Listeners from individualistic cultures focus more on the achievement of a single person. Emphasize how your information can help them as individuals. Collectivistic cultures tend to emphasize the accomplishments of a group or team. Point out the benefits of your information to their community.
- **High or low context**—High-context listeners pay closer attention to a variety of nonverbal cues than low-context ones, who will focus mainly on your words.
- **Tolerance of uncertainty and need for certainty**—People with low tolerance for uncertainty need your speech to be clearly organized and may prefer a linear, step-by-step structure.
- **High or low power**—People from high-power cultures are more likely to perceive people in leadership roles—including speakers—as credible. They will also be more comfortable with proposals or solutions that identify or acknowledge differences in social class. Those from low-power cultures often favor more shared approaches to leadership and governance.
- **Long-term or short-term time orientation**—Listeners with a short-term orientation consider time an important resource. Show the immediate impact of any ideas you propose. In contrast, appeal to persistence and benefits to future generations for listeners who are concerned with the long term.

QUICK CHECK

Adapt to a Culturally Diverse Audience

- Tailor your speech primarily to your target audience.
- Avoid generalizations; assess a variety of cultural variables.
- Use a variety of strategies.
- Identify listeners' common values and assumptions.
- Use stories and examples that span cultures.
- Use visual aids with universal appeal.

STUDY GUIDE

MEET YOUR OBJECTIVES

7.1 Explain how to read nonverbal cues to understand listeners' reactions to your speech.

While speaking, pay attention to your listeners' eye contact with you, their facial expressions and amount of movement, and their verbal and nonverbal responses to you.

7.2 Describe several adaptations you can make to respond to listeners' nonverbal cues.

When you receive clues that listeners are bored, don't understand, or disagree with you, change what you are doing. You can try many strategies to communicate more effectively.

7.3 List several ways you can customize your message to your audience.

Adapt to your specific audience by using audience members' names or mentioning the group they belong to; relating your speech to the location where you are speaking or to a historical or recent event; and relating statistics to your specific audience.

7.4 Discuss strategies for adapting to diverse groups of listeners.

Adapt your speech to your listeners' cultural orientations toward individualism or collectivism, time, power, need for certainty, and attention to context. Consider directing your message toward a target audience.

THINK ABOUT THESE QUESTIONS

1. **Self Assessment** Consider a recent speech you gave. How did you adapt it to your specific audience? How could you have better customized the speech?
2. **Ethics Assessment** How can you ethically address the interests of all audience members if you direct your message toward a target audience?
3. **Critical Assessment** In the middle of a presentation, Brandon notices a few of the audience members losing eye contact with him, shifting in their seats, and glancing at their phones. What is happening, and what should Brandon do?

DEVELOPING YOUR SPEECH

SELECT YOUR TOPIC

8.1   Select and narrow a topic for a speech.

Your first task is to choose a topic for your speech. You will then need to narrow this topic to fit your time limits. But how do you go about choosing an appropriate, interesting topic?

Consider the Audience

As you search for potential speech topics, keep in mind each audience's interests and expectations. Your topic should be relevant to the *interests* and *expectations* of your listeners, and it should take into account the *knowledge* listeners already have about the subject.

Choose topics that are important—topics that matter to your listeners, as well as to yourself. Table 8.1 offers examples of topics appropriate for the interests, expectations, knowledge, and concerns of given audiences.

Consider the Occasion

To be successful, a topic must be appropriate to the occasion. For example, you may not want to give a bawdy, humorous after-dinner speech at the birthday party of a dignified elder, or criticize an organization while speaking at the opening of its new headquarters.

Consider Yourself

The best public-speaking topics are those that reflect your personal experience or especially interest you. You can select a topic with which you are already familiar or one you would like to learn more about. Your interest will motivate both your research and your eventual delivery of the speech.

Table 8.1 Sample Audience-Centered Topics

Audience	Topic
Retirees	Prescription drug benefits
Civic organizations	The Special Olympics
Church members	Starting a community food bank
First graders	What to do in case of a fire at home
Teachers	Building children's self-esteem
College fraternities	Campus service opportunities

Strategies for Selecting a Topic

Contemplating your audience, yourself, and your occasion does not automatically yield a good topic. The following strategies can also help.

BRAINSTORM   Follow the guidelines in the How To box to use the time-tested technique of **brainstorming** to generate ideas for speech topics.[1]

LISTENING AND READING FOR TOPIC IDEAS   Often, something you see, hear, or read triggers an idea for a speech. A current news story or social trend or issue you see on TV, read in your favorite news source, or receive via social media may suggest a topic. You can also consider randomly browsing the categories of a Web directory such as DMOZ (*dmoz.org*) until you see a topic that piques your interest. Chances are that a topic covered in one medium has been covered in another as well, allowing for extended research.

Just as you jotted down possible topics generated by brainstorming sessions, remember to write down topic ideas you get from what's trending among your Facebook friends or on your Twitter feed, other media, class lectures, or informal conversations.

DON'T PROCRASTINATE!   For most brief classroom speeches (less than 10 minutes), you should allow at least one week to develop and research your speech. A week gives you enough time to develop and research your speech. The whole process will be far easier than if you delay work until the night before you are supposed to deliver your speech.

Brainstorm Speech Topics

- Write down the first topic that comes to mind. Do not allow yourself to evaluate it. Just write it down in a word or a phrase.
- Now jot down a second idea—again, anything that comes to mind.
- One topic may remind you of another possibility. Write it down. Such "piggybacking" of ideas is okay.
- Continue without restraint. At this stage, anything goes.
- Make as long a list as you can think up in the time you have.
- Later, evaluate the list to choose a viable topic.

Narrow the Topic

Now that you have a topic, you need to narrow it so that it fits within the time limits set by your assignment. Write your general topic—perhaps it is *Music*—at the top of a list. Add entries to the list, making each one more specific than the previous entry. Under "Music," for example, you might write, "Folk music," then "Irish folk music," and so on. Eventually, you will have a topic specific enough for the length of your speech. Be careful not to narrow your topic so much that you cannot find enough information for even a 3-minute talk. If you do, just go back a step to a broader topic.

QUICK CHECK

Selecting a Topic

- Is the topic relevant and important to your audience?
- How much does your audience know about the topic?
- Is the topic appropriate to the occasion?
- Is the topic of interest and importance to you?

Determine Your General Purpose

The **general purpose** of virtually any speech is either to inform, to persuade, or to entertain.

- Informative speakers give listeners information. They define, describe, or explain a thing, person, place, concept, process, or function to increase the knowledge of their listeners.
- Persuasive speakers try to get you to believe or do something. They may offer information, but they use the information to try to change or reinforce an audience's beliefs or to urge some sort of action.
- Entertaining speakers aim to get listeners to relax, smile, perhaps laugh, and generally enjoy themselves.

DETERMINE YOUR SPECIFIC PURPOSE

8.2 Write an audience-centered specific-purpose statement for a speech.

Now that you have a topic and you know generally whether your speech should inform, persuade, or entertain, it is time you decided on its specific purpose. A **specific purpose** is a concise audience-centered statement of what your listeners should be able to do by the time you finish your speech.

Formulating the Specific Purpose

Specific-purpose statements begin with the same nine words: "At the end of my speech, the audience will…." The next word should be a verb that names an observable, measurable action that the audience should be able to do by the end of the speech.

Use verbs such as *list, explain, describe,* or *write.* Do not use words such as *know, understand,* or *believe.* You can discover what your listeners know, understand, or believe only by having them show you by performing some measurable activity.

Clarify the Specific Purpose

After you write your specific-purpose statement, make sure it follows these guidelines:

- Your specific purpose reflects the interests, expectations, and knowledge level of your audience.
- Your specific-purpose statement expresses only one single idea. The purpose, "At the end of my speech, the audience will write a simple computer program and play the latest video game," has more than one idea. If you try to achieve more than one specific purpose, you will have trouble covering all your ideas, and your speech may seem unfocused.
- Your specific-purpose statement does not say what you, the *speaker*, will do. It says what your *audience* will do.

Using the Specific Purpose

Everything you do while preparing and delivering the speech should contribute to your specific purpose. The specific purpose can help you assess the information you are gathering for your speech. For example, you may find that an interesting statistic, although related to your topic, does not help you achieve your specific purpose. In that case, you can substitute material that directly advances your purpose.

DEVELOP YOUR CENTRAL IDEA

8.3   State a central idea for a speech.

The **central idea** is a one-sentence summary of your speech. The central idea (sometimes called the *thesis statement*), like the purpose statement, restates the speech topic. But whereas a purpose statement focuses on audience behavior, the central idea focuses on the content of the speech.

- The central idea should be a complete declarative sentence—not a phrase (such as *toxic waste dumping*) or clause (such as *stop dumping toxic waste*), and not a question ("Why is toxic waste a problem?").
- The central idea should use direct, specific language. An example of a good central idea is, "Toxic waste dumping is a major environmental problem in the United States today." Avoid qualifiers such as *in my opinion.* Avoid a central idea that is too vague, such as "Toxic waste is a reason to worry."
- The central idea should be a single idea. More than one central idea, like more than one idea in a purpose statement, only leads to confusion and a lack of coherence in a speech.
- The central idea should reflect consideration of the audience. You considered your audience when selecting and narrowing your topic and when composing your purpose statement. In the same way, you should consider your audience's needs, interests, expectations, and knowledge when stating your central idea. If you do not consider your listeners, you run the risk of losing their attention before you even begin developing the speech.

GENERATE AND PREVIEW YOUR MAIN IDEAS

8.4 Apply three ways of generating main ideas from a central idea.

Write the central idea at the top of a clean sheet of paper. Then ask these three questions:

1. Does the central idea have *logical divisions*? (These may be indicated by such phrases as "three types" or "four means.")
2. Can you think of several *reasons* why the central idea is true?
3. Can you support your central idea with a series of *steps* or a chronological progression?

You should be able to answer yes to one or more of these questions. These are your **main ideas**. Main ideas might, for example, be three *types* of birds of prey, four *reasons* the local park needs new lighting, or four *steps* in writing your own wedding vows.

Consult your specific-purpose statement as you generate your main ideas. If these main ideas do not help you achieve your purpose, you need to rethink your speech. You may change either your purpose or your main ideas. Whichever you do, be sure to synchronize these two elements. Remember, it is much easier to make changes at this stage than after you have done your research and produced a detailed outline.

Once you have generated your main ideas, you can produce a **blueprint** for your speech by adding a preview of those main ideas to your central idea. An example of a blueprint is, "Toxic waste dumping is a major environmental problem in the United States today. It endangers animals and poisons the water that humans drink." Preview the ideas in the same order you plan to discuss them in the speech.

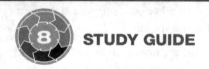 **STUDY GUIDE**

MEET YOUR OBJECTIVES

8.1 Select and narrow a topic for a speech.
Brainstorm, read, and listen to find topic ideas. Effective speech topics are appropriate for your audience, yourself, and your occasion.

8.2 Write an audience-centered specific-purpose statement for a speech.
A specific-purpose statement begins, "At the end of my speech, the audience will…" and describes a single measurable action the audience should take. It should guide you during all speech preparation activities.

8.3 State a central idea for a speech.
A central idea summarizes the topic of your speech with direct, specific language in a complete declarative sentence.

8.4 Apply three ways of generating main ideas from a central idea.

Divide your central idea into main ideas by asking yourself if the central idea has logical divisions, if there are several reasons the central idea is true, and if the central idea can be supported with a series of steps.

THINK ABOUT THESE QUESTIONS

1. **Self Assessment** Refer to Table 8.1. For each of the audiences listed in the left-hand column, generate at least one additional audience-centered topic.

2. **Ethics Assessment** You overhear another student describing her paper about abolishing the death penalty and the book she used to research it. Would it be ethical to "borrow" her topic and consult the book she mentioned to prepare a speech for your public-speaking class?

3. **Critical Assessment** Use information from this chapter to critique and rewrite, if needed, the following specific-purpose statements. After you have made necessary corrections, pick one statement and use it to practice generating a central idea and main points.

    (1) At the end of my speech, the audience will know more about the Mexican Free-Tailed Bat.

    (2) I will explain some differences in nonverbal communication between Asian and Western cultures.

    (3) At the end of my speech, the audience will be able to list some reasons for xeriscaping one's yard.

    (4) At the end of my speech, the audience will be able to prepare a realistic monthly budget.

    (5) The advantages and disadvantages of living in a college dormitory.

GATHERING SUPPORTING MATERIAL

OBJECTIVES

9.1 Describe how personal knowledge and experience can serve as a source of supporting material for a speech.

9.2 Locate and evaluate Internet resources for a speech.

9.3 Explain how to use online databases to find supporting material for a speech.

9.4 Describe traditional library holdings that can provide supporting material for a speech.

9.5 Summarize how to conduct an effective interview.

9.6 Explain five strategies for a methodical research process.

Creating a successful speech requires knowledge of both the sources and the types of supporting material that speechmakers typically use.

PERSONAL KNOWLEDGE AND EXPERIENCE

9.1 Describe how personal knowledge and experience can serve as a source of supporting material for a speech.

You might give a speech about a skill or hobby in which you are an expert. Or you might talk on a subject with which you have had some personal experience. In these cases, you may be able to provide some effective supporting materials from your own knowledge and experience. As an audience-centered speaker, you should realize that personal knowledge often has the additional advantage of heightening your credibility in the minds of your listeners.

THE INTERNET

9.2 Locate and evaluate Internet resources for a speech.

When facing a research task, most people turn first to the Internet. Understanding how to locate and evaluate various types of Internet resources can help make your search for supporting material more productive.

Locating Internet Resources

You have undoubtedly used Google to access material on the Web. If you feel overwhelmed by the number of sites a Google search can yield, a more specialized **vertical search engine** can help you narrow your search. For example, Google Scholar indexes academic sources, and Indeed indexes job sites. You can also use various strategies to narrow your results. For example, try enclosing your search phrase in quotation marks or parenthesis so that your search yields only those sites on which the exact phrase appears.

Exploring Internet Resources

As you begin to explore the search results you've generated, you will discover a wide variety of sites—from Web pages that try to sell you something, to the official sites of government agencies and news organizations. One clue to the type of site you have found is the **domain**, indicated by the last three letters of the site's URL (for example, *.com* or *.org*).

The following are common categories of Web sites.[1]

- **Commercial.**   The purpose of this type of Web site is to sell products or services. The domain is often *.com*. News and entertainment sites also often have *.com* domains.
- **Country codes.**   Web sites from countries other than the United States include a country code. For example, Great Britain is *.uk* and Canada is *.ca*.
- **Educational.**   This type of site provides information about an educational entity. The domain is usually *.edu*.
- **Government.**   The purpose of this type of Web site is to provide information produced by government agencies, offices, and departments. The domain is usually *.gov*.
- **Military.**   Information about or from the military is usually indicated by Internet addresses that end in *.mil*.
- **Organizational.**   The purpose of this type of Web site is to advocate a group's point of view. The domain is usually *.org*.

Evaluating Internet Resources

No search strategy can ensure the quality of the sites you discover. As you begin to explore sites, you need to evaluate them according to a consistent standard. The following six criteria can serve as such a standard.[2]

ACCOUNTABILITY   Find out what individual or organization is responsible for the Web site.

- The individual or organization responsible for the site may be clear from the title of the site and/ or its URL.
- See whether the site is signed.
- Follow links or search the author's name to determine his or her expertise and authority.
- If the site is unsigned, search for a sponsoring organization. Follow links, search the organization's name, or consider the domain to determine reputability.
- If you cannot identify or verify the author or sponsor of a Web site, be extremely wary of the site.

ACCURACY   It may be difficult to determine whether the information a site contains is accurate unless you are an expert in the area the site addresses. These steps can help.

- Consider whether the author or sponsor is a credible authority. If so, the information is more likely to be accurate.

- Assess the care with which the site has been written. A site should be relatively free of writing errors.
- Conduct additional research into the information on the site. You may be able to verify or refute the information by consulting another resource.

OBJECTIVITY   Objectivity is related to accountability. Once you know who is accountable for a site, consider the interests, philosophical or political biases, and the source of financial support for the author or sponsor of the site. The more objective the author, the more credible the facts and information presented. Consider, too, any advertisements on the site that might influence its content.

TIMELINESS   Look for evidence that the site has recent posts or has been kept current. At the bottom of many sites, you will find a statement specifying when the site was created and when it was last updated. When you are concerned with factual data, the more recent, the better.

USABILITY   The site should load fairly quickly. The layout and design of the site should facilitate its use. Also consider whether there is a fee to gain access to any of the information on the site.

DIVERSITY   An inclusive Web site will be free of material that communicates bias against any gender, ethnicity, race, culture, or sexual orientation; and against people with disabilities.[3]

No discussion of evaluating Internet resources would be complete without mentioning *Wikipedia*, the resource that often appears as the first hit from a Web search. *Wikipedia* can be useful for general information about current events and new technology that may not find its way into print resources for years. But keep in mind that because anyone, regardless of expertise, can add to or change the content of a *Wikipedia* entry, the site's reliability and appropriateness for academic use are limited. For this reason, many instructors consider *Wikipedia* an inappropriate source of information for student speeches.

QUICK CHECK

Evaluate Internet Resources

- I know who is accountable for the Web site.
- I can verify the accuracy of the information.
- The site is objective.
- The site is current.
- The site is easy to use and provides links to other sites.
- The site is culturally diverse and free of bias.

ONLINE DATABASES

9.3   Explain how to use online databases to find supporting material for a speech.

Online databases provide access to bibliographic information, abstracts, and full texts for a variety of resources. Like Web sites, online databases are reached via a networked computer. Unlike

Web sites, however, most databases are restricted to the patrons of libraries that subscribe to them. Your library may subscribe to several or all of the following popular full-text, searchable databases:

- **ABI/Inform Global.**   This resource offers many full-text articles in business and trade publications from 1971 to the present.
- **Academic Search Complete.**   This popular database offers many full-text articles from 1887 to the present, covering a wide variety of subjects.
- **JSTOR.**   This is a multi-subject, full-text database of journal articles from the first volume to the present.
- **LexisNexis Academic.**   Focusing on business and law, this database provides many full-text articles from newspapers, magazines, journals, newsletters, and wire services. Dates of coverage vary.
- **Newspaper Source.**   This database offers many full-text articles from more than 40 U.S. and international newspapers; television and radio news transcripts from CBS News, CNN, CNN International, FOX News, NPR, and others; and selected full-text articles from more than 330 regional (U.S.) newspapers.

TRADITIONAL LIBRARY HOLDINGS

9.4   Describe traditional library holdings that can provide supporting material for a speech.

Despite the rapid development of Internet and database resources, the more traditional holdings of libraries, both paper and electronic, remain rich sources of supporting material.

The key to finding library materials is the *card catalog*. You can access the computerized card catalog of most libraries from your own computer before you even enter the library. The catalog will supply each book's *call number*, which you will need to find the book. Once you have the call number, you are ready to venture into the library to obtain the item you want. It is a good idea to become familiar with your library's layout before you have to do research under the pressure of a deadline.

- **Books**   Libraries' collections of books are called the **stacks**. The stacks are organized by call numbers. Many libraries offer a location guide or map to help you find the floor or section of the stacks housing the books with the call numbers you are interested in.

    Do not wait until the last minute to conduct library research for your speech. Increasing numbers of libraries are beginning to house some of their stacks off-site. You may have to fill out a request form and allow some wait time before a book becomes available to you.
- **Reference resources**   The call numbers of print reference resources will have the prefix *ref*, indicating that they are housed in the reference section of the library. Print reference resources are usually available only for in-house research and cannot be checked out. Reference librarians are often able to suggest print or electronic resources that you might otherwise overlook. Try to visit the library during hours when a librarian is available to help you.

INTERVIEWS

9.5 Summarize how to conduct an effective interview.

Consider interviewing a person who might know the answers to some of the important questions raised by your speech topic. But before you decide that an interview is necessary, be sure that your questions cannot be answered by doing online or library research.

Preparing for the Interview

If you decide that only an interview can give you the material you need, you should prepare for it in advance.

DETERMINE YOUR PURPOSE   Specifically, what do you need to find out?

ARRANGE A MEETING   Once you have a specific purpose for the interview, decide whom you need to speak with, and arrange a meeting.

Using your electronic device to record audio or video of the interview can free you from having to take copious notes and make it easy to refer to the interviewee's exact words. If you are considering recording the interview, ask for the interviewee's okay during this initial contact. If the person does not grant permission, be prepared to gather your information without electronic assistance.

PLAN YOUR QUESTIONS   Before your interview, find out as much as you can about both your subject and the person you are interviewing. Prepare questions that take full advantage of the interviewee's specific knowledge of your subject.

Combine closed-ended and open-ended questions. Open-ended questions often follow closed-ended questions: When the person you are interviewing answers a closed-ended question with a simple "yes" or "no," you may wish to follow up by asking "Why?"

Conduct the Interview

Follow the suggestions in the How To box to conduct effective interviews.

Conduct an Effective Interview

- **Dress appropriately.** Conservative, businesslike clothes show that you are serious about the interview.
- **Bring note-taking supplies.** Even if you plan to record the interview, you may want to turn off the recording at some point or your device may malfunction.
- **Arrive a few minutes ahead of schedule.** Be prepared, however, to wait patiently, if necessary.
- **Prepare your equipment.** If you have decided to use a recorder, set up your device as needed. If you are going to take written notes, get your supplies ready.
- **Follow your plan.** Use the questions you have prepared as a guide. Listen carefully to the person's answers, and ask follow up questions. Request clarification if needed.
- **Be ready to adjust the plan.** Listen closely to the person's words and their intended meaning. If the interviewee mentions something you did not think of, don't be afraid to pursue the point.

After an Interview

As soon as possible after the interview, read through your notes carefully and revise any portions that may be illegible or unclear. If you recorded the interview, save and label the file with the date and the interviewee's name. Send a note of thanks to your interviewee.

RESEARCH STRATEGIES

9.6 Explain five strategies for a methodical research process.

Methodical research strategies will make finding supporting material easier and more efficient. You need to develop a preliminary bibliography, locate potential resources, evaluate their usefulness, take notes, and identify possible visual aids.

Develop a Preliminary Bibliography

Creating a **preliminary bibliography** or list of promising resources should be your first goal. You will probably discover more resources than you will actually look at or refer to in your speech; at this stage, the bibliography simply serves as a menu of possibilities. How many resources should you list in a preliminary bibliography for, say, a 10-minute speech? A reasonable number might be 10 or 12. If you have many more, you may feel overwhelmed. If you have fewer, you may have too little information.

You will need to develop a system for keeping track of your resources. Web browsers let you bookmark pages for future reference and ready access. If you are searching an online catalog or database, you can compile a record of the references you find. Also consider using a Web-based **citation manager** to collect, organize, and format citation information for the resources you discover. RefWorks and EndNote are examples of popular citation managers that may be available through your university library.

Locate Resources

You should have no trouble obtaining full texts of resources from the Web and online databases. If you have used a citation manager, you can locate resources by simply clicking on your entries. For other items in your preliminary bibliography, you will need to locate the resources yourself. Refer back to the discussion earlier in this chapter on traditional library holdings.

Evaluate the Usefulness of Resources

It makes sense to gauge the potential usefulness of your resources before you begin to read more closely and take notes. The instructions in the How To box can help you.

Evaluate Source Material

Before you read in depth and take notes from your resources, take a little time to figure out which ones are likely to be of most use for your speech.

- Glance over the tables of contents of books.
- Flip quickly through books or scroll Web sites or database articles to note any charts, graphs, or other materials that could be used as visual aids.
- Skim a key chapter or two. Skim Web sites and articles as well.

Take Notes

Once you have located, previewed, and ranked your resources, you are ready to begin more careful reading and note-taking.

- Beginning with the resources that you think have the greatest potential, record any examples, statistics, opinions, or other supporting material that might be useful to your speech. Depending on the resource, you can save supporting material on your computer, photocopy it, or print it out.
- If you copy a phrase, sentence, or paragraph verbatim from a source, be sure to put quotation marks around it. You may need to know later whether it is a direct quote or a paraphrase. (This information will be obvious, of course, on printouts or photocopies.)
- To avoid the possibility of committing unintentional plagiarism, keep track of your sources as you take notes.

Identify Possible Presentation Aids

In addition to discovering verbal and written supporting material in your sources, you may also find charts, graphs, photographs, and other potentially valuable visual material.

QUICK CHECK
Research Strategies

- Develop a preliminary bibliography.
- Locate sources.
- Assess the usefulness of sources.
- Take notes.
- Identify possible presentation aids.

STUDY GUIDE

MEET YOUR OBJECTIVES

9.1   Describe how personal knowledge and experience can serve as a source of supporting material for a speech.

Personal experiences and knowledge can provide some of your source material and can raise your credibility with the audience.

9.2   Locate and evaluate Internet resources for a speech.

Vertical search engines can narrow results of an Internet search. Use the domain to help you evaluate the accountability, accuracy, objectivity, timeliness, usability, and diversity of Internet materials.

9.3   Explain how to use online databases to find supporting material for a speech.

Online databases offer abstracts and full-text of articles, news, and more. They are typically available through libraries that subscribe to them.

9.4   Describe traditional library holdings that can provide supporting material for a speech.

Books, stored in the library's stacks, and references, stored in the reference room, can provide information unavailable online. Be sure to allow plenty of time for library research.

9.5   Summarize how to conduct an effective interview.

Prepare carefully for an interview by researching and creating a list of questions. Treat interviewees' time with respect, and listen carefully to their responses to questions in order to follow up with clarification questions.

9.6   Explain five strategies for a methodical research process.

To conduct an efficient search, you need to develop a preliminary bibliography, locate resources, evaluate the usefulness of resources, take notes, and identify possible presentation aids.

THINK ABOUT THESE QUESTIONS

1.   **Self Assessment** Explain how you might use each of the five key sources of supporting material to help you develop an informative speech on how to choose a new computer.
2.   **Ethics Assessment** Electronic and print indexes and databases sometimes include abstracts of books and articles rather than full texts. If you have read only the abstract of a source, is it ethical to include that source in your preliminary bibliography?
3.   **Critical Assessment** You neglected to record complete bibliographic information for one of your best information sources, a journal article you found on a database. You discover your omission as you are reviewing your outline just before you deliver your speech, and now you have no way to look up the information. How can you solve your problem in an ethical way? What are some ways you could have avoided this problem?

SUPPORTING YOUR SPEECH

OBJECTIVES

10.1 Explain the importance and best practices for using illustrations in a speech.

10.2 Differentiate how descriptions and explanations are used in speeches.

10.3 Summarize how to give definitions in a speech.

10.4 Describe how to use analogies in a speech.

10.5 Recap effective ways to present statistics in a speech.

10.6 Describe the value of using opinions in a speech.

10.7 Select the best supporting material for a speech.

Once you have gathered a variety of appropriate supporting material, you will need to decide how to use your information to best advantage in your speech. Be sure to use oral or written citations as described in Chapter 4 to properly acknowledge sources of supporting material.

USE ILLUSTRATIONS

10.1 Explain the importance and best practices for using illustrations in a speech.

A story or anecdote—an **illustration**—almost always guarantees audience interest by appealing to their emotions.

- **Brief illustrations** are often no longer than a sentence or two. A series of brief illustrations can sometimes have more impact than either a single brief illustration or a more detailed, extended illustration. In addition, although an audience could dismiss a single illustration as an exception, two or more strongly suggest a trend or norm.
- **Extended illustrations** are longer and more detailed than brief illustrations; they resemble a story. They are vividly descriptive, and they have a plot—which includes an opening, complications, a climax, and a resolution. Longer stories take more time, but they can be dramatic and emotionally compelling. Extended illustrations can work well as speech introductions.
- A **personal illustration**—sharing an experience with the audience—can help a speaker gain conviction and credibility. If you have had personal experience with your topic, consider relating that experience to the audience.
- **Hypothetical illustrations** describe situations or events that have not actually occurred but that *might* happen. Remember from Chapter 4 that ethical speakers introduce hypothetical illustrations with a phrase such as, "Imagine that ..."

To use illustrations effectively, be certain that your stories are directly relevant to the idea or point they are supposed to support. They should be typical of a situation or represent a trend. The best illustrations are personal ones that your listeners can imagine experiencing themselves. Include enough details to make the story vivid and specific to listeners.

USE DESCRIPTIONS AND EXPLANATIONS

10.2   Differentiate how descriptions and explanations are used in speeches.

A **description** provides the details that allow audience members to develop a mental picture of what a speaker is talking about. Good descriptions are vivid, accurate, and specific; they make people, places, and events come alive for the audience.

An **explanation** is a statement that clarifies how something is done or why it exists in its present form or existed in its past form. Speakers who discuss or demonstrate processes of any kind rely at least in part on explanations of *how* those processes work. Explaining *why* involves giving causes or reasons for a policy, principle, or event. Explaining why some condition or event exists provides an analysis that often leads to better solutions.

Use Descriptions and Explanations

● Avoid overuse. Alternate descriptions and explanations with other types of support.
● Keep them brief. Supply only the necessary details.
● Be specific. Use vivid, concrete language that appeals to the senses.

PROVIDE DEFINITIONS

10.3   Summarize how to give definitions in a speech.

Definitions have two uses in speeches. First, a speaker should be sure to define any and all specialized, technical, or little-known terms in his or her speech. Such definitions are usually achieved by *classification*, the kind of definition you would find in a dictionary. Second, a speaker may define a term by showing how it works or how it is applied in a specific instance—what is known as an *operational definition*. For example, a speaker may define a disease such as rickets by explaining the effects on people who develop it, rather than using a dictionary definition.

Use Definitions Effectively

● Use a definition only when needed.
● Make definitions immediately and easily understandable to your audience.
● Be certain that your definition and your use of a term are consistent throughout a speech.

USE ANALOGIES

10.4   Describe how to use analogies in a speech.

An **analogy** is a comparison. Like a definition, an analogy increases understanding; unlike a definition, it deals with relationships and comparisons—between the new and the old, the unknown and the known, or any other pair of ideas or things. Analogies can help your listeners understand unfamiliar ideas, things, and situations by showing how these are similar to something they already know.

Literal Analogies

A **literal analogy** is a comparison between two similar things. For example, one speaker compared crustaceans, such as shrimp, to insects, noting that both are arthropods.[1] Literal analogies can help listeners from a different culture understand terms they may not be familiar with. To help the audience understand, make sure the two things you compare in a literal analogy are very similar.

Figurative Analogies

If you describe the relationships among a group of coworkers as a seething snake pit, filled with hissing gossip and sharp-fanged attacks, you are using a **figurative analogy**. A figurative analogy relies on imaginative insights, rather than on facts or statistics, so it is not considered hard evidence. Be sure that the essential similarity between the two objects in a figurative analogy is readily apparent. For example, the main similarity between the snake pit and the work group is the strife between those in the same group. If the comparison is unclear, your audience can end up wondering what in the world you are talking about.

USE STATISTICS AS SUPPORT

10.5   Recap effective ways to present statistics in a speech.

Just as three or four brief examples may be more effective than just one, a statistic that represents hundreds or thousands of individuals may be more persuasive still. **Statistics** can help a speaker express the magnitude or seriousness of a situation. Or statistics can express the relationship of a part to the whole.

Use Reliable Sources

Statistics can be exploited to support almost any conclusion desired. As an ethical speaker, your goal is to cite *reputable, authoritative*, and *unbiased* sources.

- Reputable sources are those known to have expertise in research or the subject of the statistics.
- The most authoritative source is the *primary source*—the original collector and interpreter of the data. Go to the primary source as often as possible. Do not assume that a secondhand account, or *secondary source*, has reported the statistic accurately and fairly.

- Unbiased sources have no special interest in their statistics supporting any particular viewpoint. Government statistics and those from independent sources are generally considered unbiased.

As you evaluate your sources, try to find out how the statistics were gathered. For example, if a statistic relies on a sample, how was the sample taken? Sample sizes and survey methods do vary widely, but most legitimate polls involve samples of 500 to 2,000 people, selected at random from a larger population.

Interpret Statistics Accurately

People are often swayed by statistics that sound good but have, in fact, been wrongly calculated or misinterpreted. Both as a user of statistics in your own speeches and as a consumer of statistics in articles, books, and speeches, be constantly alert to what the statistics actually mean.

Making Statistics Understandable and Memorable

You can make your statistics easier to understand and more memorable in several ways.

- Dramatize a statistic by strategically choosing the perspective from which you present it. Does a genetic condition protect 10 percent of people from high blood pressure or, more dramatically, make it easier for 90 percent to develop high blood pressure?[2]
- Compact a statistic, or express it in units that are more meaningful or more easily understandable to your audience. For example, you might express the amount of the national debt as the number of dollars per American adult.[3]
- Explode statistics. Exploded statistics are created by adding or multiplying related numbers—for example, cost per unit times number of units. Because it is larger, the exploded statistic seems more significant than the original figures from which it was derived.
- Compare statistics. Comparing your statistic with another heightens its impact.
- Use visual aids to present your statistics. Displaying numbers in a table or graph in front of your listeners enables them to more easily grasp the statistics.

QUICK CHECK

Select Effective Statistics

- Are the data from primary sources?
- Are the sources reputable, unbiased, and authoritative?
- Did you interpret the statistics accurately?
- Are the statistics easy to understand?
- Are they memorable?
- Can you convert the statistics into visual aids?

USE OPINIONS

10.6 Describe the value of using opinions in a speech.

Expert testimony, the testimony of a recognized authority, can add a great deal of weight to your arguments. You may quote experts directly or paraphrase their words, as long as you are careful not to alter the intent of their remarks.

Like illustrations, **lay testimony**, the opinions of nonexperts, can stir an audience's emotions. And, although neither as authoritative nor as unbiased as expert testimony, lay testimony is often more memorable.

Another way to make a point memorable is to include a **literary quotation** in your speech. You can easily access quotation dictionaries on the Web and in the reference sections of most libraries. Brief, pointed quotations usually have greater audience impact than longer ones.

Here are a few suggestions for using opinions effectively in your speeches.

- Be certain that any authority you cite is unbiased and an expert on the subject you are discussing.
- Cite your source properly, and be sure to quote accurately.
- Use opinions that are representative of prevailing opinion.
- Limit quotations to one or two per speech.

SELECT THE BEST SUPPORTING MATERIAL

10.7 Select the best supporting material for a speech.

As previously discussed, you should consider accountability, accuracy, objectivity, timeliness, usability, and diversity in evaluating any supporting material you hope to use. How do you decide what to use and what to eliminate?

- **Magnitude.** Bigger is better. The larger the numbers, the more convincing your statistics will be. The more experts who support your point of view, the more your expert testimony will command your audience's attention.
- **Relevance.** The best supporting material is whatever is the most relevant to your listeners, or the "closest to home."
- **Concreteness.** If you need to discuss principles and theories, explain them using concrete examples and specific statistics.
- **Variety.** A mix of illustrations, opinions, definitions, and statistics is much more interesting and convincing than the exclusive use of any one type of supporting material.
- **Humor.** Unless the topic is serious or somber, audiences usually appreciate a touch of humor in an example or opinion.
- **Suitability.** Your final decision about whether to use a certain piece of supporting material will depend on its suitability to you, your speech, the occasion, and your audience.

STUDY GUIDE

MEET YOUR OBJECTIVES

10.1 Explain the importance and best practices for using illustrations in a speech.

Illustrations catch listeners' interest. Brief, extended, personal, and hypothetical illustrations can also help your audience understand your message.

10.2 Differentiate how descriptions and explanations are used in speeches.

Use vivid descriptions to help listeners visualize people, places, things, or events. Use specific, concrete explanations to show *how* something works or the reasons *why* something occurs or exists.

10.3 Summarize how to give definitions in a speech.

Use easily understandable dictionary and operational definitions to help audiences understand unfamiliar terms.

10.4 Describe how to use analogies in a speech.

Use literal analogies to compare two similar things and imaginative figurative analogies to help listeners understand things that share fewer similar characteristics.

10.5 Recap effective ways to present statistics in a speech.

Use statistics from reliable sources, interpret them accurately, and make them understandable to listeners by dramatizing, compacting, exploding, comparing, or showing visuals of them.

10.6 Describe the value of using opinions in a speech.

Expert and lay testimony and literary quotations can help you use the opinions of others to support your own message.

10.7 Select the best supporting material for a speech.

The best supporting materials are those with the most magnitude, relevance to the audience, concreteness, variety, and suitability to the audience. Some humor is usually welcome.

THINK ABOUT THESE QUESTIONS

1. **Self Assessment** Describe how you can use each of the six types of supporting material described in this chapter in your next speech.
2. **Ethics Assessment** Before adding to your speech an illustration that shares personal information about a friend, should you ask your friend for permission?
3. **Critical Assessment** Tony found just the statistics he needs on the Internet. What information does he need to evaluate the statistics?

PART 4
Crafting a Speech

ORGANIZING YOUR SPEECH

You must organize your ideas in logical patterns to ensure that your audience can follow, understand, and remember what you say.

ORGANIZE YOUR MAIN IDEAS

11.1 List and describe five patterns for organizing the main ideas of a speech.

In Chapter 8, you learned how to generate a preliminary plan for your speech by determining whether your central idea had logical divisions, could be supported by several reasons, or could be explained by identifying specific steps.

Now you are ready to decide which of your main ideas to discuss first, second, and so on. Five organizational patterns are most common:

- topical
- chronological
- spatial
- cause and effect
- problem–solution

Organize Ideas Topically

If your central idea has natural divisions, you can often organize your speech topically. Speeches on such diverse topics as factors to consider when selecting a mountain bike, types of infertility treatments, and the various classes of ham-radio licenses all could reflect **topical organization**.

Natural divisions are often basically equal in importance. It may not matter which point you discuss first, second, or third. You can simply arrange your main points as a matter of personal preference.

At other times, you may wish to emphasize one point more than the others. You can use one of the following guidelines.

- **Primacy** To use the principle of **primacy**, discuss your most important or convincing idea *first*. The beginning of your speech can be the most important position if your listeners are either unfamiliar with your topic or hostile toward your central idea.

- **Recency** According to the principle of **recency**, the point discussed *last* is the one audiences will remember best. If your audience is at least somewhat knowledgeable about and generally favorable toward your topic and central idea, you should probably organize your main points according to recency.

- **Complexity** If your main points range from simple to complicated, it makes sense to arrange them in order of **complexity**, progressing from the simple to the most complex.

Order Ideas Chronologically

When your central idea can be supported by a series of steps, chronological organization often makes sense. **Chronological organization** is organization by time or sequence; your steps are ordered according to when each occurred or should occur. Historical and how-to speeches are usually organized chronologically.

You can choose to organize your main points either from earliest to most recent (forward in time) or from recent events back into history (backward in time). The progression you choose depends on your personal preference and on whether you want to use the principles of primacy or recency to emphasize the beginning or the end of the sequence. However, how-to explanations are usually arranged forward in time, as a sequence or series of steps to follow from beginning to end.

Arrange Ideas Spatially

A speaker who relies on **spatial organization** arranges ideas according to their physical locations or directions. Speeches on such diverse subjects as the National Museum of the American Indian, the travels of Robert Louis Stevenson, and the structure of an atom can all be organized spatially. It does not usually matter whether the speaker chooses to progress up or down, east or west, forward or back, as long as ideas are developed in a logical order.

Organize Ideas to Show Cause and Effect

A speech using a **cause-and-effect organization** might first identify a situation and then discuss the effects that result from it (cause→effect). For example, a speaker might describe a recent drought and then discuss its effects.

A speech could also present a situation and then seek its causes (effect→cause). Such a speaker might describe the recent drought and then talk about factors that created it.

According to the recency principle, the cause–effect pattern emphasizes the effects; the effect–cause pattern emphasizes the causes.

Organize Ideas by Problem and Solution

If you want to emphasize how best to *solve* a problem, you will probably use a **problem–solution organization**. Like causes and effects, problems and solutions can be discussed in either order:

- If listeners are already fairly aware of a problem but uncertain how to solve it, you will probably discuss the problem first and then the solution(s).
- If your audience knows about an action or program that has been implemented but does not know the reasons for its implementation, you might select a solution–problem pattern of organization.

Combine Multiple Patterns

You can combine several of these patterns. For example, you may use an overall cause–effect pattern, discussing a drought and then its effects. However, you may order your points about the effects topically—talking first about effects on crops, then on animals, and then on people—or spatially, talking about effects in different geographical areas.

Acknowledge Cultural Differences in Organization

Although the five patterns discussed so far in this chapter are typical in regard to the way speakers in the United States are expected to organize and process information, they are not necessarily typical of all cultures.[1] In fact, each culture teaches its members patterns of thought and organization that are considered appropriate for various occasions and audiences.

In general, U.S. speakers tend to be more linear and direct than speakers from other cultures. Semitic speakers may support their main points by pursuing tangents that could seem "off topic" to many U.S. speakers. Speakers in some Asian cultures may only allude to a main point through a circuitous route of illustration and parable. And speakers from Romance and Russian cultures tend to begin with a basic principle and then move to facts and illustrations that they only gradually connect to a main point.

Of course, these are broad generalizations. But as an audience-centered speaker, you might acknowledge or even adapt elements of your organizational strategy when presenting to listeners from a culture other than your own.

And as a listener who recognizes the existence of cultural differences, you can better appreciate and understand that a speaker from another culture may not be disorganized but simply using organizational strategies different from those presented in this chapter.

ORGANIZE YOUR SUPPORTING MATERIAL

11.2 Explain how to integrate supporting material into a speech.

Suppose you have decided what supporting material to use and have identified the ideas in your speech that require support. Now you realize that in support of your second main idea you have an illustration, two statistics, and an opinion. In what order should you present these items?

You can sometimes use the five standard organizational patterns to arrange your supporting material. Illustrations, for instance, may be organized chronologically, as one speaker did when discussing technology:

> …miracle has followed upon miracle—from a television in every home in the 1950s, to the launching of the first communications satellite in the 1960s, to the introduction of cable TV in the 1970s, the rise of personal computers in the 1980s, the Internet in the 1990s, and social media in the 2000s.[2]

At other times, however, none of the five patterns may seem suited to the supporting materials you have. In those instances, you may need to turn to an organizational strategy more specifically adapted to your supporting materials. These strategies include (1) primacy or recency, (2) specificity, (3) complexity, and (4) "soft" to "hard" evidence.

Primacy or Recency

As we've discussed, the principles of primacy and recency can help you determine whether to put a main idea at the beginning or the end of your speech. You can use these principles to order your supporting material, too.

Suppose that you have several statistics to support a main point. All are relevant and significant, but one is especially gripping. You might opt to arrange the statistics in your speech according to recency, saving the most dramatic one for last.

Specificity

Sometimes your supporting material will range from very specific examples to more general overviews of a situation. You may either offer your specific information first and end with your general statement or make the general statement first and support it with specific evidence.

Complexity

You've seen that moving from the simple to the complex is one way you can organize your main ideas. The same method of organization may also be applied to supporting material. In many situations, it makes sense to start with the simplest ideas, which are easy to understand, and work up to more complex ones. For example, you might give a definition of an unfamiliar term before presenting a graph of statistics related to that term.

Soft to Hard Evidence

Supporting material can also be arranged from "soft" to "hard."

- **Soft evidence** rests on opinion or inference. Hypothetical illustrations, descriptions, explanations, definitions, analogies, and opinions are usually considered soft.
- **Hard evidence** includes factual examples and statistics.

QUICK CHECK

Organizing Your Supporting Material

- Primacy: most important material first
- Recency: most important material last
- Specificity: from specific information to general overview or from general overview to specific information
- Complexity: from simple to more complex material
- Soft to hard evidence: from opinion or hypothetical illustration to fact or statistic

To organize supporting materials in this order, you might tell a brief story about your own experience trying to use less water during a drought and then present expert opinions about the best ways to use less water, followed by statistics about which methods actually do use the least water. Soft to hard organization of supporting material relies chiefly on the principle of recency—that the last statement is remembered best. In this example, your listeners would be likely to remember the most effective ways they can save water.

ORGANIZING YOUR PRESENTATION FOR THE EARS OF OTHERS: SIGNPOSTING

11.3 Use verbal and nonverbal signposts to organize a speech for the ears of others.

You have a logically ordered, fairly complete plan for your speech. But if you delivered the speech at this point, your audience might become frustrated or confused as they tried to figure out your organizational plan. So your next task is to develop **signposts**—organizational cues for your audience's ears. Signposts include previews, transitions, and summaries.

One significant difference between writing and public speaking is that public speaking is more repetitive. Audience-centered speakers need to remember that listeners, unlike readers, cannot go back to review a missed point. Using signposts like previews, summaries, and transitions not only helps your audience follow the organization of your speech but also builds repetition of key points into your speech, so that audience members are less likely to miss them.

Previews

As its name indicates, a **preview** is a statement of what is to come. Previews help to ensure that audience members will first anticipate and later remember the important points of a speech. Two types of previews are usually used in speeches: initial previews and internal previews.

INITIAL PREVIEWS   An **initial preview** is a statement of what the main ideas of the speech will be. As discussed in Chapter 8, it is usually presented in conjunction with the central idea at or near the end of the introduction, as a *blueprint* for the speech. For example, your blueprint might be, "The recent drought is the cause of severe problems for all living things in our area. It has produced ill effects on crops, animals, and people."

INTERNAL PREVIEWS   In addition to using previews near the beginning of their speeches, speakers also use them at various points throughout. These **internal previews** introduce and outline ideas that will be developed as the speech progresses. Sometimes speakers phrase internal previews in the form of questions they plan to answer. The question in this example provides an internal preview.

> …the question remains, what can we do, as potential travelers and potential victims, to protect ourselves?[3]

Just as anticipating an idea helps audience members remember it, mentally answering a question helps them plant the answer firmly in their minds.

Transitions

A **transition** is a verbal or nonverbal signal that a speaker has finished discussing one idea and is moving to another.

VERBAL TRANSITIONS   A speaker can sometimes make a **verbal transition** simply by repeating a key word from a previous statement or by using a synonym or a pronoun that refers to a prior key word or idea. This type of transition is often used to make one sentence flow smoothly into the next. (The previous sentence itself is an example: "This type of transition" refers to the sentence that precedes it.)

Other verbal transitions are words or phrases that show relationships between ideas. Note the italicized transitional phrases in the following examples:

- *In addition to* transitions, previews and summaries are *also* considered to be signposts.
- *Not only* does plastic packaging use up our scarce resources, but it contaminates them *as well.*
- *In other words*, as women's roles have changed, they have *also* contributed to this effect.
- *In summary*, Fanny Brice is probably the best-known star of Ziegfeld's Follies.
- *Therefore*, I recommend that you sign the grievance petition.

Simple enumeration (*first, second, third*) can also point up relationships between ideas and provide transitions.

HOW TO   Transition to Your Conclusion

One type of transitional signpost that can occasionally backfire and do more harm than good is one that signals the end of a speech. The words *finally* and *in conclusion* give the audience implicit permission to stop listening, and they often do. Better strategies for moving into your conclusion include the following:

- Repeat a key word or phrase.
- Use a synonym or pronoun that refers to a previous idea.
- Offer a final summary.
- Refer back to the introduction of your speech.

NONVERBAL TRANSITIONS   A **nonverbal transition** can occur in several ways, sometimes alone and sometimes in combination with a verbal transition. A change in facial expression, a pause, an altered vocal pitch or speaking rate, and a movement all may indicate a transition.

For example, a speaker talking about the value of cardiopulmonary resuscitation began his speech with a powerful anecdote about a man suffering a heart attack at a party. No one knew how to help, and the man died. The speaker then looked up from his notes and paused, while maintaining eye contact with his audience. His next words were, "The real tragedy of Bill Jorgen's death was that it should not have happened." His pause, as well as the words that followed, indicated a transition into the body of the speech.

Most good speakers use a combination of verbal and nonverbal transitions to move from one point to another through their speeches. You will learn more about nonverbal communication in Chapter 17.

Summaries

Like a preview, a **summary**, or recap of what has been said, provides your listeners with additional exposure to your ideas and can help ensure that they will grasp and remember your message. Most speakers use two types of summaries: *the final summary* and *the internal summary*.

FINAL SUMMARY   A **final summary** restates the main ideas of a speech and gives an audience their *last* exposure to those ideas. It occurs just before the end of a speech, often doing double duty as a transition between the body and the conclusion. Your final summary should leave listeners in no doubt as to the important points of your speech.

INTERNAL SUMMARY   As the term suggests, an **internal summary** occurs within the body of a speech; it restates the ideas that have been developed up to that point. You can use an internal summary after discussing two or three points, to keep those points fresh in the minds of the audience as the speech progresses.

Speakers often combine an internal summary and internal preview to form a transition. For example, you might say, "Now that I've detailed the devastating crop losses caused by the drought and the large losses in animal populations, I want to tell you what the drought has done to us humans."

QUICK CHECK

Types of Signposts

Initial previews
Internal previews
Verbal transitions
Nonverbal transitions
Final summaries
Internal summaries

11 STUDY GUIDE

MEET YOUR OBJECTIVES

11.1   List and describe five patterns for organizing the main ideas of a speech.
For North American audiences, the five most common patterns of organization include topical, chronological, spatial, cause and effect, and problem–solution. These patterns are sometimes combined. Other organizational patterns may be favored in different cultures.

11.2 Explain how to integrate supporting material into a speech.

You can organize the supporting material for each main idea according to one of the five common patterns: primacy, recency, specificity, complexity, or soft-to-hard evidence.

11.3 Use verbal and nonverbal signposts to organize a speech for the ears of others.

Signposts include verbal and nonverbal transitions, previews, and summaries. They are used to help you communicate your organization to your audience.

THINK ABOUT THESE QUESTIONS

1. **Self Assessment** Take notes while listening to either a live or recorded speech. Try to determine the speaker's organizational strategy, the reasons for it, and its effectiveness. Note whether the speaker used signposts to help you follow the organization.

2. **Ethics Assessment** Is there an ethical distinction between primacy and recency? If a speaker has a statistic that offers overwhelming evidence of the severity of a given problem, for example, is it ethical for the speaker to save that statistic for last? Should the speaker reveal immediately to the audience how severe the problem really is?

3. **Critical Assessment** Which organizational pattern is most appropriate for the main points suggested in the following central ideas?
   - There are at least three distinct theories about what happened to the dinosaurs.
   - The new university multipurpose sports center will be divided into several zones to serve students' activity needs.

OUTLINING AND REVISING YOUR SPEECH

OBJECTIVES

12.1   Develop a preparation outline for a speech.

12.2   Prepare speaking notes for a speech.

DEVELOP A PREPARATION OUTLINE

12.1   Develop a preparation outline for a speech.

Although few speeches are written in paragraph form, most speakers develop a detailed **preparation outline** that includes the following:

- central idea
- main ideas
- supporting material
- the speech's specific purpose
- introduction
- conclusion
- signposts
- references (optional)

To begin your preparation outline, you might turn to the strategy of clustering, which is a visual mapping strategy. Write down all of your main ideas, subpoints, and supporting material for the speech. Then use geometric shapes and arrows to indicate the logical relationships among them.

Whatever technique you choose to begin your outline, your ultimate goal is to produce a plan that lets you judge the unity and coherence of your speech, determine how well the parts fit together, and see how smoothly the speech flows. The following suggestions will help you complete your preparation outline. However, keep in mind that different instructors may have different expectations for what an outline must include and how it is formatted. Be sure to understand and follow your own instructor's guidelines.

Write Your Preparation Outline in Complete Sentences

Unless you write your preparation outline in complete sentences, you will have trouble judging the coherence of the speech. Moreover, complete sentences will help during your early rehearsals. If you write cryptic phrases, you may not remember what they mean.

Use Standard Outline Form

Although you did not have to use standard outline form when you began to outline your ideas, you need to do so now. **Standard outline form** lets you see at a glance the exact relationships among the various main ideas and supporting material in your speech. It is an important tool for evaluating your speech. To produce a correct outline, follow the instructions in the How To box and the model in Figure 12.1.

HOW TO — Use Standard Outline Form

- Properly indent main ideas, subpoints, and supporting material, as shown in Figure 12.1.
- Use at least two subpoints, if any, for each main idea. Logic dictates that you cannot divide anything into one part.
- If you have only one piece of supporting material, incorporate it into the subpoint or main idea that it supports.
- If you have only one subpoint, incorporate it into the main idea above it.
- If you have more than five subpoints, you may want to place some of them under another point. An audience will remember your ideas more easily if they are divided into blocks of no more than five.

Write and Label Your Specific Purpose at the Top of Your Outline

Do not work the specific purpose into the outline itself. Instead, label it and place it at the top of the outline. Your specific purpose can serve as a yardstick by which to measure the relevance of each main idea and piece of supporting material. Everything in the speech should contribute to your specific purpose.

Add the Blueprint, Key Signposts, Introduction, and Conclusion to Your Outline

Place the introduction after the statement of your specific purpose, the blueprint immediately following the introduction, the conclusion after the outline of the body of the speech, and other signposts within the outline.

Figure 12.1   Standard Outline Form. It is unlikely that you will subdivide beyond the level of lowercase letters (a, b, c) in most speech outlines, but next would come numbers in parentheses and then lowercase letters in parentheses.

```
I.  First main idea
    A.  First subpoint of I
    B.  Second subpoint of I
        1.  First subpoint of B
        2.  Second subpoint of B
            a.  First subpoint of 2
            b.  Second subpoint of 2
II. Second main idea
```

Analyze Your Preparation Outline

Once you have completed your preparation outline, you can use it to help you analyze and possibly revise the speech. The following questions can help you in this critical thinking task.

- **Does the speech as outlined fulfill the purpose you have specified?** If not, revise the specific purpose or change the direction and content of the speech itself.
- **Are the main ideas logical extensions (natural divisions, reasons, or steps) of the central idea?** If not, revise either the central idea or the main ideas.
- **Do the signposts enhance the flow of one idea into the next?** If not, change or add previews, summaries, or transitions.
- **Does each subpoint provide support for the point under which it falls?** If not, then either move or delete the subpoint.
- **Is your outline form correct?** For a quick reference, refer to the How To box and Figure 12.1.

Having considered these questions, you are ready to rehearse your speech, using the preparation outline as your first set of notes.

PREPARE SPEAKING NOTES

12.2 Prepare speaking notes for a speech.

As you rehearse your speech, you will find that you need your preparation outline less and less. Both the structure and the content of your speech will become set in your mind. At this point, you are ready to prepare a shorter outline to serve as your **speaking notes**.

This shorter outline should provide enough clearly formatted details to ensure that you can make your presentation as you have planned in your preparation outline. However, your speaking notes should not be so detailed that you will be tempted to read them word for word to your audience. Use the following suggestions for developing speaking notes.

Choose Your Technology

You may decide to display your outline on a smartphone or electronic tablet—perhaps using one of several apps available for speaking notes—or you may opt to use old-fashioned note cards. Regardless of which technology you select, make sure your letters and words are large enough to be read easily.

Even if you plan to use an electronic option, you may want to have a backup outline on note cards in case of technical difficulty. Note cards don't rustle like paper does, and they are small enough to hold in one hand. Write on one side only, and number your note cards in case they get out of order just before or during your speech.

Use Standard Outline Form

Make your introduction, each main idea, and your conclusion distinct. Standard outline form will help you find your exact place when you glance down at your speaking notes. You will know, for example, that your second main idea is indicated by "II."

Include Shortened Versions of Your Introduction and Conclusion

Even if your instructor does not require you to include your introduction and conclusion on your preparation outline, include abbreviated versions of them in your speaking notes. You might feel more comfortable delivering the presentation if you have your first and last sentences written out in front of you.

Include Your Central Idea, Not Your Purpose Statement

Be sure to include your central idea. But as you will not actually say your specific-purpose statement during your presentation, do not put it in your speaking notes.

Include Supporting Material and Signposts

Write out in full any statistics and direct quotations and their sources. Write your key signposts—your initial preview, for example—to ensure that you will not have to flounder awkwardly as you move from one idea to another.

Include Delivery Cues

Write in your speaking notes such cues as "Louder," "Pause," or "Walk two steps left." However, be sure to write or format your delivery cues in a different color or font so you don't confuse them with your verbal content.

QUICK CHECK

Preparation Outline and Speaking Notes

Preparation	**Delivery**
Use complete sentences.	Use single words and phrases.
Write out full introduction and conclusion.	Write first and last sentences only.
Add blueprint, all signposts.	Keep only statistics, direct quotations, and key signposts.
Place specific-purpose statement at the top.	Omit specific-purpose statement.

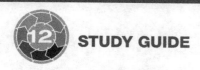 **STUDY GUIDE**

MEET YOUR OBJECTIVES

12.1 Develop a preparation outline for a speech.

A preparation outline includes your carefully organized main ideas, subpoints, and supporting material; it may also include your specific purpose, introduction, blueprint, internal previews and summaries, transitions, and conclusion. Write each of these elements in complete sentences and standard outline form. Use the preparation outline to begin rehearsing your speech and to help you revise it, if necessary.

12.2 Prepare speaking notes for a speech.

Speaking notes are less detailed than a preparation outline and usually include supporting material, signposts, and delivery cues.

THINK ABOUT THESE QUESTIONS

1. **Self Assessment** Different instructors have different expectations for outline content and format. Obtain your own instructor's guidelines and compare them to the advice in this chapter.
2. **Ethics Assessment** Can a speaker legitimately claim that a speech is extemporaneous if he or she has constructed a detailed preparation outline?
3. **Critical Assessment** Myorka thinks it is silly to worry about using correct outline form for either her preparation outline or her speaking notes. Do you agree with her? Why or why not?

DEVELOPING AN INTRODUCTION

PURPOSES OF INTRODUCTIONS

13.1   Explain the functions of a speech introduction.

Many speakers think that drafting an introduction is the first task in preparing a speech, but it is actually more often the last. A key purpose of your introduction is to provide an overview of your message. How can you do that until you know what the message is going to be? Nonetheless, the introduction is too important to the overall success of your speech to be left to chance or last-minute preparation.

The introduction provides your audience with important first impressions of you and your speech, and its main job is to convince your audience to listen to you. Specifically, a good introduction must perform five important functions:

1. Get the audience's attention.
2. Introduce the subject.
3. Give the audience a reason to listen.
4. Establish your credibility.
5. Preview your main ideas.

Get the Audience's Attention

A key purpose of the introduction is to gain favorable attention for your speech. Because listeners form their first impressions of a speech quickly, the introduction must capture their attention and cast the speech in a favorable light or the rest of the speech may be wasted on them.

We emphasize *favorable* attention for a good reason. It is possible to gain an audience's attention with words or presentation aids that alienate or disgust them so that they become irritated instead of interested in what you have to say.

Be creative in your speech introductions. But also use common sense in deciding how best to gain the favorable attention of your listeners. Alienating them is even worse than boring them.

Introduce the Subject

The most obvious purpose of an introduction is to introduce the subject of a speech. Within a few seconds after you begin your speech, the audience should have a pretty good idea of what you are going to talk about.

The best way to ensure that your introduction does indeed introduce the subject of your speech is to include a statement of your central idea in the introduction.

Give the Audience a Reason to Listen

After you have captured the attention of your audience and introduced the topic, you have to give the audience some reason to want to listen to the rest of your speech. An unmotivated listener quickly tunes out.

You can help establish listening motivation by showing the members of your audience how the topic affects them. One criterion for determining the effectiveness of your supporting material is *proximity*, the degree to which the information affects your listeners directly. Just as proximity is important to supporting materials, it is also important to speech introductions. "This concerns me" is a powerful reason to listen.

It does not matter so much *how* or *when* you demonstrate proximity. But it is essential that you do at some point establish that your topic is of vital personal concern to your listeners.

HOW TO

Establish Credibility during Your Introduction

1. **Be well prepared.**   Thorough research and good organization help give the audience confidence that you know what you are talking about.
2. **Appear confident.**   Speaking fluently while maintaining eye contact does much to convey a sense of confidence. If you seem to have confidence in yourself, your audience will have confidence in you.
3. **Tell the audience of your personal experience with your topic.**   Instead of considering you boastful, most audience members will listen to you with respect.

Establish Your Credibility

Credibility is a speaker's believability. A credible speaker is one whom listeners judge to be a believable authority and a competent speaker. A credible speaker is also someone listeners believe they can trust. If you can establish your credibility early in a speech, it will help motivate your audience to listen.

Preview Your Main Ideas

A final purpose of the introduction is to preview the main ideas of your speech. An initial preview statement usually comes near the end of the introduction, included in or immediately following a statement of the central idea. This preview statement allows your listeners to anticipate the main ideas of your speech, which in turn helps ensure that they will remember those ideas after the speech.

As we discussed in Chapter 11, an initial preview statement is an organizational strategy called a *signpost*. Just as signs posted along a highway tell you what is coming up, a signpost in your

QUICK CHECK

Purposes of Introductions

Purpose	Method
Get the audience's attention.	Avoid alienating, disgusting, or irritating listeners.
Introduce the subject.	Present your central idea to your audience.
Give the audience a reason.	Tell your listeners how the topic directly affects them.
Establish your credibility.	Prepare, look confident, and offer your credentials.
Preview your main ideas.	Tell your audience what you are going to tell them.

speech tells the listeners what to expect by enumerating the ideas or points that you plan to present. Identifying your main ideas helps organize the message and enhances listeners' learning.

EFFECTIVE INTRODUCTIONS

13.2 List and discuss methods for introducing a speech.

There are several effective methods for developing speech introductions. Not every method is appropriate for every speech, but chances are that you can discover among these alternatives at least one type of introduction to fit the topic and purpose of your speech, whatever they might be.

Use Illustrations or Anecdotes

An illustration or **anecdote** can provide the basis for an effective speech introduction. In fact, if you have an especially compelling illustration that you had planned to use in the body of the speech, you might do well to use it in your introduction instead. A relevant and interesting anecdote will introduce your subject and almost invariably gain an audience's attention.

Provide Startling Facts or Statistics

A second method of introducing a speech is to use a startling fact or statistic. Grabbing an audience's attention with the extent of a situation or problem invariably catches listeners' attention, motivates them to listen further, and helps them remember afterward what you had to say.

Use Quotations

Using an appropriate quotation to introduce a speech is a common practice. Often another writer or speaker has expressed an opinion on your topic that is more authoritative, comprehensive, or memorable than what you can say. However, only use quotes if they are extremely interesting, compelling, or very much to the point. Using a quotation to open every speech can become a lazy habit.

Use Humor

Humor, handled well, can be a wonderful attention-getter. It can help relax your audience and win their goodwill for the rest of the speech.

If your audience is linguistically diverse or composed primarily of listeners whose first language is not English, you may want to choose an introduction strategy other than humor. Much humor is created by verbal plays on words and may not translate well with people who do not speak the same language.

Certain subjects are also inappropriate for humor. It would hardly be appropriate to open a speech on world hunger, Sudden Infant Death Syndrome, or rape, for example, with a funny story. Used with discretion, however, humor can provide a lively, interesting, and appropriate introduction for many speeches.

Ask Questions

Questions are commonly combined with another method of introduction. Either by themselves or in tandem with another method of introduction, questions can provide effective openings for speeches. For example, you may ask, "Do you know how many of today's college graduates hold more than $100,000 in student debt?" and then present a startling statistic that answers your question.

When using a question to open a speech, you will generally use a **rhetorical question**, the kind to which you don't expect an answer. A rhetorical question can prompt your listeners' mental participation in your introduction, getting their attention and giving them a reason to listen.

Refer to Historical Events

Perhaps you could begin a speech by drawing a relationship between a historic event that happened on this day and your speech objective. An Internet search for "this date in history" will reveal many possible events. Be sure the historical reference you choose is clearly linked to the purpose of your speech.

Refer to Recent Events

If your topic is timely, a reference to a recent event can be a good way to open your speech. An opening taken from a recent news story can take the form of an illustration, a startling statistic, or even a quotation. Referring to a recent event increases your credibility by showing that you are knowledgeable about current affairs.

"Recent" does not necessarily mean a story that broke just last week or even last month. An event that occurred within the past year or so can be considered recent. Even a particularly significant event that is slightly older can qualify.

Use Personal References

A reference to yourself can take several forms. You might reveal your reason for interest in the topic. You might express appreciation at having been asked to speak. Or you might share a personal experience. Whatever form of personal reference you use, the purpose is to establish a bond between you and your audience.

Refer to the Occasion

References to the occasion are often made at weddings, birthday parties, dedication ceremonies, and other such events. A reference to the occasion can also be combined with other methods of introduction, such as an illustration or a rhetorical question.

Refer to Preceding Speeches

If your speech is one of several being presented on the same occasion, you will usually not know until shortly before your own speech what other speakers will say. Few experiences will make your stomach sink faster than hearing a speaker just ahead of you speak on your topic. Worse still, that speaker may even use some of the same supporting materials you had planned to use. When this situation occurs, it may be wise to refer to a preceding speech. If the other speaker has spoken on a topic closely related to your own, you can draw an analogy. In a sense, your introduction becomes a transition from that earlier speech to yours.

QUICK CHECK

Effective Introduction Techniques

- Use an illustration or anecdote.
- Present startling facts or statistics.
- Use an appropriate quotation.
- Use humor.
- Begin with a rhetorical question.
- Refer to historical events or recent events.
- Use personal references.
- Refer to the occasion or to preceding speeches.

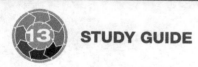 **STUDY GUIDE**

MEET YOUR OBJECTIVES

13.1 Explain the functions of a speech introduction.
A good introduction captures the audience's attention, gives the audience a reason to listen, introduces your subject, establishes your credibility, and previews your main ideas.

13.2 List and discuss methods for introducing a speech.

Effective introduction methods include illustrations, startling facts or statistics, quotations, humor, questions, references to historical events, references to recent events, personal references, references to the occasion, or references to preceding speeches, used alone or in combination.

THINK ABOUT THESE QUESTIONS

1. **Self Assessment** How could you motivate your classroom audience to listen to you on each of these topics: cholesterol, Elvis Presley, the history of greeting cards, ozone depletion, distracted driving?

2. **Ethics Assessment** Mardi tells her public-speaking classmate Shanna about an illustration she thinks will make an effective introduction. Shanna thinks it would make a great introduction for her own speech, which is on a different topic. Shanna learns that she is scheduled to speak before Mardi. She badly wants to use the illustration that Mardi discovered. Can she ethically do so?

3. **Critical Assessment** Nikai is planning an informational speech in which he will demonstrate Native American musical instruments. What is a good way for Nikai to introduce his speech?

DEVELOPING A CONCLUSION

PURPOSES OF CONCLUSIONS

14.1 Explain the functions of a speech conclusion.

Just as most fireworks displays end with a grand finale, your speech should end, not necessarily with fireworks, but with a conclusion worthy of your well-crafted message. Long after you finish speaking, your audience is likely to remember the effect, if not the content, of your closing remarks. An effective conclusion will serve two purposes: It will summarize the speech, and it will provide closure.

Summarize the Speech

The end of your speech is your last chance to impress the central idea on your audience, and it provides you the opportunity to do it in such a way that they cannot help but remember. The conclusion is also your last chance to repeat your main ideas for the audience.

REEMPHASIZE THE CENTRAL IDEA IN A MEMORABLE WAY   Many of the most memorable quotations from famous speakers were the conclusions of their speeches. When on July 4, 1939, New York Yankees legend Lou Gehrig addressed his fans in an emotional farewell to a baseball career cut short by a diagnosis of amyotrophic lateral sclerosis (ALS), he concluded with the memorable line, "I may have had a tough break, but I have an awful lot to live for."[1] With practice, most people can prepare similarly effective conclusions. Begin by using the ideas in Chapter 15 for using language to make your statements more memorable. The end of your speech is your last chance to impress the central idea on your audience. Do it in such a way that they cannot help but remember it.

RESTATE THE MAIN IDEAS   Most speakers summarize their main ideas in the first part of the conclusion or as part of the transition between the body of the speech and its conclusion.

Provide Closure

Probably the most obvious purpose of a conclusion is to provide **closure**—to let the audience know that the speech has ended. Use verbal and nonverbal signals, such as those described in the How To box, to let your audience know you are closing your speech.

Signal the End of Your Speech

Verbal Signals

- Use such transition words and phrases as *finally*, *for my last point*, *in conclusion*, and so on.
- Avoid giving listeners permission to "tune out" too soon.
- Follow transition quickly with the final statement of the speech.

Nonverbal Signals

- Pause between the body of your speech and its conclusion.
- Slow your speaking rate.
- Move out from behind the podium to make a final impassioned plea.
- Use a falling vocal inflection for your final statement.

MOTIVATE THE AUDIENCE TO RESPOND   At the beginning of your speech, your goal was to motivate your audience to listen to you. At the end, you want to motivate listeners to respond to your message. If your speech is informative, you may want the audience to think about the topic or to research it further. If your speech is persuasive, you may want your audience to take some sort of appropriate action—write a letter, buy a product, make a telephone call, or get involved in a cause. In fact, an *action* step is essential to the persuasive organizational strategy called the *motivated sequence*, discussed in Chapter 24. When audience members feel they are or could be personally involved or affected, they are more likely to respond to your message.

QUICK CHECK

Purposes of Conclusions

Summarize the Speech

- Reemphasize the central idea in a memorable way.
- Restate your main ideas.

Provide Closure

- Give verbal or nonverbal signals of the end of the speech.
- Motivate the audience to respond.

EFFECTIVE CONCLUSIONS

14.2   List and discuss methods for concluding a speech.

Effective conclusions may employ illustrations, quotations, personal references, or any of the other methods used for introductions. In addition, there are at least two other distinct ways of concluding a speech: with a reference to the introduction and with an inspirational appeal or challenge.

Refer to the Introduction

The following are excellent ways to provide closure in the conclusion:

- Finish a story from your introduction.
- Answer your opening rhetorical question.
- Remind the audience of the startling fact or statistic you presented in the introduction.

Like bookends, a related introduction and conclusion provide unified support for the ideas in between.

Issue an Inspirational Appeal or Challenge

Another way to end your speech is to issue an inspirational appeal or challenge to your listeners, rousing them to a high emotional pitch. Dr. Martin Luther King Jr. stirred his audience with the famous inspirational closing to his "I Have a Dream" speech. When you use this method, the conclusion becomes the climax toward which your entire speech builds.

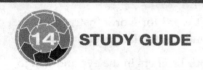

STUDY GUIDE

MEET YOUR OBJECTIVES

14.1 Explain the functions of a speech conclusion.
The two main purposes of the conclusion are to summarize your speech in a memorable way and to provide closure.

14.2 List and discuss methods for concluding a speech.
Conclusions may take any one of the forms used for introductions. In addition, you can refer to the introduction or make inspirational appeals or challenges in your conclusion.

THINK ABOUT THESE QUESTIONS

1. **Self Assessment** Knowing that you have recently visited the Vietnam Veterans Memorial in Washington, D.C., your American history professor asks you to make a brief presentation to the class about the Wall: its history; its symbolic meaning; and its impact on the families, comrades, and friends of those memorialized there. Write both an introduction and a conclusion for this speech.
2. **Ethics Assessment** You believe the closing words used by a famous speaker would provide the most effective conclusion for your own speech. How could you ethically use the famous speaker's inspirational words?
3. **Critical Assessment** Many public-speaking instructors advise against saying, "in conclusion."[2] Why might you want to avoid this transitional phrase?Study Guide

USING WORDS WELL

15

OBJECTIVES

15.1 Describe three differences between oral and written language styles.

15.2 List and explain three ways to use words effectively.

15.3 Discuss how to adapt your language style to diverse listeners.

15.4 List and explain three types of memorable word structures.

ORAL VERSUS WRITTEN LANGUAGE STYLE

15.1 Describe three differences between oral and written language styles.

Your instructor has probably told you not to write your speech out word for word. Instructors say this because there are at least three major differences between oral and written language styles.

- **Oral style is more personal.**   When speaking, you can look your listeners in the eye and talk to them directly. That personal contact affects your speech and your verbal style. As a speaker, you are likely to use more pronouns (*I, you*) than you would in writing. You are also more likely to address specific audience members by name.

- **Oral style is less formal.**   Memorized speeches usually sound as if they were written because the words and phrases are longer, more complex, and more formal than those used by most speakers. Oral style, on the other hand, is characterized by "looser construction, repetition, rephrasing, and comment clauses ('you know')...."[1]

- **Oral style is more repetitious.**   When you're listening to a speech, you don't have opportunities to stop and reread, look up unfamiliar words, or ask for help if you don't understand. For this reason, an oral style is and should be more repetitious. Speakers build in repetition in previews, transitions, and summaries to make sure that listeners will grasp their messages.

USE WORDS EFFECTIVELY

15.2 List and explain three ways to use words effectively.

Although your speech will be more personal, less formal, and more repetitive than a term paper written on the same topic, you will still want to ensure that your message is clear, accurate, and memorable. Your spoken words should be specific, concrete, simple, and correct.

Use Specific, Concrete Words

Specific words are often concrete words, which appeal to one of our five senses, whereas general words are often abstract words, which refer to ideas or qualities. A linguistic theory known as *general semantics* holds that the more concrete your words are, the clearer your communication will be.[2]

Specific, concrete nouns create memorable images; likewise, specific, concrete verbs can be especially effective. It is more memorable, for example, to say, "The leaves of plants in the fields are shredded to tatters," than to say, "The hailstorm severely damaged crops."

Use Simple Words

The best language is often the simplest. Your words should be immediately understandable to your listeners. Don't try to impress them with jargon and pompous wording.

Use Words Correctly

Your effectiveness with your audience depends in part on your ability to use the English language correctly. If you are unsure of a grammatical rule, refer to a good English usage handbook. If you are unsure of a word's pronunciation, use a dictionary. Major online dictionaries provide recordings of the correct pronunciation of words. Consult dictionaries to confirm word meanings, too, but remember that language operates on two levels.

1. The **denotation** of a word is its literal meaning, the definition you find in a dictionary. For example, the denotation of the word *notorious* is "famous."

2. The **connotation** of a word is the meaning we associate with the word, based on our past experiences. *Notorious* connotes fame for some dire deed. *Notorious* and *famous* are not really interchangeable. It is just as important to consider the connotations of the words you use as it is to consider the denotations. When considering connotations, remember these two points:

   - Audience members may have their own personal connotations for words, based on their own experiences. Personal meanings are difficult to predict, but as a public speaker you should be aware of the possibility of triggering audience members' personal connotations, especially when you are discussing highly emotional or controversial topics.

   - If your audience includes people whose first language is not English, to whom the nuances of connotation may not be readily apparent, explain your intentions in more detail, rather than relying on word associations.

Use Words Concisely

Your goal should be to use only as many words as are necessary to convey your message. The How To box offers suggestions for using language concisely.

- Eliminate phrases that add no meaning to your message, such as "In my opinion" (just state the opinion) or "Before I begin, I'd like to say" (you've already begun—just say it).
- Avoid narrating your speaking technique. There is no need to say, "Here's an interesting story that I think you will like." Just tell the story.
- Avoid using a long phrase when a short one will do. Here are some examples:

Instead of saying...	Say...
So, for that reason	So
Due to the fact	Because
But at the same time	But
In the final analysis	Finally

ADAPT YOUR LANGUAGE STYLE TO DIVERSE LISTENERS

15.3 Discuss how to adapt your language style to diverse listeners.

To communicate successfully with the diverse group of listeners who comprise your audience, make sure your language is understandable, appropriate, and unbiased.

Use Understandable Language

Even if you and all your public-speaking classmates speak English, you probably speak many varieties of the language, including the following.

- **Ethnic vernacular**, such as "Spanglish," African American Vernacular English (AAVE), or Cajun
- **Regionalisms**, words or phrases specific to one part of the country but rarely used in quite the same way in other places
- **Jargon**, the specialized language of a particular profession or interest group

If you give a speech to others who share your ethnic, regional, or professional background, you can communicate successfully with them using these specialized varieties of English. However, if you give a speech to a more diverse audience, use **Standard American English (SAE)**. SAE is the language taught by schools and used in the media, business, and the government in the United States. *Standard* does not imply that SAE is inherently right and all other forms are wrong, but only that it conforms to a standard most speakers of American English can readily understand.

Use Respectful Language

Be careful to avoid any language that could be found offensive to people of particular ethnic, racial, and religious backgrounds; sexual orientations; women; or people with disabilities. A speaker whose language defames any group, or whose language might be otherwise considered offensive or risqué, is not only speaking unethically but also running a great risk of antagonizing audience members.

Use Unbiased Language

Even speakers who would never dream of using overtly offensive language may find it difficult to avoid language that stereotypes or discriminates more subtly. Sexist language falls largely into this second category.

For example, not many years ago, a sentence such as, "Everyone should bring *his* book to class tomorrow" was considered appropriate to refer to people of all genders. Now we use both pronouns ("Everyone should bring *his* or *her* book to class tomorrow") or reword the sentence so that it is plural and thus gender neutral ("All students should bring *their* books to class tomorrow").

The use of a masculine noun to refer generically to all people is also considered sexist. Instead of masculine nouns such as *waiter, chairman, fireman,* and *congressman,* choose gender-neutral alternatives such as *server, chair, firefighter,* and *member of Congress.*

In addition, you should avoid sexist language that patronizes or stereotypes people. It is not always easy to avoid biased language. For example, suppose that Dr. Pierce is a young, African American, female M.D. If you avoid mentioning her age, race, and gender when referring to her, you may reinforce your listeners' stereotypical image of a physician as middle-aged, white, and male. But if you *do* mention these factors, you may be suspected of implying that Dr. Pierce's achievement is unusual. There is no easy answer to this dilemma or others like it. You will have to consider your audience, your purpose, and the occasion when deciding how best to identify Dr. Pierce.

QUICK CHECK

Use Words Well

- Are your words specific and concrete?
- Do you use the English language correctly?
- Are your words concise?
- Is your language immediately understandable to your listeners?
- Is your language respectful to your audience?
- Is your language unbiased?

CRAFT MEMORABLE WORD STRUCTURES

15.4   List and explain three types of memorable word structures.

Memorable speeches are stylistically distinctive. They create arresting images. And they have what a marketing-communication specialist has termed "ear appeal."[3] In Chapter 25 you will learn about strategies for creating humor in a speech.

Create Figurative Images

Figurative language deviates from the ordinary, expected meanings of words to make a description or comparison unique, vivid, and memorable. Common figurative language includes metaphors, similes, and personification.

Use Metaphors and Similes   A **metaphor** is an implied comparison. For example, "He is a snake." A **simile** is a less direct comparison that includes the word *like* or *as*. For example, "His lies make him as slippery as a snake."

Use Personification   **Personification** is the attribution of human qualities to inanimate things or ideas. If, for example, you say that the sun smiles upon your city, you are personifying the sun.

Speakers often turn to figurative language in times that are especially momentous or overwhelming; times when literal language seems insufficient. In the hours and days after the September 11, 2001, terrorist attacks on the United States, various speakers used metaphorical phrases, including "one more circle of Dante's hell," "nuclear winter," and "the crater of a volcano" to describe the site of the destroyed World Trade Center in New York City.[4] Such language is sometimes referred to as **crisis rhetoric**.

Create Drama

Another way you can make phrases and sentences memorable is to use them to create drama in your speech—to keep the audience in suspense or to catch them slightly off guard by phrasing something in a way that differs from the way they expect you to say it.

Sentence Length   Use a short sentence to express a vitally important thought. Short, simple sentences can have much the same power as short, simple words.

Omission   Use **omission**. Leave out a word or phrase that the audience expects to hear. For example, a speaker might omit the words *mountain climbers* to add drama, saying, "Only 5 of the 16 who set out to scale the peak would ever return." When you use omission, be sure listeners will understand the words you leave out.

Inversion   Use **inversion**. Reverse the expected word order of a phrase or sentence. John F. Kennedy used inversion by changing the usual subject-verb-object sentence pattern to object-subject-verb in this brief declaration from his inaugural speech: "This much we pledge."[5]

Suspension   When you read a mystery novel, you are held in suspense until you reach the end and learn "who did it." The stylistic technique of verbal suspension does something similar, using a key word or phrase at the end of a phrase or sentence, rather than at the beginning.

Some years ago, the Coca-Cola Company used **suspension** as the cornerstone of its worldwide advertising campaign by making *Coke* the last word in the slogan, "Things go better with Coke," rather than the expected order, "Coke goes better with everything."

Create Cadence

Cadence is the rhythm of language. Take advantage of language rhythms, not by speaking in singsong patterns, but by using such stylistic devices as repetition, parallelism, antithesis, and alliteration.

Repetition   Using a key word or phrase more than once gives rhythm and power to your message and makes it memorable. Perhaps the best-known modern example of **repetition** in a speech is the declaration that became the title of Martin Luther King Jr.'s most famous civil rights speech.

Parallelism **Parallelism** occurs when two or more clauses or sentences have the same grammatical pattern. In a 2013 speech to Israeli students in Jerusalem, President Barack Obama used parallelism by starting sentences with the words *we are*:

> We are enriched by faith. We are governed not simply by men and women, but by laws. We are fueled by entrepreneurship and innovation. And we are defined by a democratic discourse....[6]

Antithesis The word *antithesis* means "opposition." In language style, a sentence that uses **antithesis** has two parts with parallel structures but contrasting meanings. Speakers have long realized the dramatic potential of antithesis. For example, Journalist David Brooks once wrote, "Don't think about what you want from life, think about what life wants from you."[7] An antithetical statement is a good way to end a speech. The cadence will make the statement memorable.

Alliteration **Alliteration** is the repetition of a consonant sound (usually an initial consonant) several times in a phrase, clause, or sentence (for example, *discipline and direction; confidence and courage*).

Onomatopoeia **Onomatopoeia** is when a word is pronounced like its meaning (for example, *buzz* or *murmur*).

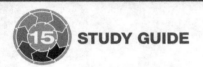 **STUDY GUIDE**

MEET YOUR OBJECTIVES

15.1. Describe three differences between oral and written language styles.
Oral language is more personal and less formal than written language. Speakers must also provide their audiences with more repetition than writers need to use.

15.2. List and explain three ways to use words effectively.
Effective speakers use specific, concrete words to evoke clear mental images in their listeners. They also choose simple, respectful, unbiased words. As a speaker, be sure to use words correctly and to keep in mind the connotations of words, as well as their dictionary definitions. And, finally, eliminate unnecessary words and phrases.

15.3. Discuss how to adapt your language style to diverse listeners.
Use language your listeners can understand. Use respectful language to avoid offending your audience. Use unbiased language to communicate in a sensitive way.

15.4. List and explain three types of memorable word structures.
Create arresting images through such figures of speech as metaphors, similes, and personification. Create drama by using short sentences for important ideas, strategically omitting words, and structuring sentences with key words at the end to create suspense. Use repetition, alliteration, parallelism, antithesis, and onomatopoeia to create memorable rhythm or cadence.

THINK ABOUT THESE QUESTIONS

1. **Self Assessment** A friend asks for advice on making the word choices in her speech as effective as possible. Offer her at least three suggestions, based on this chapter, for using words effectively.

2. **Ethics Assessment** Is it ethical to change your variety of English in order to adapt to your listeners' expectations? Why or why not?

3. **Critical Assessment** How would a 750-word paper and a 3- to 5-minute speech that both have the same topic, central idea, main idea, and supporting material differ?

METHODS OF DELIVERY

OBJECTIVES

16.1 Explain how to effectively deliver a manuscript speech.

16.2 Summarize the advantages and disadvantages of memorizing a speech.

16.3 Describe how to deliver an effective impromptu speech.

16.4 Explain the benefits of delivering a speech extemporaneously.

There are four basic methods of delivery from which a speaker can choose: manuscript speaking, memorized speaking, impromptu speaking, and extemporaneous speaking. Table 16.1 found at the end of this chapter offers an overview of the advantages and disadvantages of each method.

MANUSCRIPT SPEAKING

16.1 Explain how to effectively deliver a manuscript speech.

Reading from a manuscript word-for-word is usually a poor way to deliver a speech. Although it may provide some insurance against forgetting part of the speech, **manuscript speaking** is rarely done well enough to be interesting.

However, in a few situations some speeches should be read. For example, during times of crisis, statements to the press by government or business leaders should be crafted precisely, rather than

HOW TO

Deliver a Manuscript Speech

- Mark your manuscript to remind yourself where to pause or to emphasize certain words.
- Type your speech in short, easy-to-scan phrases so you can maintain as much eye contact with the audience as possible. Look directly at them, not over their heads.
- Use your index finger to keep your place in the manuscript when you look up.
- Do not read your speech too quickly; use your normal, natural speed of delivery.
- Vary the rhythm and inflection of your voice to sound natural.
- Use appropriate and natural gestures and movement.

tossed off casually. One advantage of reading from a manuscript is that you can choose words very carefully when dealing with a sensitive and critical issue.

The key to giving an effective manuscript speech is to sound as though you are not giving a manuscript speech. Use the tips in the How To box to help you.[1]

MEMORIZED SPEAKING

16.2 Summarize the advantages and disadvantages of memorizing a speech.

Memorized speaking sounds stiff, stilted, and over-rehearsed. You also run the risk of forgetting parts of your speech and awkwardly searching for words in front of your audience. And you won't be able to make on-the-spot adaptations to your listeners if your speech is memorized. Memorized speaking does, however, have the advantage of allowing you to have maximum eye contact with the audience.

If you are accepting an award, introducing a speaker, making announcements, or delivering other brief remarks, a memorized delivery style is sometimes acceptable. But, as with manuscript speaking, you must take care to make your presentation sound lively and interesting.

IMPROMPTU SPEAKING

16.3 Describe how to deliver an effective impromptu speech.

You have undoubtedly already delivered many impromptu presentations. Your response to a question posed by a teacher in class and your unrehearsed rebuttal to a comment made by a colleague during a meeting are examples of impromptu presentations. The impromptu method is often described as "thinking on your feet" or "speaking off the cuff." The advantage of **impromptu speaking** is that you can speak informally and maintain direct eye contact with the audience. But unless you are extremely talented or have learned and practiced the techniques of impromptu speaking, an impromptu speech usually lacks logical organization and thorough research. When you are called on to deliver an improvised or impromptu speech, the guidelines in the How To box can help ease you through it.

HOW TO   Make an Impromptu Speech

- **Consider your audience.** Who are the members of your audience? What do they expect you to say? What is the occasion of your speech?
- **Be brief.** One to three minutes is a realistic time frame for most impromptu situations. Some spur-of-the-moment remarks, such as press statements, may be even shorter.
- **Organize!** Effective impromptu speakers organize their ideas into an introduction, body, and conclusion. Consider using a simple organizational strategy such as chronological order or a topical pattern. A variation on the chronological pattern is discussing (1) what has happened in the past, (2) what is happening now, and (3) what may happen in the future.

Because there is no opportunity to conduct any kind of research before delivering an impromptu speech, you will have to speak from your own experience and knowledge. Remember, audiences almost always respond favorably to personal illustrations, so use any appropriate and relevant ones that come to mind. Do not make up information or provide facts or figures you're not certain about. An honest "I don't know" or a very brief statement is more appropriate. No matter how much knowledge you have, if your subject is at all sensitive or your information is classified, be careful when discussing it during your impromptu speech. If asked about a controversial topic, give an honest but noncommittal answer. You can always elaborate later, but you can never take back something rash you have already said. It is better to be careful than sorry!

EXTEMPORANEOUS SPEAKING

16.4   Explain the benefits of delivering a speech extemporaneously.

In **extemporaneous speaking**, you speak from a written or memorized general outline, but you do not have the exact wording in front of you or in your memory. You have rehearsed the speech so you know the key ideas and their organization, but not to the degree that the speech sounds memorized. An extemporaneous style is conversational; it gives your audience the impression that the speech is being created as they listen to it, and to some extent it is.

You develop an extemporaneous style by first rehearsing your speech, using as many notes as you need to help you remember your ideas. However, each time you rehearse, rely less and less on your notes. If you find yourself using the same words each time you rehearse, you're memorizing your speech; either stop rehearsing or consider other ways of expressing your ideas. By your final rehearsal, revise your speaking notes so you only need brief notes or notes for only lengthy quotations.

Table 16.1   Advantages and Disadvantages of Methods of Delivery

	Advantages	Disadvantages
Manuscript: reading a speech from a prepared text	You can craft the message carefully when dealing with sensitive or critical issues; you can be precise.	It takes considerable skill and practice to make the message sound interesting.
Memorized: giving a speech from memory without using notes	This method enables you to maintain direct eye contact with the audience. You can also move around freely.	May sound mechanical and over-rehearsed; you may forget parts of your speech; you cannot make on-the-spot adaptations.
Impromptu: delivering a speech without preparing in advance	You can speak informally and maintain direct eye contact with the audience. You can also easily adapt the speech to your audience.	May lack logical organization and thorough research; may be unimpressive.
Extemporaneous: knowing the major ideas, which have been outlined, but not memorizing the exact wording	Your speech is well organized and researched. It sounds spontaneous, yet appropriately polished.	It takes time to prepare and skill to deliver the speech well.

STUDY GUIDE

MEET YOUR OBJECTIVES

16.1 Explain how to effectively deliver a manuscript speech.

When precise wording is important, you may need to read a speech from a prepared text. Make your voice and gestures as natural as possible, and make eye contact with your audience, especially at the ends of sentences.

16.2 Summarize the advantages and disadvantages of memorizing a speech.

Giving a speech from memory allows maximum eye contact with the audience, but you risk sounding stiff, forgetting part of the speech, and being unable to adapt the speech to the audience.

16.3 Describe how to deliver an effective impromptu speech.

An unrehearsed speech allows informality and eye contact. Consider the audience, and organize your remarks accordingly. Keep your talk brief, use your own knowledge, and share information cautiously.

16.4 Explain the benefits of delivering a speech extemporaneously.

Because it seems spontaneous and is customized to the audience, the extemporaneous method is the most desirable in most situations. Speak from an outline without memorizing the exact words.

THINK ABOUT THESE QUESTIONS

1. **Self Assessment** Imagine you are an executive for a corporation. What business situations would call for you to deliver each of the four types of speeches described in this chapter?

2. **Ethics Assessment** Is it ethical to present a manuscript or memorized speech when you have been asked to present an extemporaneous speech?

3. **Critical Assessment** Roger was so nervous about his first speech that he practiced it until he could have given it in his sleep. He had some great examples, and his instructor had praised his outline. But as he gave his speech, he saw his classmates tuning out. What might he have done wrong, and how could he have rescued his speech?

NONVERBAL COMMUNICATION

OBJECTIVES

17.1 Make effective eye contact during a speech.

17.2 Use gestures effectively while speaking.

17.3 Move purposefully in ways that enhance your message while speaking.

17.4 Display an appropriate posture while delivering a speech.

17.5 Use facial expressions to enhance verbal messages.

17.6 Choose appropriate attire for making a speech.

EYE CONTACT

17.1 Make effective eye contact during a speech.

Of all the aspects of speech delivery discussed in this chapter, the most important one in a public-speaking situation for North Americans is eye contact.[1] Eye contact with your audience opens communication, keeps your audience interested, and makes you more believable. Each of these functions contributes to the success of your delivery. Eye contact also provides you with feedback about how your speech is coming across, so you can adapt it if needed. The How To box offers advice for effective eye contact.

GESTURES

17.2 Use gestures effectively while speaking.

Important points are emphasized with gestures. You also gesture to indicate places, enumerate items, and describe objects. Sometimes a gesture takes the place of a word.

Using Gestures Effectively

Here are some guidelines to consider when working on your delivery.

- **Stay natural.** Gestures should be *relaxed*, not tense or rigid. Your gestures should flow with your message. Avoid sawing or slashing through the air with your hands unless you are trying to emphasize a particularly dramatic point.

- **Be definite.** Gestures should appear *definite* rather than as accidental brief jerks of your hands or arms. If you want to gesture, go ahead and gesture. Avoid minor hand movements that will be masked by the lectern.

Make Eye Contact with Your Audience

- When it's time to speak, calmly walk to the lectern or to the front of the audience, pause briefly, and look at your audience before you say anything.
- Have your opening sentence well enough in mind that you can deliver it without looking at your notes or away from your listeners.
- Establish eye contact with the entire audience, not just with those in the front row or only one or two people.
- Look to the back as well as the front and from one side of your audience to the other, but avoid following a predictable pattern.
- Look at individuals, establishing person-to-person contact with them—not so long that it will make a listener feel uncomfortable, but long enough to establish the feeling that you are talking directly to that individual.
- Don't look over your listeners' heads; establish eye-to-eye contact.
- If your speech is being recorded and there is an audience present, look at your audience rather than only at the camera lens. If no audience is present, look into the camera lens as you deliver your speech.

- **Use gestures that are consistent with your message.** If you are excited, for example, gesture more vigorously.

- **Vary your gestures but don't overdo it.** Strive for *variety* and versatility in your use of gestures. Try not to use just one hand or one all-purpose gesture; try to use gestures for a variety of purposes.

- **Make your gestures appropriate to your audience and situation.** Gestures must be adapted to the audience. In more formal speaking situations, particularly when speaking to a large audience, bolder, more sweeping, and more dramatic gestures are appropriate. A small audience in a less formal setting calls for less formal gestures. When delivering a speech via video, such as in a videoconference, it's especially important not to use overly dramatic gestures. The camera lens is generally only a few feet away from you, which tends to amplify the intensity of your gestures and movements.

- **Adapt your gestures to audience cultural expectations.** Consider toning down your gestures for predominantly high-context listeners. Some Asian cultures place considerable emphasis on unspoken messages. Many European listeners are accustomed to speakers who are less animated in their use of gestures, movement, and facial expressions than is typical for Americans.

Keep one important principle in mind: Use gestures that work best for you. Don't try to be someone you are not. Your gestures should fit your own personality. It may be better to use no gestures—to just put your hands comfortably at your side—than to use awkward, distracting gestures or to try to counterfeit someone else's gestures. Your nonverbal delivery should flow from *your* message.

Gestures

The most effective gestures are

- natural and relaxed
- definite and varied
- consistent with your message
- unobtrusive
- coordinated with what you say
- appropriate to your audience and situation

MOVEMENT

17.3   Move purposefully in ways that enhance your message while speaking.

Should you walk around during your speech, or should you stay in one place? If there is a lectern, should you stand behind it, or would it be acceptable to stand in front or to the side of it? Is it all right to sit down while you speak? Can you move among the audience? The following discussion may help you answer these questions.

Move Purposefully

Your movement should be consistent with the verbal content of your message. It should make sense rather than appear as aimless wandering. Your movement should not detract from your message. If the audience focuses on your movement rather than on what you are saying, it is better to stand still.

Reduce Physical Barriers

Eliminate physical barriers between you and the audience. For more formal occasions, you will be expected to remain standing behind a lectern to deliver your message. But even on those occasions, it can be appropriate to move from behind the lectern to make a point, signal a change in mood, or turn to another idea.

Establish Immediacy

Movements such as standing, moving closer to listeners, or coming out from behind a lectern can help to create a perception of closeness or **immediacy** between you and your audience, which may enhance your credibility and help you effectively communicate your message.[2] Pay close attention to your listeners to determine the appropriate amount of immediacy so that you do not violate cultural expectations or make listeners uncomfortable.

How to Move Effectively

Your use of movement during your speech should make sense to your listeners. Avoid random pacing and overly dramatic gestures.

POSTURE

17.4   Display an appropriate posture while delivering a speech.

Although there have been few formal studies of posture in relation to public speaking, there is evidence that the way you carry your body communicates significant information.[3] Whereas your face and voice play a major role in communicating a specific emotion, your posture communicates the *intensity* of that emotion.

In general, avoid slouching your shoulders, shifting from foot to foot, or drooping your head. Your posture should not call attention to itself. Instead, it should reflect your interest in the speaking event and your attention to the task at hand.

FACIAL EXPRESSION

17.5   Use facial expressions to enhance verbal messages.

Your face plays a key role in expressing your thoughts and especially your emotions and attitudes.[4] Your audience sees your face before they hear what you are going to say. Thus, you have an opportunity to set the emotional tone for your message before you start speaking. Try for a pleasant facial expression that helps establish a positive emotional climate, but do not adopt a phony smile that looks insincere and plastered on your face.

According to cross-cultural studies by social psychologist Paul Ekman, nearly all people around the world agree on the general meanings of facial expressions for six primary emotions: happiness, anger, surprise, sadness, disgust, and fear.[5] Humans are physically capable of producing thousands of different facial expressions, but our faces most often express one of these six primary emotions or a blend of expressions. Even a culturally diverse audience will usually be able to read your emotional expressions clearly.

Consider these tips for monitoring your facial expression:

- As you rehearse, be mindful of the emotion that you wish your audience members to feel. Monitor your expression so that it communicates the emotion you intend.
- Unless you are presenting sad or bad news, have a naturally pleasant, positive facial expression to signal your interest in communicating with your listeners.
- When presenting a speech that will be seen only on video, take care not to overly exaggerate your facial expression. Close-ups can amplify the intensity of your emotional expressions.
- Remember that listeners from high-context cultures, such as people from Asia, often prefer less dramatic and subtler facial expressions.

PERSONAL APPEARANCE

17.6   Choose appropriate attire for making a speech.

There is considerable evidence that your personal appearance affects how your audience will respond to you and your message, particularly during the opening moments of your presentation. If you violate their expectations about appearance, you will be less successful in achieving your purpose. Appropriate wardrobe varies depending on climate, custom, culture, and audience expectations. Most people have certain expectations about the way a speaker should look. Use your audience analysis to identify and avoid violating your audience's expectations.

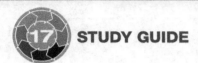

STUDY GUIDE

MEET YOUR OBJECTIVES

17.1 Make effective eye contact during a speech.
To communicate effectively with North American audiences, make eye contact with the entire audience before and during your speech.

17.2 Use gestures effectively while speaking.
Use natural, definite, and varied gestures that fit your personality and help you communicate your message to your particular audience.

17.3 Move purposefully in ways that enhance your message while speaking.
Use movement to emphasize your verbal messages, to make your audience feel closer to you, and to help listeners understand the transitions and organization of your speech.

17.4 Display an appropriate posture while delivering a speech.
Posture communicates the intensity of your emotions and your interest in your audience and speech. Avoid slouching and drooping.

17.5 Use facial expressions to enhance verbal messages.
Rehearse using universally recognized facial expressions that match the emotions of your verbal messages.

17.6 Choose appropriate attire for making a speech.
Analyze your audience and speaking situation to determine what to wear when you deliver your speech.

THINK ABOUT THESE QUESTIONS

1. **Self Assessment** Record and analyze a video of yourself rehearsing your next speech. Did you follow the advice given in this chapter? How can you improve your eye contact, gestures, posture, and use of movement and facial expressions?
2. **Ethics Assessment** Many politicians hire image consultants to coach them in nonverbal skills. Is it ethical for a speaker to use such consultants to attempt to gain more credibility with voters?
3. **Critical Assessment** Monique is self-conscious about her hand gestures, and she often just puts her hands behind her back. What advice would you give Monique to help her use gestures more effectively?

VERBAL COMMUNICATION

OBJECTIVES

18.1 Use effective vocal delivery when giving a speech.

18.2 Explain how to use a microphone when speaking in public.

18.3 Describe the steps to follow when rehearsing your speech.

VOCAL DELIVERY

18.1 Use effective vocal delivery when giving a speech.

Your credibility as a speaker and ability to communicate ideas clearly to your listeners will in large part depend on your vocal delivery. It is primarily through the quality of our voices, as well as our facial expressions, that we communicate whether we are happy, sad, bored, or excited. If your vocal clues suggest you are bored with your topic, your audience will probably also be bored.

Vocal delivery includes pitch, speaking rate, volume, pronunciation, articulation, pauses, and general variation of the voice. A speaker has at least two key vocal obligations to an audience: Speak to be understood, and speak with vocal variety to maintain interest.

Speak to Be Understood

To be understood, consider four aspects of vocal delivery: volume, articulation, dialect, and pronunciation.

VOLUME   The fundamental goal in vocal delivery is to speak loudly enough so that your audience can hear you. The **volume** of your speech is determined by the amount of air you project through your larynx, or voice box. More air equals more volume of sound.

Your diaphragm, a muscle that lies between your lungs and your abdomen, helps control sound volume by increasing airflow from your lungs through your voice box. Breathing from your diaphragm—consciously expanding and contracting your abdomen as you breathe in and out—can increase the volume of sound, as well as enhance the quality of your voice.

ARTICULATION   The process of producing speech sounds clearly and distinctly is **articulation**. Without distinct enunciation or articulation of the sounds that make up words, your listeners may not understand you or may fault you for simply not knowing how to speak clearly and fluently. Here are some commonly misarticulated words:[1]

Dint	instead of	*didn't*
Lemme	instead of	*let me*
Mornin	instead of	*morning*
Seeya	instead of	*see you*
Soun	instead of	*sound*
Wanna	instead of	*want to*
Wep	instead of	*wept*
Whadayado	instead of	*what do you do*

The best way to improve your articulation of sounds is first to identify words or phrases that you have a tendency to slur or chop. Once you have identified them, practice saying the words correctly. Consult an online dictionary to make sure you can hear the differences between the improper and proper pronunciations. A speech teacher can help you check your articulation.

DIALECT   A **dialect** is a consistent style of pronouncing words that is common to an ethnic group or a geographic region. In the southern part of the United States, people prolong some vowel sounds when they speak. And in the northern Midwest, the word *about* sometimes sounds a bit like "aboat." Research suggests that listeners tend to prefer a dialect similar to their own.[2]

Although a speaker's dialect may pigeonhole that person as being from a certain part of the country, it won't necessarily affect the audience's comprehension of the information unless the dialect is so pronounced that the listeners can't understand the speaker's words. We don't recommend that you eliminate your own mild dialect, but if your word pronunciation is significantly distracting to your listeners, you might consider modifying it, using the suggestions in the How To box.

HOW TO — Modify a Dialect

You can adapt your dialect by changing your intonation pattern, vowel production, consonant production, or speaking rate.

- **Use proper intonation.** A typical North American intonation pattern is predominantly a rising and falling pattern. The pattern looks something like this:

  "Good ^{morn}ing. How ^{are} you?"

  Intonation patterns of other languages, such as Hindi, may remain on almost the exact same pitch level; North American ears find the monotone pitch distracting.
- **Pronounce vowels clearly.** Clipping or shortening vowel sounds can make comprehension more challenging. If you need to stretch or elongate your vowels, consider recording your speech and then comparing it with the standard American pronunciation you hear on the TV or radio.
- **Pronounce consonants appropriately.** Consonant production varies, depending on which language you are speaking. It is sometimes difficult to produce clear consonants that are not overdone. Consonants that are so soft as to be almost unheard may produce a long blur of unintelligible sound rather than a crisply articulated sound.
- **Use an appropriate speaking rate.** A rate that is too fast can contribute to problems with clipped vowels, soft or absent consonants, and an intonation pattern that is on one pitch level rather than comfortably varied. Slowing the rate just a bit often enhances comprehension.

PRONUNCIATION   Whereas articulation relates to the clarity of sounds, **pronunciation** concerns the degree to which the sounds conform to those assigned to words in standard English. Mispronouncing words can detract from a speaker's credibility. If you are uncertain about how to pronounce a word, look it up in an online dictionary. Most popular dictionaries provide recordings of the correct pronunciations of words. Often, however, we are not aware that we are not using standard pronunciation unless someone points it out.

Some speakers reverse speech sounds, saying "aks" instead of "ask," for example. Some allow an *r* sound to intrude into some words, saying "warsh" instead of "wash," or leave out sounds in the middle of a word, as in "ackchally" instead of "actually" or "Febuary" instead of "February." Some speakers also accent syllables in nonstandard ways; they say "po´lice" instead of "po lice´" or "um´brella" rather than "um brel´la."

If English is not your native language, you may have to spend extra time working on your pronunciation and articulation. Here are two useful tips to help you. First, make an effort to prolong your vowel sounds. Speeeeak tooooo prooooolooooong eeeeeeach vooooooowel soooooound yooooooooou maaaaaaaake. Second, to reduce choppy-sounding word pronunciation, blend the end of one word into the beginning of the next. Make your speech flow from one word to the next, instead of separating it into individual chunks of sound.[3]

Speak with Variety

Appropriate variation in vocal pitch and rate, as well as appropriate use of pauses, can add zest to your speech and help maintain audience attention.

PITCH   Vocal **pitch** is how high or low your voice sounds. Everyone has a habitual pitch. This is the range of your voice during normal conversation. Some people have a habitually high pitch, whereas others have a low pitch.

Your voice has **inflection** when you raise or lower the pitch as you pronounce words or sounds. The best public speakers appropriately vary their inflection. We're not suggesting that you need to imitate a top-forty radio disk jockey when you speak. But variation in your vocal inflection and overall pitch helps you communicate the subtlety of your ideas.

Record your speech as you rehearse and evaluate your use of pitch and inflection. If you are not satisfied with your inflection, consider practicing your speech with exaggerated variations in vocal pitch. Although you would not deliver your speech this way, it may help you explore the expressive options available to you.

RATE   How fast do you talk? Most speakers average between 120 and 180 words per minute. There is no one "best" speaking rate. The best rate depends on two factors: your speaking style and the content of your message.

One symptom of speech anxiety is the tendency to rush through a speech to get it over with. You can use feedback from others or record and listen critically to your message to help you assess whether you are speaking at the proper speed.

Fewer speakers have the problem of speaking too slowly, but a turtle-paced speech will almost certainly make it more difficult for your audience to maintain interest. Remember, your listeners can grasp information much faster than you can speak it.

PAUSES   An appropriate pause can often do more to accent your message than any other vocal characteristic. President Kennedy's famous line, "Ask not what your country can do for you; ask what you can do for your country," was effective not only because of its language, but also because it was delivered with a pause dividing the two thoughts. Try delivering that line without the pause; without it, the statement just doesn't have the same power.

Effective use of pauses, also known as *effective timing*, can greatly enhance the impact of your message. Whether you are trying to tell a joke, a serious tale, or a dramatic story, your use of a pause can determine the effectiveness of your anecdote. A well-timed pause, coupled with eye contact, can also powerfully accent a particular word or sentence. Silence is a way of saying to your audience, "Think about this for a moment."

Beware, however, of the vocalized pause. Many beginning public speakers are uncomfortable with silence, and so, rather than pausing where it seems natural and normal, they vocalize sounds such as "umm," "er," "you know," and "ah." However, such vocalized pauses will annoy your audience and detract from your credibility.

QUICK CHECK

Good Vocal Delivery

- Use adequate volume.
- Articulate speech sounds clearly and distinctly.
- Pronounce words accurately.
- Vary your pitch and speaking rate.
- Pause to emphasize ideas.

USING A MICROPHONE

18.2 Explain how to use a microphone when speaking in public.

No matter how polished your gestures or well-intoned your vocal cues are, if you are inaudible or use a microphone awkwardly, your speech will not have the desired effect.

There are three kinds of microphones. The **lavaliere microphone** is the clip-on type often used by newspeople and interviewees. Worn on the front of a shirt, jacket, or dress, it requires no particular care other than not to thump it or to accidentally knock it off. The **boom microphone**, used by makers of movies and TV shows, hangs over the heads of the speakers and is remote-controlled.

The most common microphone is the **stationary microphone**. This type is most often attached to a lectern, sitting on a desk, or standing on the floor. Generally, the stationary microphones used today are multidirectional. You do not have to remain frozen in front of a stationary mike while delivering your speech. However, you do need to take some other precautions when using one.

- First, check to make sure the microphone is indeed multidirectional and can pick up your voice even if you aren't speaking directly into it.

- Second, speak clearly and crisply. You may need to pronounce *B, P,* and *S* sounds with less intensity than usual.

- Third, if you must test a microphone, count or ask the audience whether they can hear you. Blowing on a microphone produces an irritating noise! Do not tap, pound, or shuffle anything near the microphone. If you are using note cards, quietly slide them aside as you progress through your speech.

- Fourth, continue to speak at your normal volume. Some people speak more quietly when they have a microphone in front of them, becoming inaudible.

- Finally, make sure your microphone is turned off before having personal conversations with others.

If you have the chance to rehearse with the microphone you will use, figure out where to stand for the best sound quality and how sensitive the microphone is to extraneous noise. Practice will accustom you to any voice distortion or echo that might occur so that these sound qualities do not surprise you during your speech.

REHEARSING YOUR SPEECH: SOME FINAL TIPS

18.3 Describe the steps to follow when rehearsing your speech.

Rehearsal is the key to effective verbal and nonverbal delivery of your speech. The following suggestions can help you make the most of your rehearsal time.

- Finish drafting your speech outline at least two days before your speech performance.

- Before you prepare the speaking notes to use in front of your audience, rehearse your speech aloud to help determine where you will need notes to prompt yourself.

- Revise your speech as necessary to keep it within the time limits set by your instructor or whoever invited you to speak.

- Prepare your speaking notes. Use whatever system works best for you to maintain an extemporaneous delivery style. Some speakers use pictorial symbols to remind themselves of a story or an idea. Others use complete sentences or just words or phrases in an outline pattern to prompt them. Many teachers advocate using note cards for speaking notes. Some speakers use a smartphone, an iPad, or other electronic display. If you do use electronic notes, it is wise to have a hard-copy backup.

- Rehearse your speech standing up so that you can get a feel for your use of gestures as well as your vocal delivery. Do not try to memorize your speech or plan specific gestures. As you rehearse, you may want to modify your speaking notes to reflect appropriate changes.

- If you can, present your speech to someone else so that you can practice establishing eye contact. Seek feedback from your captive audience about both your delivery and your speech content.

- If possible, make an audio or video recording of your speech during the rehearsal stage. Most smartphones, computers, and tablets have a built-in camera and microphone. When listening to or viewing the recording, observe your vocal and physical mannerisms and make necessary changes. Many speakers still find it useful to practice before a mirror so they can observe their body language—it's low-tech, but it still works.

- Rehearse using all your presentation aids. Don't wait until the last minute to plan, prepare, and rehearse with computer-generated slides or other aids you will need to manipulate as you speak.

- Your final rehearsals should re-create, as much as possible, the speaking situation you will face. If you will be speaking in a large classroom, find a large classroom in which to rehearse your speech. If your audience will be seated informally in a semicircle, then this should be the context in which you rehearse your speech. Keep in mind that realistic rehearsal results in more confidence and a better performance.

- Practice good delivery skills while rehearsing. Remember this maxim: Practice *makes* perfect if practice *is* perfect.

 STUDY GUIDE

MEET YOUR OBJECTIVES

18.1 Use effective vocal delivery when giving a speech.

To be effective, speak to be understood, with enough volume, clear articulation, and correct pronunciation, modifying your dialect only if necessary. Maintain your listeners' interest by speaking with vocal variety, including proper pitch and inflection, an appropriate rate, and effective use of pauses.

18.2 Explain how to use a microphone when speaking in public.

Try to rehearse with your microphone before your speech to determine how much you can move. Avoid making annoying sounds, but use your normal speaking volume.

18.3 Describe the steps to follow when rehearsing your speech.

Allow at least two days after finishing your speech outline to practice your speech delivery and develop your speaking notes. As much as possible, re-create the speech environment when you rehearse. Record your rehearsal or recruit a listener to provide feedback on your performance.

THINK ABOUT THESE QUESTIONS

1. **Self Assessment** Review the tips for rehearsing your speech presented in this chapter. Rate yourself on a scale of 1 to 5 (1 = poor; 5 = excellent) on each of the suggestions. Use your self-ratings to develop a plan to improve your rehearsals.

2. **Ethics Assessment** Is it ethical to cultivate a highly emotional vocal delivery style to use when attempting to persuade listeners?

3. **Critical Assessment** Professor Murray speaks slowly and in a monotone; consequently, many of her students do not enjoy her music history lectures. What can she do to give her voice some variety?

DELIVERING YOUR SPEECH

OBJECTIVES

19.1 Take steps to prepare for a successful speech delivery.

19.2 Prepare to answer questions after delivering a speech.

SUCCESSFULLY DELIVER YOUR SPEECH

19.1 Take steps to prepare for a successful speech delivery.

When you are ready to deliver your speech, your task is to calmly and confidently communicate with your audience. Consider the following suggestions to help you prepare for a successful performance.

- **Be well rested.** Get plenty of sleep before your speech. Last-minute, late-night final preparations can take the edge off your performance.

- **Review the suggestions in Chapter 2 for becoming a confident speaker.** Re-create the speech environment when you rehearse. Use deep-breathing techniques to help you relax. Make sure you are especially familiar with your introduction and conclusion. Act calm so that you will feel calm.

- **Arrive early for your speaking engagement.** If the room is in an unfamiliar location, give yourself plenty of time to find it. You may also want to rearrange the furniture or make other changes to the speaking environment.

- **Check your equipment.** After checking your equipment, set up your presentation aids carefully.

- **Visualize success.** Picture yourself delivering your speech in an effective way. Also, remind yourself of the effort you have spent preparing for your speech. A final mental rehearsal can boost your confidence and help ensure success.

Keep in mind that speech delivery is an art rather than a science. Adapt these tips and your delivery to reflect your personality and individual style.

RESPONDING TO QUESTIONS

19.2 Prepare to answer questions after delivering a speech.

A question-and-answer (Q&A) session may be scheduled after your speech. During this Q&A period, your delivery method changes from extemporaneous to impromptu speaking. Here are some tips to make the Q&A period less challenging. Chapter 26 offers additional suggestions for answering questions after group presentations.

- **Prepare.** Analyze your audience. Think of possible questions those particular listeners might ask you, and then rehearse your answers.

- **Repeat or rephrase the questions.** Repeating a question makes sure that everyone can hear the question. It also ensures that you understand the question. It lets you succinctly summarize a rambling question. And repeating the question gives you just a bit of time to think about your answer.

- **Stay on message.** Keep bringing the audience back to your central idea. If a listener asks a question unrelated to your talk, gently guide your questioner back to the message you have prepared.

- **Give a "double-barreled" talk.** Some seasoned speakers suggest that you save a bit of your speech to deliver during the Q&A session.[1] You present your speech, and then when an appropriate question is asked, you give your second, much briefer speech as your answer.

- **Respond to the entire audience, not just the person who asked the question.** Although you can start your response by having eye contact with the person who asked you a question, make sure that you stay audience-centered. Look at all audience members and keep in mind that your response should be relevant to them.

- **Ask the first question yourself.** As you transition between the end of your speech and the Q&A, prime the audience by asking and answering an initial challenging question.

- **Listen nonjudgmentally.** Give your full attention to the questioner. Listen politely and respond courteously.

- **Neutralize hostile questions.** Restate the question and acknowledge the questioner's emotions. Focus your answer on the heart of the questioner's issue or problem.

- **When you don't know the answer, admit it.** You can promise to find out more information and then get back to the person later. When you make a promise, follow through on it.

- **Be brief.** Even if you've planned a "double-barreled" talk, make your answers short and to the point.

- **Use organized signposts.** Use verbal signposts to help listeners understand your answer. For example, you can say, "I have two responses to that question. First,...." Then, when you get to your second point, say, "My second point is...."

- **Indicate when the Q&A period is ending.** For example, warn your audience, "I only have time for two more questions."

 STUDY GUIDE

MEET YOUR OBJECTIVES

19.1 Take steps to prepare for a successful speech delivery.

Rest well before a speech. Take steps to boost your confidence. Arrive early, and visualize your successful speech.

19.2 Prepare to answer questions after delivering a speech.

Consider your audience and plan for questions they might ask. Listen politely to questions and repeat or rephrase them, especially hostile questions. Keep answers brief, organized, and to the point.

THINK ABOUT THESE QUESTIONS

1. **Self Assessment** Review the tips for getting ready to deliver your speech. Rank the suggestions in order of how much they can help you before your next speech.
2. **Ethics Assessment** Many politicians deliver their message using a teleprompter. Is it ethical to disguise the fact that you are using extensive notes when delivering a speech?
3. **Critical Assessment** Muriel, who has been a church organist for 35 years, is planning on speaking to her music club about her experiences playing the pipe organ. How would you advise Muriel to prepare for questions after her speech?

SELECTING PRESENTATION AIDS

OBJECTIVES

20.1 Discuss five ways in which presentation aids help communicate ideas to an audience.

20.2 Describe six types of presentation aids and how to use them effectively.

20.3 Describe how computers may be used to generate high-quality presentation aids.

20.4 Use criteria to choose presentation aids to include in a speech.

THE VALUE OF PRESENTATION AIDS

20.1 Discuss five ways in which presentation aids help communicate ideas to an audience.

A **presentation aid** is any image, object, or sound that reinforces your point visually or aurally so that your audience can better understand it. Presentation aids can help your listeners do all of the following:[1]

- **Focus**—Presentation aids gain and maintain the attention of your listeners and keep their interest when words alone might not.
- **Understand**—Presentation aids can enhance understanding.
- **Remember**—It is well known that you remember most what you understand best.
- **Organize**—Listing your major ideas on a computer-generated slide, chart, or poster can help your audience grasp your main ideas and follow your transitions.
- **Illustrate**—Of your five senses, you learn more from sight than from all the others combined.[2] Demonstrating or showing procedures or events step-by-step is an especially effective way to enhance understanding.[3]

TYPES OF PRESENTATION AIDS

20.2 Describe six types of presentation aids and how to use them effectively.

There are six types of presentation aids: images, text, video, audio, objects, and people.

Images

The most common presentation aids are two-dimensional images such as drawings, photographs, maps, graphs, and charts.

DRAWINGS   Drawings are easy and inexpensive to make, and they can be tailored to your specific needs. As a rule, large and simple line drawings are more effective for stage presentations than detailed images. One way to view drawings at large sizes is to incorporate them into computer-generated presentation aids.

PHOTOGRAPHS   Photographs can show objects or places that cannot be illustrated with drawings or that an audience cannot view directly. Photos can easily be incorporated into computer-generated slides. If you must use a printed photograph, enlarge it or scan and project it.

MAPS   Most maps are designed to be read from a distance of no more than two feet. To make a map large enough for your audience to see, you can enlarge it using a color copier, draw a simplified large-scale version, or embed it in a computer-generated slide.

GRAPHS   A **graph** is a pictorial representation of statistical data in an easy-to-understand format. Most listeners find that graphs help make data more concrete. Graphs are particularly effective in showing overall trends and relationships among data. The four most common types of graphs are bar graphs, pie graphs, line graphs, and picture graphs.

- A **bar graph** consists of flat areas—bars—whose various lengths represent information.
- A **pie graph** shows the individual shares of a whole. Pie graphs are especially useful in helping your listeners to see quickly how data are distributed in a given category or area.
- **Line graphs** show relationships between two or more variables. Like bar graphs, line graphs organize statistical data to show overall trends. A line graph can cover a greater span of time or numbers than a bar graph without looking cluttered or confusing. A simple line graph communicates better than a cluttered one.
- **Picture graphs** look somewhat less formal and less intimidating than other kinds of graphs. One of the advantages of picture graphs is that they need few words or labels, which makes them easier for your audience to read.

CHARTS   **Charts**, or tables, summarize and present a great deal of information in a small amount of space. They are easy to use, reuse, and enlarge. They can also be displayed in a variety of ways. You can use a flipchart, a poster, or a computer-generated slide, which can project a giant image of your chart on a screen. Charts must be simple and easy to read. Do not try to put too much information on one chart.

Text

In addition to images, many speakers use text, which could be just a word or two, or a very brief outline of the key points. The key to using text as a presentation aid is to not overdo it. To use text effectively, consider these principles:

- Use no more than seven lines of text on any single visual, especially on a computer-generated visual.
- Use *brief* bullet points to designate individual items or thoughts.
- Use parallel structure in bulleted lists (for example, begin each bulleted phrase with the same word, as we do in this list).

- Use the heading of each slide to summarize the essential point of the visual so listeners can follow the key point you are making.[4]

If you're using a computer, you'll be able to choose from dozens of typefaces and **fonts**. But make an informed choice rather than selecting a typeface just because it strikes your fancy. Graphic designers divide typefaces into four types: serif, sans serif, script, and decorative. Several types of fonts are shown in Figure 20.1. Serif fonts are easier to read for longer passages. Although interesting and dramatic, script fonts should be used sparingly because they are hard to read. Use decorative fonts only when you want to communicate a special tone or mood. Regardless of which font style you use, don't use more than one or two on a single visual.

Video

It's now easy to record video to support speech ideas. Digital video cameras are inexpensive, widely available, and a standard feature of smartphones. If you use video clips from movies or TV to support your talk, you'll likely get them from YouTube or other Internet sources, or from commercially prerecorded digital video discs (DVDs).

Before you decide to use a video clip, think about whether or not it will really enhance your speech. Short, well-selected clips are most likely to be effective.

You can use a variety of technologies to store your videos and play them back during your speech:

- **DVD player.** Simply play back part of a prerecorded movie or TV show.
- **Computers and other electronic devices.** You can store and play video clips on your computer, smartphone, computer tablet, or MP4 player. Embedding video in computer-generated presentation aids can give you more control over precisely what clip you are showing, as well as the visual context and timing when you play it. Unless the audience is very small, all of these options require you to

Figure 20.1 Typefaces grouped by font type.

Font Types

Serif	Sans Serif
Poster	Abadi
Bodoni	**Herald**
Garamond	**Denmark**
Americana	**Garrison Sans**

Script	Decorative
Quill	*Pablo*
Kaufflinn	Curlz
Mariah	PAPER CLIP
Kunstler Script	**Stars and Stripes**

connect your device to a monitor or a projection system. Make sure monitors are available and compatible with your device, or bring your own.

- **The Internet.** If the room where you are delivering your speech has Internet access, you can skip storing your video and instead stream it directly from YouTube or another Internet source. You can also retrieve your video or audio material from the "cloud," computer storage that is in a remote location. Playing video directly from the Internet or from cloud storage does, however, carry the risk of losing an Internet connection before or during your speech.

When using any of these technologies, you'll want to practice using your video and make sure all of the equipment you need is available. We also recommend that, before you give your speech, you do a technical run-through, ensuring that your video clip will be ready when you want it to be.

Audio

Audio can be used to complement visual displays. As with video, you can either create your own audio content or use prerecorded sources. You also have a number of options for storage and playback. As with video, be sure to rehearse with and master any technology involved with audio aids, and don't let your soundtrack overwhelm or distract from your own speech.

Objects and Models

Listeners like looking at real, tangible items that can be touched, smelled, heard, and even tasted, as well as seen. Using an object or, if the object is too big or illegal to bring to your speech, using a model, can enhance audience interest.

OBJECTS   If you use an object to illustrate an idea, make sure you can handle the object with ease. If an object is too large, it can be unwieldy and difficult to show to your audience. Tiny objects can be seen only close up. Avoid objects that are dangerous to handle.

MODELS   If it is not possible to bring the object you would like to show your audience, consider showing them a **model**. Make sure, however, that any model you use is large enough to be seen by all members of your audience.

People

Using people to illustrate your message can be tricky. Before your presentation, choose someone you trust so that you can fully inform him or her about what needs to be done. Rehearse your speech using your live presentation aid.

If you don't need the person to demonstrate something during your opening remarks, wait and introduce the person to your audience when needed. Remember, your presentation aids are always subordinate to your speech. You must remain in control.

USING COMPUTER-GENERATED PRESENTATION AIDS

20.3   Describe how computers may be used to generate high-quality presentation aids.

You are probably already familiar with the basic elements of developing a computer-generated image. And because you've undoubtedly seen many computer-generated presentations, you also know that you can incorporate video clips as well as digital photos into a slide. But, as with any presentation aid, the images or clips you use must help develop your central idea; otherwise, they will distract your audience from it.

Basic Principles of Using Computer-Generated Presentation Aids

Most audiences, especially those in the corporate world, expect a speaker to use computer-generated presentation aids.[5] PowerPoint, which is the most popular presentation software, helps you create and present images, photos, words, charts, and graphs. PowerPoint can also incorporate video and sound. Prezi is another increasingly popular presentation software program that is cloud-based—information is accessed on demand via the Internet rather than on your own computer. Prezi also allows users to zoom in and out of slides. Keynote, which was developed for Apple™ computers and devices, is another type of presentation software. Like other programs, it permits users to easily maintain consistency in fonts and colors. Some people prefer its sleek, contemporary appearance.

Tips for Using Computer-Generated Presentation Aids

Although computer-generated graphics can be overused and, like any presentation aid, can distract from your message if used improperly, they nonetheless open up professional-looking possibilities for illustrating your speech.

Be sure to consider your audience when you use computer-generated presentation aids.[6] As with any presentation aid, the images or clips you choose to display must help develop your central idea; otherwise, they will distract your audience from it. The following tips can help.[7]

KEEP SIGHTS AND SOUNDS SIMPLE   Many users attempt to shovel too much information into their slides, which can overwhelm listeners. Keep in mind that presentation aids *support* your message; they are not your message.

- Limit the number of words on each slide.
- Use slides to present images rather than merely repeat your words.
- Resist the urge to add sound effects. *You* should be the soundtrack, not your computer.

CONTROL COMPUTER IMAGES   When using computer-generated slides, there may be times when you want to speak to your audience and not refer to a slide or image. During these times, use a blank slide or use the projector's remote control to temporarily project no image.

REPEAT VISUAL ELEMENTS TO UNIFY YOUR PRESENTATION   Use a common visual element, such as a bullet or other symbol, at the beginning of each word or phrase in a list. Use common color schemes and spacing to give your visuals coherence. Use fonts consistently, rather than mix them. Use a similar visual style for each of your images to achieve a professional, polished look. Use repetition of key words (such as *use* at the beginning of each sentence in this paragraph).

The most significant advantage of computer graphics is the ease with which they allow you to display attractive visual images. Both color and black-and-white images are available as **clip art**. Copyright-free clip art and photos are available at no cost from many Internet sources. Presentation software allows you to easily incorporate these images into your visual aids.

MAKE INFORMED DECISIONS ABOUT USING COLOR   Color communicates. Choose colors that will support and reinforce the topic and purpose of your speech. To unify your presentation, use the same background color on all visuals and no more than two colors for words. Using a dark background with lighter-colored words can have a pleasing effect and make the words easy to see.

ALLOW PLENTY OF TIME TO PREPARE YOUR PRESENTATION AIDS   Prepare your presentation aids well in advance of your speaking date so that you can make them as attractive and polished looking as possible. A sloppy, amateurish presentation aid will convey the impression that you are not a credible speaker, even if you have spent many hours preparing the verbal part of your speech.

QUICK CHECK

Design Effective Computer-Generated Presentation Aids

- Keep sights and sounds simple.
- Repeat elements to unify your presentation.
- Use clip art to give your visuals a professional touch.
- Choose a typeface with care.
- Avoid mixing many different fonts.
- Make informed decisions about using color.
- Finish preparing your presentation aids early.

SELECT THE RIGHT PRESENTATION AIDS

20.4   Use criteria to choose presentation aids to include in a speech.

Because there are so many choices, you may wonder, "How do I decide which presentation aid to use?" Use the suggestions in the How To box to help you.

Choose Presentation Aids

- **Consider your audience.** The age, interests, and attitudes of your audience should affect your selection of audiovisual support.
- **Estimate the size of the audience.** Choose presentation aids that everyone will be able to see clearly.
- **Think of your speech objective.** Don't select a presentation aid until you have decided on the purpose of your speech.
- **Evaluate your own skill and experience.** Use only equipment with which you are comfortable or have had practical experience.
- **Know the room in which you will speak.** If the room has large windows with no shades and no other way to dim the light, do not consider using visuals that require a darkened room.

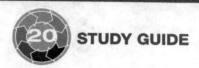 **STUDY GUIDE**

MEET YOUR OBJECTIVES

20.1   Discuss five ways in which presentation aids help communicate ideas to an audience.

Presentation aids help you gain and maintain the audience's attention and communicate the organization of your ideas. They can improve listeners' understanding and recollection of those ideas.

20.2   Describe six types of presentation aids and how to use them effectively.

There are six types of presentation aids: images, text, video, audio, objects, and people. The most common presentation aids are two-dimensional images such as drawings, photographs, maps, graphs, and charts. Many speakers also use text, which could be just a word or two, or a very brief outline of the key points. Video and audio can also be used to help communicate ideas to listeners. Using objects and models as well as people can also enhance audience interest.

20.3   Describe how computers may be used to generate high-quality presentation aids.

To design effective computer-generated presentation aids keep sights and sounds simple, repeat elements to unify your presentation, use clip art to give your visuals a professional touch, choose a typeface with care, avoid mixing too many different fonts, make informed decisions about using color, and finish preparing your presentation aids early.

20.4   Use criteria to choose presentation aids to include in a speech.

Consider the audience, your topic and purpose, your own skills, and the location of your speech when choosing presentation aids.

THINK ABOUT THESE QUESTIONS

1. **Self Assessment** Identify several public-speaking situations that would lend themselves well to using presentation aids. What are some situations in which using presentation aids would *not* be beneficial?

2. **Ethics Assessment** Tom is preparing a speech on driver safety. He plans to begin his speech with a series of graphic pictures showing traffic accident victims. Is it ethical to show graphic images that arouse audience fears?

3. **Critical Assessment** Professor Chou uses only the chalkboard to illustrate her anthropology lectures and then only occasionally writes a word or two. What other types of visual or auditory aids could Professor Chou use in teaching?

PREPARING AND USING PRESENTATION AIDS

GUIDELINES FOR PREPARING PRESENTATION AIDS

21.1 Follow three guidelines for developing effective presentation aids.

A speech should be more than just what a speaker says, with a few PowerPoint slides or other visual aids added as an afterthought. Spend time carefully developing your **visual rhetoric** as well as your words. The following commonsense and research-based strategies can help you prepare effective presentation aids for your speeches.

Make Them Easy to See

To communicate your ideas clearly, everyone in the audience must be able see your presentation aids clearly. Our most important advice is this: *Write big!*

Keep Them Simple

Simple presentation aids usually communicate best. Some students think the visuals accompanying a speech must be as complicated as a Broadway production, complete with lights and costumes. Resist making them complicated. Text should be limited to key words or phrases. Simple images are better than overly detailed graphics. Don't cram too much information on one chart or computer slide. If you have a lot of information, it is better to use two or three simple charts or slides than to attempt to put all your words on one.

Keep Them Safe!

While demonstrating how to string a bow during a speech on archery, one student accidentally launched the bow over the heads of his startled audience. Not only did he lose credibility because he was not able to string the bow successfully, but he also endangered his audience.

We cannot emphasize this point enough: Do not use dangerous or illegal presentation aids! They are never worth the risk of a ruined speech or an injured audience member. Substitute a picture, chart, or other representational device.

USING PRESENTATION AIDS

21.2   Identify guidelines for effectively using presentation aids.

Here are some tips to help you use presentation aids for maximum audience impact.

Rehearse with Your Presentation Aids

Your appearance before an audience should not be the first time you deliver your speech while holding up an object, turning on a video monitor, operating a remote control to show your slides, clicking on a YouTube video, or using a flipchart. Practice with your presentation aids until you feel at ease with them.

Make Eye Contact with Your Audience, Not with Your Presentation Aids

Of course, you will need to glance at your visual aid to make sure that it isn't upside down or that it is the proper one. But do not face the image or object while giving your talk. Keep looking your audience in the eye.

Explain Your Presentation Aids

Always set your visuals in a verbal context. Don't just unceremoniously announce, "Here are the recent statistics on birth rates in the United States," and hold up your visual without further explanation. Tell the audience how to interpret the data.

Do Not Pass Objects among Members of Your Audience

What can you do if your object is too small to be seen without passing it around? If no other speaker follows your speech, you can invite audience members to come up and see your object when your speech is over. If your audience is only two or three rows deep, you can even hold up the object and move in close to the audience to show it while you maintain control. Or you can take photos of the object, embed the photos in presentation software, and project the images at a size even a large audience can see.

Use Animals with Caution

Most actors are unwilling to work with animals—and for good reason. At best, they may steal the show. And most often, they are unpredictable. You may think you have the smartest, best-trained dog in the world, but you really do not know how your dog will react to a strange environment and an unfamiliar audience. The risk of having an animal detract from your speech may be too great to make planning a speech around one worthwhile.

Use Handouts Effectively

Many public-speaking instructors believe you should not distribute handouts during a speech. Handing out papers in the middle of your presentation will only distract your audience. However, many audiences in business and other types of organizations expect a summary of your key ideas in written form. If you do find it necessary to use written material to reinforce your presentation, consider using the suggestions in the How To box.

HOW TO: Use Handouts

- Don't distribute your handout *during* the presentation unless your listeners need to refer to the material while you're talking about it.
- Control listeners' attention by telling them where in the handout you want them to focus.
- Clearly number the pages on your handout material to make it easy for you to direct audience members to specific pages.
- If your listeners do not need the information during your presentation, tell them that you will distribute a summary of the key ideas at the end of your talk.

Time the Use of Visuals to Control Your Audience's Attention

A skillful speaker knows when to show a supporting visual and when to put it away. For example, it's not wise to begin your speech with all your charts, graphs, and drawings in full view, unless you are going to refer to them in your opening remarks. Time the display of your visuals to coincide with your discussion of the information contained in them.

- **If possible, use a remote control device to advance computer-generated images.**   You do not need to stay anchored near the computer to advance each slide, you can move around.
- **Show a blank slide to return the audience's focus to you.**   You could also turn off the projection altogether. Just don't allow an image or bulleted list of words unrelated to your message to compete with you for your listeners' attention when you are making a point or telling a story.
- **Consider arranging for someone to help you.**   The person can be a presentation aid, hold other aids, turn the pages of your flipchart, or change the slides on the projector. Make sure you rehearse with your assistant so that all goes smoothly during your presentation.

Use Technology Effectively

Some novice speakers are tempted to overuse presentation aids simply because they can quickly produce eye-catching visuals. Resist this temptation.

Also, don't assume that the hardware and software you need will be available in the room where you are speaking. Be sure to ask what kinds of technology exist.

Remember Murphy's Law

According to Murphy's Law, if something can go wrong, it will. When you use presentation aids, you increase the chances that problems or snags will develop when you present your speech. The chart may fall off the easel, you may not find the chalk, or the computer in the room may not be compatible with your software. Be prepared. Bring backup supplies and have an alternative plan in case your original plans go awry.

If something doesn't go as you planned, do your best to keep your speech on track. If the chart falls, pick it up and keep talking; don't offer lengthy apologies. If you can't find the chalk, ask a friend to go on a chalk hunt in another room. No computer-generated slides as you had planned? Have all key pieces of information in your notes rather than relying on your computer slides. A thorough rehearsal, a double-check of your equipment, backup images, and extra supplies such as extension cords and masking tape can help repeal Murphy's Law.

QUICK CHECK

Use Presentation Aids Effectively

- Rehearse until you feel at ease with your presentation aids.
- Make eye contact with the audience, not with your presentation aids.
- Explain your presentation aids.
- Do not pass objects among members of your audience.
- Use animals with caution.
- Use handouts effectively.
- Time your visuals to control your audience's attention.
- Use technology effectively.
- Remember Murphy's Law.

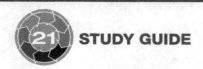 **STUDY GUIDE**

MEET YOUR OBJECTIVES

21.1 Follow three guidelines for developing effective presentation aids.
Effective presentations are to easy to see, are simple, and are safe to use.

21.2 Identify guidelines for effectively using presentation aids.
As you present your speech, remember to look at your audience, not at your presentation aid; talk about your visual, don't just show it; avoid passing objects among your audience; use handouts to reinforce the main points in your speech; time your visuals carefully; and be sure to have backup supplies and a contingency plan.

THINK ABOUT THESE QUESTIONS

1. **Self Assessment** You have prepared handouts, several charts, and a short video clip to support your speech. What steps should you take to make sure your presentation is effective?
2. **Ethics Assessment** Ceally wants to play sound clips of offensive lyrics to demonstrate to his college classmates the increased use of profanity in contemporary music. Would you advise Ceally to play these songs, even though doing so might offend several members of his audience?
3. **Critical Assessment** Nikki plans to give a talk encouraging listeners to support funding for a new library. She wants to make sure they understand how cramped and inadequate the current library is. What type of visual support could she use to make her point?

INFORMATIVE SPEAKING

22.1 Describe three goals and five different types of informative speeches.

22.2 Effectively and appropriately use three strategies to enhance audience understanding.

22.3 Effectively and appropriately use three strategies to maintain audience interest.

22.4 Effectively and appropriately use four strategies to enhance audience recall of information presented in an informative speech.

22.5 Develop an audience-centered informative speech.

GOALS AND TYPES OF INFORMATIVE SPEECHES

22.1 Describe three goals and five different types of informative speeches.

When you inform someone, you assume the role of a teacher. A **speech to inform** shares information with others to enhance their knowledge or understanding of the information, concepts, and ideas you present. The skill of teaching and enhancing understanding is important to virtually any profession. When you speak to inform, you typically attempt to achieve these three goals:

- *You speak to enhance understanding.*   Understanding occurs when a listener accurately interprets the intended meaning of a message.
- *You speak to maintain interest.*   If your listeners are bored and not focusing on your message, you won't achieve your informative-speaking goal.
- *You speak to be remembered.*   The day after hearing a presentation, most listeners remember only about 50 percent of what they were told. By two days later, they recall only about 25 percent. Your job as an informative speaker is to improve those statistics.

Informative speeches can be classified according to the subject areas they cover. As Table 22.1 shows, classifying your speech can help you decide how to organize the information you want to present. Good organization will help your audience process your message.

Table 22.1 Types of Informative Speeches

Topic	Purpose	Typical Organization Patterns	Examples
Objects	Present information about tangible things	Topical Spatial Chronological	The Rosetta Stone Museums The Mars Rover Religious icons

Procedures	Review how something works or describe a process	Chronological
		Topical
		Complexity
			How to…
			    Use a smartphone app to help you lose weight
			    Operate a nuclear-power plant
			    Buy a quality used car
			    Trap lobsters

People	Describe famous people or personal acquaintances	Chronological Topical	Sojourner Truth Nelson Mandela J. R. R. Tolkien Your grandmother Your favorite teacher
Ideas	Present abstract information or discuss principles, concepts, theories, or issues	Topical Complexity	Communism Immigration Buddhism Reincarnation
Events	Describe an event that either has happened or will happen	Chronological Topical Spatial	May Day in Oxford, England Inauguration Day Cinco de Mayo

STRATEGIES TO ENHANCE AUDIENCE UNDERSTANDING

22.2 Effectively and appropriately use three strategies to enhance audience understanding.

How do you enhance someone's knowledge or understanding? We can suggest several powerful strategies.

Speak with Clarity

To speak with clarity is to express ideas so that the listener understands the intended message accurately. Speaking clearly is an obvious goal of an informative speaker. What is not so obvious is *how* to speak clearly. As a speaker you may think you're being clear, but only the listener can tell you whether he or she has received your message.

Give careful thought to how you will help listeners understand your message. Communication researcher Joseph Chesebro has summarized several research-based strategies you can use to enhance message clarity and turn information into communication.[1]

- Preview your main ideas in your introduction.
- Tell your listeners how new information relates to a previous point.
- Frequently summarize key ideas.
- Provide a visual outline to help listeners follow your ideas.

Use Adult-Learning Principles

- **Give adults information they can use right away.** Listeners are more likely to focus on and understand information they can apply immediately to their mental "in-basket" or to-do list.
- **Actively involve adult learners in the learning process.** Consider asking them questions to think about or, in some cases, to respond to on the spot.
- **Connect learners' life experiences with new information.** First, know the kinds of experiences that your listeners have had, and then refer to those experiences as you present your ideas.
- **Explain how new information is relevant to listeners' needs and their busy lives.** Show how the ideas you share are relevant to them.
- **Seek ways to relate the ideas you present to listeners' problems.** People will be more likely to pay attention to information that helps them better understand and solve their problems.

- Provide a handout prior to your talk with the major points outlined; leave space so that listeners can jot down key ideas.
- Once you announce your topic and outline, stay on message.

Use Principles and Techniques of Adult Learning

Andragogy is the art and science of teaching adults. The How To box summarizes some effective andragogical, or adult-learning, principles found by researchers and scholars.[2]

Clarify Unfamiliar Ideas or Complex Processes

Research suggests you can demystify a complex process if you first provide a simple overview of the process with an analogy, a vivid description, or a word picture.[3]

ANALOGIES   *Analogies*, or comparisons, can help listeners understand unfamiliar ideas or processes by comparing them to something they already know. To comprehend the vastness of the Milky Way galaxy, for instance, you might point out that if the Milky Way were the size of North America, our entire solar system would fit inside a coffee cup.[4]

USE A VIVID, DESCRIPTIVE WORD PICTURE   When you *describe*, you provide more detail than when you just define something. One way to describe a situation or event is with a word picture. A **word picture** is a lively description that helps your listeners form a mental image by appealing to their senses of sight, taste, smell, sound, and touch. To create an effective word picture, begin by forming your own clear mental image of the person, place, object, or process before you try to describe it. See it with your "mind's eye."

- What would a listener see if he or she were looking at it?
- What would listeners hear?
- If they could touch the object or participate in the process, how would it feel to them?
- If your listeners could smell or taste it, what would that be like?

To describe these sensations, choose the most specific and vivid words possible. Onomatopoeic words—words that resemble the sounds they name—such as *buzz, snort, hum, crackle,* or *hiss,* are powerful. So are similes and other comparisons. "The rock was as rough as sandpaper" and "the pebble was as smooth as a baby's skin" appeal to both the visual and the tactile senses.

Be sure to describe the emotions that a listener might feel if he or she were to experience the situation you relate. If you experienced the situation, describe your own emotions. Use specific adjectives rather than general terms such as *happy* or *sad.*

One speaker, talking about her first speech assignment, described her reaction this way: "My heart stopped. Panic began to rise up inside. For the next week, I lived in dreaded anticipation of the event."[5] Note how effectively her choices of such words and phrases as "my heart stopped," "panic," and "dreaded anticipation" describe her terror at the prospect of making a speech—much more so than if she had said, "I was scared." The more vividly and accurately you can describe emotion, the more intimately involved in your description the audience will become.

As you develop your speech and supporting materials, consider how you can appeal to a variety of learning styles at the same time. Because you'll be giving a speech, your auditory learners will like that. Visual learners like and expect an informative talk to be illustrated with PowerPoint™ images. They will appreciate seeing pictures or having statistics summarized using bar or line graphs or pie charts. Visual print learners will like handouts, which you could distribute after your talk. Kinesthetic learners will appreciate movement, even small actions such as raising their hands in response to questions.

QUICK CHECK

Strategies to Enhance Audience Understanding

- Speak with clarity.
- Use principles and techniques of adult learning.
- Clarify complex processes.

STRATEGIES TO MAINTAIN AUDIENCE INTEREST

22.3 Effectively and appropriately use three strategies to maintain audience interest.

Before you can inform an audience, you must gain and maintain their interest. No matter how carefully crafted your definitions, skillfully delivered your description of a process, or visually reinforcing your presentation aid, if your listeners aren't paying attention, you won't achieve your goal. Strategies for gaining and holding interest are vital in achieving your speaking goal.

Motivate Your Audience to Listen to You

Most audiences probably will not be waiting breathlessly for you to talk to them. You will need to motivate them to listen to you. Unless you hold the power to reward or punish your listeners, you will need to find more creative ways to get your audience to listen to you. Pique their interest with a story. Explain how the information you present will be of value to them. Use an unexpected twist or rhetorical question.

Tell a Story

Good stories with interesting characters and riveting plots have fascinated listeners for millennia; the words "Once upon a time" are usually a surefire attention getter. Stories are also a way of connecting your message to people from a variety of cultural backgrounds.[6]

The characteristics of a well-told tale are simple yet powerful. A good story includes conflict, incorporates action, creates suspense, and may also include humor.

- **Conflict.** Stories that pit one side against another and describe opposing ideas and forces in government, religion, or personal relationships foster attention.
- **Action.** An audience is more likely to listen to an action-packed message than to one that listlessly lingers on an idea too long. The key to maintaining interest is a plot that moves along to hold attention. Good stories have a beginning that sets the stage, a heart that moves to a conclusion, and an ending that ties up all the loose ends.
- **Suspense.** Keeping people on the edge of their seats because they don't know what will happen next is an element in good storytelling.
- **Humor.** Using a bit of humor makes the point while holding the listener's attention. Not all stories have to be funny. Stories may be sad or dramatic without humor. But adding humor when appropriate usually helps maintain interest and attention.

Present Information That Relates to Listeners

Being an audience-centered informative speaker means being aware of information that your audience can use. If, for example, you are going to teach your audience about recycling, be sure to talk about specific recycling efforts on your campus or in your community. Adapt your message to the people who will be in your audience.

Use the Unexpected

Advertisers know that listeners will focus on the unexpected. If you add a surprise twist to a quotation or story, audience members will increase their attention. You can also create a "mini-mystery" by asking a rhetorical question to get listeners to actively process your words.[7]

STRATEGIES TO ENHANCE AUDIENCE RECALL

22.4 Effectively and appropriately use four strategies to enhance audience recall of information presented in an informative speech.

Some speakers are better than others at presenting information in a memorable way. Here are some strategies that will help your audiences remember you and your message.

Build in Redundancy

When you speak, repeat key points. Provide a clear preview at the beginning of your talk as well as a summary statement in your conclusion. Include internal summaries—short summaries after key points during your speech—to help audiences remember key ideas. Use numeric signposts (numbering key ideas verbally by saying, "My first point is….My second point is….") to make sure your audience can identify and remember key points.

A reinforcing visual aid that displays your key ideas can also enhance recall. If you really want to ensure that listeners come away from your speech with essential information, consider preparing a handout or an outline of key ideas.

Make Your Key Ideas Short and Simple

Don't bombard listeners with lengthy lists. One classic research study concluded that people can hold only about seven pieces of information in their short-term memories.[8] Remember to crystallize the central idea of your speech into a one-sentence statement. Phrase your central-idea statement, as well as your main points, as simply as possible. Try to make them short enough to fit on a bumper sticker.

Pace Your Information Flow

Organize your speech so that you present an even flow of information, rather than bunching up a number of significant details around one point. If you present too much new information too quickly, you may overwhelm your audience.[9]

Make sure your audience has time to process any new information. Use supporting materials both to help clarify new information and to slow down the pace of your presentation. Do not try to see how much detail and content you can cram into a speech.

Reinforce Key Ideas

Reinforcing key ideas is one of the most powerful techniques of all.

REINFORCE IDEAS VERBALLY You can reinforce an idea by using such phrases as "This is the most important point" or "Be sure to remember this next point." Suppose you have four suggestions for helping your listeners avoid serious sunburns, and your last suggestion is the most important. How can you make sure your audience knows that? Just tell them. "Of all the suggestions I've given you, this last tip is the most important one. The higher the SPF level on your sunscreen, the better." Be careful not to overuse this technique. If you claim that every other point is a key point, soon your audience will not believe you.

REINFORCE IDEAS NONVERBALLY You can also signal the importance of a point with nonverbal emphasis. Gestures serve the purpose of accenting or emphasizing key phrases, as italics do in written communication.

- A well-placed pause can provide emphasis and reinforcement to set off a point. Pause just before or just after making an important point to focus attention on it.
- Raising or lowering your voice can also reinforce a key idea.
- Movement can help emphasize major ideas. Moving from behind the lectern to tell a personal anecdote can signal that something special and more intimate is about to be said.
- Your movement and gestures should be meaningful and natural, rather than seemingly arbitrary or forced.

DEVELOPING AN AUDIENCE-CENTERED INFORMATIVE SPEECH

22.5 Develop an audience-centered informative speech.

Use the audience-centered speaking model, shown in Figure 3.1, to guide you step-by-step through the process of preparing an informative speech.

Consider Your Audience

As with any type of speech, you need to consider three general questions about audience analysis when preparing an informative talk:

- *To whom are you speaking?*
- *What are their interests, attitudes, beliefs, and values?*
- *What do they expect from you?*

When your general purpose is to inform, you should focus on specific aspects of these three general questions. Part of considering who your audience is will include figuring out, as best you can, their preferred learning styles. Determining listeners' interests, attitudes, beliefs, and values can help you balance your use of strategies to enhance understanding and recall with your need to maintain their interest. For example, you won't need to work as hard to maintain the interest of an audience who is already highly interested in your topic. Careful consideration of audience members' expectations can also help you maintain their interest, perhaps by surprising them with something they do not expect.

Once your topic and purpose are clearly established, continue to consider your audience when developing your central idea and generating your main ideas. Interesting and appropriate supporting material will make your message clear, engaging, and memorable. Most informative speeches are primarily organized using topical, chronological, or complexity strategies. As with any speech, rehearsing several times will help you deliver a message that your audience will listen to and perceive as credible.

QUICK CHECK

Audience-Centered Informative Speaking

- **Select topic**—Consider who your listeners are, as well as their interests and needs.
- **Formulate central and main ideas**—Make them clear and simple.
- **Gather supporting material**—Decide what will help the audience maintain interest and learn.
- **Organize**—Consider topical, chronological, or complexity as the primary organizational strategy for an informative speech.
- **Rehearse**—Deliver a polished message that your audience will listen to and perceive as credible.

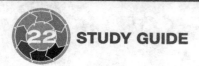

STUDY GUIDE

MEET YOUR OBJECTIVES

22.1   Describe three goals and five different types of informative speeches.

Informative speakers must enhance listeners' understanding, maintain their interest, and be remembered. They can make speeches about objects, procedures, people, events, and ideas.

22.2   Effectively and appropriately use three strategies to enhance audience understanding.

To enhance your listeners' understanding of a message: (1) define ideas clearly, (2) use principles and techniques of adult learning, and (3) clarify unfamiliar ideas or complex processes.

22.3   Effectively and appropriately use three strategies to maintain audience interest.

To gain and maintain listeners' interest, you must motivate your audience to listen to you. Tell a story, present information that relates to listeners, or use the unexpected.

22.4   Effectively and appropriately use four strategies to enhance audience recall of information in an informative speech.

Help your listeners remember what you tell them by being redundant, keeping your ideas short and simple, pacing the flow of information, and reinforcing important points.

22.5   Develop an audience-centered informative speech.

You can apply principles of informative speaking at every step of the audience-centered method of speaking.

THINK ABOUT THESE QUESTIONS

1. **Self Assessment** What strategies do your instructors use in class to motivate students to listen, enhance listeners' understanding, and improve their recall?
2. **Ethics Assessment** In order to give your 5-minute speech about nuclear energy, you must greatly simplify a very complex process. How can you avoid misrepresenting your topic? Should you let your audience know how much you are simplifying the process?
3. **Critical Assessment** You have been asked to speak to a kindergarten class about your chosen profession. How can you make your message clear, interesting, and memorable to your audience?

UNDERSTANDING PRINCIPLES OF PERSUASIVE SPEAKING

 23

OBJECTIVES

23.1 Describe the goals of persuasive messages.

23.2 Explain classic and contemporary theories of how persuasion occurs.

23.3 Describe four ways to motivate listeners to respond to a persuasive message.

23.4 Prepare and present an audience-centered persuasive speech.

THE GOALS OF PERSUASION

23.1 Describe the goals of persuasive messages.

Persuasion is the process of changing or reinforcing attitudes, beliefs, values, or behaviors. In a persuasive speech, the speaker explicitly asks the audience to make a choice, rather than just informing them of the options. To advocate a particular view or action successfully, you must understand your listeners' positions before you speak.

Attitudes

Our attitudes represent our likes and dislikes. Stated more precisely, an **attitude** is a learned predisposition to respond favorably or unfavorably toward something. Attitudes are easier to change than either beliefs or values.

Beliefs

A **belief** is what you understand to be true or false. If you believe in something, you are convinced that it exists or is true. Beliefs are typically based on past experiences or evidence, but some beliefs are based on faith—we haven't directly experienced something, but we believe anyway. A belief is more susceptible to change than a value is, but it is still difficult to alter. Beliefs are changed by evidence. Usually it takes a great deal of evidence to change a belief and alter the way your audience structures reality.

Values

A **value** is an enduring conception of right or wrong, good or bad. If you value something, you classify it as good or desirable, and you tend to think of its opposite or its lack as bad or wrong. If you do not value something, you are indifferent to it. Speeches that focus on changing or reinforcing audience values emphasize how and why something is better than something else. Values form the basis of our life goals and the motivating force behind our behavior. Therefore listeners' values are difficult to change. Understanding what your listeners value can, however, help you adapt the content of your speech to their values.

Behavior

Persuasive messages often attempt to do more than change or reinforce attitudes, beliefs, or values—they attempt to change behavior. It seems logical that knowing someone's attitudes, beliefs, and values will help us predict precisely how that person will behave. But we are complicated creatures, and human behavior is not always neatly predictable. Sometimes our attitudes, beliefs, and values may not appear to be consistent with how we act.

HOW PERSUASION WORKS

23.2   Explain classic and contemporary theories of how persuasion occurs.

There are many theories and considerable research on how persuasion works. We'll discuss two approaches here: (1) a classic approach identified by the ancient Greek rhetorician Aristotle; and (2) the elaboration likelihood model (ELM), a contemporary theory that builds on the classic approach. Both suggest that persuasion is a complex process, and that not all of us are persuaded in the same way. Aristotle's theory emphasizes what a *speaker* should do to influence an audience, whereas ELM theory describes how *listeners* process the messages they hear.

Aristotle's Traditional Approach: Using Ethos, Logos, and Pathos to Persuade

Aristotle, a Greek philosopher and rhetorician who lived and wrote in the fourth century BCE, defined *rhetoric* as the process of discovering, in any particular case, the available means of persuasion. He identified three general methods (or, using his language, "available means") of persuasion. They are ethos, logos, and pathos.

ETHOS   To use **ethos** to persuade, an effective communicator must be credible. Not only must the information be credible, Aristotle believed the speaker also should be ethical, possess good character, have common sense, and be concerned for the well-being of the audience. The more credible and ethical a speaker is perceived to be, the greater the chances are that a listener will believe in, trust, and respond positively to the speaker's persuasive message.

LOGOS   The word **logos** literally means "the word." Aristotle used this term to refer to the rational, logical arguments a speaker uses to persuade someone. A skilled persuader not only reaches a logical conclusion, but also supports the message with evidence and reasoning.

PATHOS   Aristotle used the term **pathos** to refer to the use of appeals to emotion in persuasion. Emotion-arousing stories and examples, as well as pictures and music, all appeal to listeners' emotions.

ELM's Contemporary Approach: Using a Direct or Indirect Path to Persuade

The **elaboration likelihood model (ELM) of persuasion** has a long name but is actually a simple idea that explains how you are persuaded to do or think about something.[1]

To **elaborate** means that you *think* about the information, ideas, and issues related to the content of the message. When you elaborate on a message, you are critically evaluating what you hear by paying special attention to the arguments and evidence the speaker is using. The likelihood of whether you elaborate on a message or not (hence, the name *elaboration likelihood model*) varies from person to person and depends on the topic of the message. The theory suggests that there are two ways you can be persuaded:

1. A **direct persuasion route** that you follow when you elaborate, consciously think about, or critically evaluate a message.

2. An **indirect persuasion route**, in which you don't elaborate and are more influenced by the peripheral factors of the message and messenger. You might, for example, be persuaded by your emotional reaction to the speaker's examples or by your liking of the speaker.

ELM theory suggests that, as a speaker, you need not only to present well-reasoned arguments with credible evidence, but also to be attuned to indirect factors that can influence your listeners, such as your delivery, appearance, and your audience's general impression of how prepared you are.

QUICK CHECK

Theories of Persuasion

Aristotle

Focus is on speaker's actions:

- Logos—logic, evidence
- Ethos—speaker credibility and ethics
- Pathos—emotion

ELM

Focus is on listeners' actions:

- Direct route—elaboration on logic, evidence
- Indirect route—no elaboration, persuaded by factors such as credibility and emotion

---

HOW TO MOTIVATE LISTENERS

23.3 Describe four ways to motivate listeners to respond to a persuasive message.

Motivation is the underlying internal force that drives people to achieve their goals. Persuasion works when listeners are motivated to respond to a message. An audience is more likely to be persuaded if you help members solve their problems or otherwise meet their needs. They can also be motivated when you convince them that good things will happen if they follow your advice or bad things will occur if they don't.

Use Cognitive Dissonance

According to dissonance theory, when you are presented with information inconsistent with your current attitudes, beliefs, values, or behavior, you experience a kind of discomfort called **cognitive dissonance**.[2] The word *cognitive* refers to thoughts; *dissonance* means "lack of harmony or agreement."

So cognitive dissonance means that you are experiencing a way of thinking that is inconsistent and uncomfortable. Most people seek to avoid feelings of dissonance; thus, creating dissonance with a persuasive speech can be an effective way to change attitudes and behavior.

The first tactic in such a speech is to identify an existing problem or need. Then, the speaker ethically describes the problem to listeners in a way that arouses cognitive dissonance. Finally, the persuasive speaker suggests a solution to the problem that can help listeners reduce dissonance. Listeners can react in several ways to your use of dissonance, only one of which serves your purpose.[3]

- **Listeners may discredit the source (you).**   You need to ensure that your audience will perceive you as competent and trustworthy so that they will accept your message.
- **Listeners may reinterpret the message.**   They may choose to focus on the parts of your message that are consistent with what they already believe and ignore the unfamiliar or controversial parts. To counter this tendency, make your message as clear as possible.
- **Listeners may seek new information.**   Audience members may look for additional information to negate your position. Be sure your own evidence is trustworthy, making it harder to refute.
- **Listeners may stop listening.**   Some messages are so much at odds with listeners' current positions that they may decide to stop listening. The principle of selective exposure suggests that we tend to pay attention to messages that are consistent with our points of view and to avoid those that are not. Being aware of listeners' existing attitudes, beliefs, and values can help you ensure they don't tune out.
- **Listeners may change their attitudes, beliefs, values, or behavior—as the speaker wishes them to do.**   If listeners change their attitudes, they can reduce their dissonance and restore their sense of balance.

Use Listener Needs

Need is one of the best motivators. The more you understand what your listeners need, the greater the chances are that you can gain and hold their attention and ultimately get them to do what you want.

Abraham Maslow suggested that a hierarchy of needs, as shown in Figure 23.1, motivates everyone's behavior. Maslow suggested that we must meet basic physiological needs (such as food, water, and air) before we can be motivated to respond to higher-level needs.[4] Although research suggests that we are not limited to hierarchical order and can be motivated by several needs at the same time, Maslow's hierarchy provides a useful checklist of potential listener motivations that a persuasive speaker can activate in order to change or reinforce attitudes, beliefs, values, or behavior.

PHYSIOLOGICAL NEEDS   The most basic needs for all humans are physiological: We all need air, water, and food. According to Maslow's theory, unless those needs are met, it will be difficult to motivate a listener to satisfy other needs. Be sensitive to the basic physiological needs of your audience so that your appeals to higher-level needs will be heard.

SAFETY NEEDS   Once basic physiological needs are met, listeners are concerned about their safety. We all need to feel safe, secure, and protected. Persuasive speakers often appeal to our need to provide for our own and our loved ones' safety.

Figure 23.1   Maslow's hierarchy of needs.

SOCIAL NEEDS   We all need to feel loved and valued. We need contact with others and reassurance that they care about us. According to Maslow, these social needs translate into our need for a sense of belonging to a group (a fraternity, a religious organization, a circle of friends). Powerful persuasive appeals are based on our need for social contact.

SELF-ESTEEM NEEDS   The need for self-esteem reflects our desire to think well of ourselves. Advertisers often appeal to this need to persuade us to buy products.

SELF-ACTUALIZATION NEEDS   The need for **self-actualization** is the need to fully realize one's highest potential, which Maslow suggested could be addressed only after we met needs at the other four levels. Persuasive calls to be the best at something appeal to this need.

Use Positive Motivation

Positive motivational appeals are suggestions that good things will happen to listeners who heed the speaker's advice. A key to using positive motivational appeals effectively is to know what your listeners value. Knowing what audience members view as desirable, good, and virtuous can help you select the benefits of your persuasive proposal that will best appeal to them. Knowing that your listeners value clean air, for example, may help you persuade them to support your proposal for new limits on emissions.

Use Negative Motivation

The use of a threat to change someone's attitude or behavior is one of the most effective approaches. Negative motivation, also known as a **fear appeal**, takes the form of an "if–then" statement. If you don't do X, then awful things will happen to you. An important need will go unmet unless the desired behavior or attitude change occurs. Ethical and successful fear appeals require careful consideration of your audience. Consider the tips in the How To box.

Use Fear Appeals to Persuade

- **Threaten listeners' loved ones.** A strong threat to a loved one tends to be more successful than a fear appeal directed at the audience members themselves.
- **Establish your credibility.** The more credible your audience perceives you to be, the more likely it is that your fear appeal will be effective.
- **Make sure the threat is real.** Fear appeals are more successful if you can convince listeners that the threat will probably occur unless they take the action you are advocating.
- **Make the threat scary.** Increasing the intensity of a fear appeal increases the chances that it will be effective.[5]
- **Empower listeners.** Make sure you tell your listeners what they can do to reduce the threat—take the action you are suggesting.[6]
- **Don't exaggerate.** As an ethical speaker, you must be truthful in fear appeals.

DEVELOPING YOUR PERSUASIVE SPEECH

23.4 Prepare and present an audience-centered persuasive speech.

The process of developing a persuasive speech follows the same audience-centered path you would take to develop any speech.

Consider the Audience

Although being audience-centered is important in every speaking situation, it is vital when your objective is to persuade. It would be extremely difficult to persuade someone without knowing something about his or her interests, attitudes, beliefs, values, and behaviors.

Remember that persuasion works differently for different cultural groups. Learn as much as you can about the cultural perspectives of your listeners so that you can ethically adapt your message to use persuasive strategies listeners will find convincing.

Select and Narrow Your Persuasive Topic

The best persuasive topics are those you feel passionate about. You'll present a better speech if you select a topic you can speak about with sincere conviction. However, the ideal topic speaks to a need, concern, or issue of the audience, as well as to your interests and zeal.

Current events and controversial issues—questions about which people disagree—also make excellent sources for persuasive topics. In choosing a controversial topic, you need to be audience-centered. Know the local, state, national, or international issues that interest your listeners.

Determine Your Persuasive Purpose

When you want to persuade others, you don't always have to strive for dramatic changes in their attitudes, beliefs, values, and behavior. Your speaking goal may be only to move listeners a bit closer to your ultimate persuasive objective. **Social judgment theory** suggests that when listeners are confronted with a persuasive message, their responses fall into one of three categories: (1) a latitude of acceptance, in which they generally agree with you; (2) a latitude of rejection, in which they disagree; or (3) a latitude of noncommitment, in which they are not yet committed.[7] It is important to know which latitude category your listeners fall into before you begin so you can choose a realistic persuasive goal. If most of your listeners are in the latitude of rejection, it will be difficult to move them to the latitude of acceptance with a single speech. A more realistic goal might be to make them less certain of their rejection.

Develop Your Central Idea and Main Ideas

When persuading others, most speakers find it useful to state their central idea in the form of a proposition. A **proposition** is a statement with which you want your audience to agree. There are three categories of propositions.

PROPOSITION OF FACT   A **proposition of fact** focuses on whether something is true or false or on whether it did or did not happen. To be a good speech topic, a proposition of fact must be debatable, such as "Global climate change is (or is not) occurring." It should not be a fact, such as who won the last Super Bowl, that can be easily verified. Most persuasive speeches that focus on propositions of fact begin by identifying one or more reasons why the proposition is true.

PROPOSITION OF VALUE   A **proposition of value** is a statement that calls for the listener to judge the worth or importance of something. Value propositions often directly compare two things, or two courses of action, and suggest that one of the options is better than the other.

PROPOSITION OF POLICY   The third type of proposition, a **proposition of policy**, advocates a specific action—changing a policy, procedure, or behavior. Typically, propositions of policy include the word *should*. For example, "Public schools should encourage more physical activity."

Gather Supporting Material

Keep in mind Aristotle's three "available means" of persuasion as you gather supporting materials: (1) *ethos* includes using credible and ethical supporting material; (2) *logos* requires you to use effective logic and reasoning to support your main ideas; and (3) *pathos* suggests using appropriate emotional support.

Organize Your Speech

Your audience and your specific purpose can help you decide how to begin your message, organize your ideas, and conclude your talk. We'll discuss specific approaches and tips for organizing a persuasive speech in the next chapter.

Rehearse and Deliver Your Speech

When your goal is to persuade, make a special effort to rehearse your speech in front of another person or to run some of your ideas past others to check the overall clarity and structure of your message.

As you deliver your speech, remember that ELM predicts that the emotional energy of your delivery can, in itself, be persuasive to some of your listeners. No matter how well-reasoned your message, at least some of your listeners are likely to fail to elaborate, or critically consider it. Instead, these listeners may be persuaded by an indirect route, one based on the emotional connection you make with them in the course of delivering your speech.

STUDY GUIDE

MEET YOUR OBJECTIVES

23.1 Describe the goals of persuasive messages.
The goals of persuasion are to change or reinforce attitudes, beliefs, values, or behavior.

23.2 Explain classic and contemporary theories of how persuasion occurs.
Aristotle suggested using ethos, logos, and pathos to persuade. The elaboration likelihood model suggests that listeners either follow a direct route to persuasion, in which they elaborate (think about) the issues and evidence, or they can be persuaded via an indirect route when they don't elaborate.

23.3 Describe four ways to motivate listeners to respond to a persuasive message.
Persuasive speakers can motivate listeners through cognitive dissonance, satisfying listeners' needs, positive motivational appeals, or fear appeals.

23.4 Prepare and present an audience-centered persuasive speech.
You can apply principles of persuasion at all steps in the audience-centered speechmaking process.

THINK ABOUT THESE QUESTIONS

1. **Self Assessment** If you were attempting to sell a new computer system to the administration of your school, what persuasive principles would you draw on to develop your message?
2. **Ethics Assessment** Is it ethical to develop a persuasive message that supports an attitude or belief with which you personally disagree?
3. **Critical Assessment** Martha has been asked to speak to the Association for the Preservation of the Environment. What possible persuasive topics and propositions would be appropriate for her audience?

USING PERSUASIVE STRATEGIES

> ## OBJECTIVES
>
> **24.1** Identify strategies to improve your initial, derived, and terminal credibility.
>
> **24.2** Use principles of effective logic and evidence to develop a persuasive message.
>
> **24.3** Employ effective techniques of using emotional appeal in a persuasive speech.
>
> **24.4** Adapt your persuasive message to receptive, neutral, and unreceptive audiences.
>
> **24.5** Use strategies for effectively organizing a persuasive speech.

ESTABLISHING YOUR CREDIBILITY

24.1 Identify strategies to improve your initial, derived, and terminal credibility.

Credibility, which Aristotle referred to as *ethos*, is the audience's perception of a speaker's competence, trustworthiness, and dynamism.

- **Competence.** To be a **competent** speaker is to be considered informed, skilled, or knowledgeable about one's subject. One way to enhance your competence is to cite credible evidence to support your point.

- **Trustworthiness.** While delivering your speech, demonstrate your **trustworthiness** by conveying honesty and sincerity. One way to earn the audience's trust is by demonstrating that you have had experience dealing with the issues you talk about. Your trustworthiness may be suspect, however, if you advocate something that will result in a direct benefit to you.

- **Dynamism.** You project **dynamism**, or energy, through your delivery. **Charisma** is a form of dynamism. A charismatic person possesses charm, talent, magnetism, and other qualities that make the person attractive and energetic.

The more credible your listeners find you, the more effective you will be as a persuasive communicator. Speakers establish their credibility in three phases.

- **Initial credibility** is the impression listeners have of your credibility before you speak. Even before you open your mouth, listeners have a perception of you based on your appearance, what they may have heard about you, and the previous times they have heard you speak.

- **Derived credibility** is the perception of your credibility that listeners form as you present yourself and your message.

- The last phase of credibility, called **terminal credibility**, is the perception listeners have of your credibility when you finish your speech. The lasting impression you make on your audience is influenced by how you were first perceived (initial credibility) and what you did as you presented your message (derived credibility).

It's one thing to understand what credibility is and how it evolves, but quite another to develop it. To improve your credibility, we suggest you think about what you can do before, during, and after your speech to appear competent, trustworthy, and dynamic. Consider the following suggestions for improving your credibility.

- Make a good first impression by giving careful thought to your appearance and establishing eye contact before you begin your talk.
- Establish common ground with listeners by indicating in your opening remarks that you share their values and concerns.
- Support your arguments and conclusions with evidence.
- Present a logically organized, well-delivered message. Using appropriate internal summaries, signposts, and enumeration of key ideas can enhance your credibility as a competent and rational advocate.
- Use strategies to gain and maintain attention. Effective delivery helps you gain and maintain listener attention and affects whether listeners will like you.[1] There is some evidence that although using humor may contribute to making listeners like you, humor does not have a major impact on ultimately persuading listeners to support your message.[2]
- End with a good impression. Maintain eye contact with your audience as you deliver your conclusion. Don't start leaving the lectern or speaking area until you have finished your closing sentence. If the audience expects a question-and-answer period, be ready to listen and respond to their questions.

USE LOGIC AND EVIDENCE TO PERSUADE

24.2   Use principles of effective logic and evidence to develop a persuasive message.

Logic is a formal system of rules for making inferences. Persuasive speakers need to pay careful attention to the way they use logic, or *logos* in Aristotle's wording, to reach a conclusion. Present *evidence* and then use appropriate *reasoning* to lead your listeners to the conclusion you advocate. **Evidence** consists of facts, examples, statistics, and expert opinions you use to support and prove the points you wish to make. **Reasoning** is the process of drawing a conclusion from evidence. *Proof* consists of the evidence plus the conclusion you draw from it.

Understanding Types of Reasoning

There are three major ways to structure an argument in order to reach a logical conclusion: inductively, deductively, and causally.

INDUCTIVE REASONING   Using **inductive reasoning**, you reach a general conclusion based on specific examples, facts, statistics, and opinions. You may not know for certain that the specific instances prove the conclusion is true, but you decide that, in all probability, the specific instances support the general conclusion.

To judge the validity of a **generalization** arrived at inductively, ask these questions:

- Are there enough specific instances to support the conclusion?
- Are the specific instances typical?
- Are the instances recent?

REASONING BY ANALOGY   *Reasoning by analogy* is a special type of inductive reasoning. An *analogy* is a comparison. This form of reasoning compares one thing, person, or process with another, to predict how the second thing will perform and respond. You could reason that a law that works in one state would have the same effect if used in another state.

There are questions that you should ask in order to check the validity of conclusions reached via analogy:

- Do the ways in which the two things (such as two states) are alike outweigh the ways in which they are different?
- Is the assertion true?

REASONING BY SIGN   *Reasoning by sign,* another special type of inductive reasoning, occurs when two things are so closely related that the existence of one thing means that the other thing will happen. For example, a clap of thunder and dark, swirling clouds are signs that rain will happen. When you use or hear reasoning by sign, you must establish that there is a strong, predictive relationship between the sign and the conclusion. Multiple signs improve your ability to predict.

DEDUCTIVE REASONING   Reasoning from a general statement or principle to reach a specific conclusion is called **deductive reasoning**. This is just the opposite of inductive reasoning.

Deductive reasoning can be structured in the form of a **syllogism**, which includes three elements:

1. A **major premise** is a general statement. A classic example of a major premise is based on mythology: All gods are immortal.
2. A **minor premise** is a more specific statement about an example linked to the major premise. The minor premise in our classic example might be: Zeus is a god.
3. The **conclusion** is based on the major premise and the minor premise. Following our classic example, we could conclude: Zeus is immortal.

You need to ensure that both the major and the minor premises are true and can be supported with evidence. If they are both true, then you can state with certainty—rather than just probability—that your conclusion is also true.

CAUSAL REASONING   **Causal reasoning** relates two or more events in such a way as to conclude that one or more of the events *caused* the others. Reasoning by sign points out that one thing predicts another, but causal reasoning concludes that one thing actually *causes* another.

- Reasoning from cause to effect, you move from a known fact to a predicted result, or from something that has occurred to something that has not yet occurred. For example, "If we allow the current pollution of the river to continue, townspeople will become ill."
- Reasoning from effect to cause, you move from known effect to unknown cause. You might show that many townspeople have illnesses that are a known effect of polluted water and then point to the river as the likely cause of their illnesses.

QUICK CHECK

Types of Reasoning

- **Inductive reasoning** draws a conclusion based on specific examples, facts, statistics, and opinions. Reasoning by analogy and by sign are special types of inductive reasoning.
- **Deductive reasoning** applies a general principle to specific examples. A deductive syllogism contains a major premise, minor premise, and conclusion.
- **Causal reasoning** relates two or more events so as to conclude that one or more events caused the others. Your causal reasoning can proceed from a known cause to an unknown effect, or from a known effect to an unknown cause.

Adapt Reasoning for a Culturally Diverse Audience

Speakers from the United States typically use a straightforward, factual-inductive method of supporting ideas and reaching conclusions.[3] They identify facts and link them to support a specific proposition or conclusion. However, not all cultures assume a direct, linear, methodical approach to supporting ideas and proving a point.[4] Some cultures use a deductive pattern of reasoning, in which a speaker begins with a general premise and then links it to a specific situation. Middle Eastern speakers usually do not use standard inductive or deductive structures. They are more likely to use narrative methods, which persuade listeners by allowing them to draw their own conclusions from stories, extended analogies, and examples.[5]

Using Types of Evidence

When attempting to persuade listeners, make sure that your evidence logically supports the inductive, deductive, or causal reasoning you are using to reach your conclusion. Evidence in persuasive speeches consists of facts, examples, expert opinions, and statistics.

- A **fact** is something that has been directly observed to be true or can be proved to be true. An **inference** is a conclusion based on available evidence or partial information.
- **Examples** are illustrations that are used to dramatize or clarify a fact. Only valid, true examples can be used to help prove a point. A hypothetical example, one that is fabricated to illustrate a point, should not be used to reach a conclusion. It should be used only to clarify.
- **Opinions** can serve as evidence if they are expressed by an expert. Opinions are usually most persuasive if they are combined with other evidence, such as facts or statistics, that support the expert's position.
- A **statistic** is a number used to summarize several facts or samples.

If you use inductive reasoning (moving from specific examples to a general conclusion), you need to make sure you have enough facts, examples, statistics, and credible opinions to support your conclusion. If you reason deductively (from a generalization to a specific conclusion), you need evidence to document the truth of your initial generalization. When you are developing an argument using causal reasoning, evidence is also vital, as you attempt to establish that one or more events caused something to happen.

Once you have gathered evidence, follow these strategies to use it effectively:[6]

- **Use credible evidence.** Listeners are more likely to respond to your arguments if they determine that your evidence is from a trustworthy, knowledgeable, and unbiased source. One type of evidence that is especially powerful is reluctant testimony. **Reluctant testimony** is a statement by someone who has reversed his or her position on a given issue, or is a statement made that is not in the speaker's best interest.

- **Use new evidence.** Evidence should not only be up-to-date but also new to listeners—something they have not already heard.

- **Use specific evidence.** Avoid vague terms, such as "many people." Use specific numbers and descriptions whenever possible.

- **Use evidence to tell a story.** Your evidence will be more powerful if the facts, examples, statistics, and opinions fit together to tell a story to make your point.

- **Use culturally appropriate evidence.** Listeners from some cultures will be more persuaded by stories or eyewitness testimony, whereas others will more likely be swayed by statistics.[7] You may need to ask a sampling of audience members or someone who knows the audience well what kind of evidence will be the most convincing.

Avoid Faulty Reasoning

Many persuaders use inappropriate techniques called *fallacies*. A **fallacy** is false reasoning that occurs when someone attempts to persuade without adequate evidence or with arguments that are irrelevant or inappropriate. You will be a better and more ethical speaker and a better listener if you are aware of the following fallacies.

CAUSAL FALLACY   The **causal fallacy** involves making a causal connection without enough evidence to support the cause-and-effect conclusion. Simply because one event follows another does not mean that the two are related.

BANDWAGON FALLACY   Someone who argues that "everybody thinks it's a good idea, so you should too" is using the **bandwagon fallacy**. Simply saying that "everyone" is "jumping on the bandwagon," or supporting a particular point of view, does not make the point of view correct.

EITHER–OR FALLACY   Someone who argues that there are only two approaches to a problem is trying to oversimplify the issue by using the **either–or fallacy**.

HASTY GENERALIZATION   A person who reaches a conclusion from little or no evidence is making a **hasty generalization**. Because one person became ill after eating the meatloaf in the cafeteria, everyone eating in the cafeteria will not necessarily develop food poisoning.

AD HOMINEM   Also known as attacking the person, an **ad hominem** (Latin for "to the man") **argument** involves attacking irrelevant personal characteristics of the person who is proposing an idea, rather than attacking the idea itself.

RED HERRING   The **red herring fallacy** is used when someone attacks an issue by using irrelevant facts or arguments as distractions. This fallacy gets its name from an old trick of dragging a red herring across a trail to divert any dogs that may be following.

APPEAL TO MISPLACED AUTHORITY   Ads that use athletes to endorse automobiles make an **appeal to misplaced authority**. Although we have great respect for athletes in their own fields, they are no more expert than we are about the product they are promoting.

NON SEQUITUR   If you argue that a new parking garage should not be built on campus because the grass has not been mowed on the football field for three weeks, you are guilty of a **non sequitur**. Your conclusion simply does not follow from your statement.

USE EMOTION TO PERSUADE

24.3   Employ effective techniques of using emotional appeal in a persuasive speech.

As suggested by the two major theories of persuasion described in Chapter 23, we are often persuaded by emotion, which Aristotle called *pathos*, as well as logic. As a public speaker trying to sway your listeners to your viewpoint, your job is to ethically use emotional appeals to achieve your goal.

Your key concern as a public speaker is "How can I ethically use emotional appeals to achieve my persuasive purpose?" The How To box provides general strategies.

Another way to arouse listeners' emotions is to reference a **myth**, a belief held in common by a group of people that is based on their values, cultural heritage, or faith. Referring to a shared myth is a way for you to identify and develop a bond with your listeners and to help them see how your ideas support their ideas.

Keep in mind that listeners' cultures influence how receptive they are to emotional expressions and appeals. Some Latin American listeners, for example, expect speakers to express more emotion and passion than U.S. listeners expect. To identify listeners' expectations, you can observe other successful speakers addressing similar audiences.

Avoid Misusing Emotional Appeals: Ethical Issues

Regardless of which emotions you use to motivate your audience, you have an obligation to be ethical and forthright. Making false claims, misusing evidence to arouse emotions, or relying only on emotions without supplying any evidence to support a conclusion violates ethical standards of effective public speaking.

Use Emotion to Persuade

- Use concrete examples that help your listeners visualize what you describe.
- Use emotion-arousing words.
- Use nonverbal behavior to communicate your emotional message.
- Use visual images to evoke emotions.
- Use appropriate metaphors and similes.
- Use appropriate fear appeals.
- Consider using appeals to several emotions, including hope, pride, courage, and reverence.

STRATEGIES FOR ADAPTING IDEAS TO PEOPLE AND PEOPLE TO IDEAS

24.4 Adapt your persuasive message to receptive, neutral, and unreceptive audiences.

Audience members may hold differing views of you and your subject. Your task is to find out if there is a prevailing viewpoint held by a majority of your listeners. If they are generally friendly toward you and your ideas, you need to design your speech differently than you would if your listeners were neutral, apathetic, or hostile. We offer some suggestions to help.

Persuading the Receptive Audience

In speaking to a receptive group, you can explore your ideas in depth.

- Identify with your audience. Emphasize the similarities between you and your listeners.
- Clearly state your speaking objective. Provide an overview of your major point or purpose.
- Be explicit in directing your listeners' behavior. Tell your audience exactly what you want them to do and how you expect them to respond to your message.
- Ask listeners for an immediate show of support to help cement the positive response you have developed during your speech.
- Use emotional appeals effectively. You are more likely to move a favorable audience to action with strong emotional appeals while also reminding them of the evidence supporting your conclusion.
- Make it easy for your listeners to act. Make sure that what you're asking them to do is clear and easy.

Persuading the Neutral Audience

Many audiences will simply be neutral or indifferent. Your challenge is to make them interested in your message.

- Capture your listeners' attention early in your speech.
- Refer to beliefs that many listeners share.
- Relate your topic not only to your listeners but also to their families, friends, and loved ones.
- Be realistic about what you can accomplish. People who start with an attitude of indifference are probably not going to become as enthusiastic as you are after hearing just one speech.

Persuading the Unreceptive Audience

One of the biggest challenges in public speaking is to persuade audience members who are against you or your message. If they are hostile toward you personally, your job is to find ways to enhance your acceptability and persuade them to listen to you. If they are unreceptive to your point of view, there are several approaches that you can use.

- Don't immediately announce that you plan to change their minds.
- Begin your speech by noting areas of agreement before you discuss areas of disagreement.
- Be realistic about what you can achieve. Don't expect a major shift in attitude from a hostile audience.

- Acknowledge the opposing points of view. Your listeners will be more likely to listen to you if they know you understand their viewpoint.

- Establish your credibility. Let your audience know about the experience, interest, knowledge, and skills that give you special insight into the issues at hand.

Sometimes your audience disagrees with you because its members just don't understand your point. Or they may harbor a misconception of you and your message. For such listeners, consider explaining rather than advocating. To enhance accurate understanding or correct a misconception, experienced speakers use a four-part strategy.[8]

1. Summarize the common misconceptions about the issue or idea you are discussing.
2. State why these misconceptions may seem reasonable.
3. Dismiss the misconceptions. Provide evidence to support your point; you need sound and credible data to be persuasive.
4. State the accurate information that you want your audience to remember. With a clear summary statement, reinforce the conclusion you want your listeners to draw from the information you presented.

STRATEGIES FOR ORGANIZING PERSUASIVE MESSAGES

24.5 Use strategies for effectively organizing a persuasive speech.

How you organize your speech has a major effect on your listeners' response to your message. The How To box offers general suggestions for organizing your speech. You can also use or combine the following specific organizational patterns.

HOW TO — Organize Your Persuasive Speech

- If you think your audience will be hostile to your point of view, advance your strongest arguments first. If you save your best argument for last, your audience may have already stopped listening.

- Do not bury key arguments and evidence in the middle of your message. Your listeners are more likely to remember information presented first and last.[9]

- If you want your listeners to take some action, it is best to tell them at the end of your speech what you want them to do. Don't call for action in the middle of your speech. It will be more powerful if you wait until your conclusion.

- It is usually better to present both sides of an issue rather than just the advantages of the position you advocate. If you don't acknowledge the counterarguments—arguments against your position—that your listeners have heard, they will probably think about them anyway.

- After you mention counterarguments, refute them with evidence and logic that show how your proposal is better.

- Adapt your organization to your listeners' cultural expectations. U.S. audiences often like a highly structured message, whereas audiences from some other cultures expect a less formal structure.

Problem–Solution

The most basic organizational pattern for a persuasive speech is to make the audience aware of a problem and then to present a solution that clearly solves it. If you are speaking to an apathetic audience or if listeners are not aware that a problem exists, a problem–solution pattern works nicely.

You must provide ample evidence to document that your perception of the problem is accurate. You'll also need to convince your listeners that the solution you advocate is the most appropriate one to resolve the problem.

Refutation

Another way to persuade an audience to support your point of view is to prove that the arguments against your position are false—that is, to refute them. To use refutation, you first identify objections to your position and then refute or overcome those objections with arguments and evidence. Credible evidence, facts, and data will be more effective than emotional arguments to overcome objections to your position that your listeners hold.

Cause and Effect

As Chapter 11 describes, you can organize your persuasive cause-and-effect speech by discussing an effect, or problem, and then identifying the causes of the problem. You can also organize a message by noting the problem and then spelling out the effects of the problem. With either approach, the goal of using cause-and-effect organization is to convince your listeners that one event *causes* another. Simply because two events occur at the same time or in close succession does not prove that there is a cause-and-effect relationship.

The Motivated Sequence

The motivated sequence is a five-step organizational plan.[10] It uses the *cognitive dissonance* approach: First disturb your listeners, and then point them toward the specific change you want them to adopt.

1. **Attention.** The attention step is, in essence, the introduction to your speech. Grab your listeners' attention with a personal or hypothetical example, a startling statement, an unusual statistic, a rhetorical question, or a well-worded analogy.

2. **Need.** Next, you arouse dissonance. You must establish why your topic should concern your listeners. You must also convince listeners that there is a need for a change and that the need affects them directly.

3. **Satisfaction.** After you present the problem, identify the solution—your plan to satisfy the need. Be brief, but present enough information so that your listeners have a general understanding of how the problem may be solved.

4. **Visualization.** *Positive visualization* paints a verbal picture of how wonderful the future will be if your solution is adopted. *Negative visualization* helps listeners see how awful things will be if your solution is not adopted. Use either type alone, or both together.

5. **Action.** As the basis of your conclusion, tell your audience the specific action they can take to implement your solution. Identify exactly what you want your listeners to do. Give them simple, clear, easy-to-follow steps to achieve your goal.

The motivated sequence is a guide, not an absolute formula. Modify it to suit the needs of your topic and audience. If your audience is neutral, spend time getting their attention and inviting their interest in the problem. If you are speaking to a hostile audience, spend considerable time establishing need; if your listeners are receptive, spend less time on that step. Be audience-centered; adapt your message to your listeners.

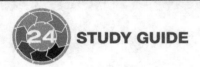

MEET YOUR OBJECTIVES

24.1   Identify strategies to improve your initial, derived, and terminal credibility.

Your competence, trustworthiness, and dynamism contribute to your credibility before, during, and after you speak.

24.2   Use principles of effective logic and evidence to develop a persuasive message.

Three general types of reasoning are inductive, which includes reasoning by analogy and by sign, deductive, and causal. Evidence includes facts, examples, opinions, and statistics.

24.3   Employ effective techniques of using emotional appeal in a persuasive speech.

Speakers can evoke persuasive levels of pleasure, arousal, and dominance among listeners by using examples, emotion-arousing words, nonverbal behavior, shared myths, and selected appeals to fear and other emotions.

24.4   Adapt your persuasive message to receptive, neutral, and unreceptive audiences.

Explore your ideas in depth when persuading a receptive audience. You must capture the interest of a neutral audience. Look for areas of agreement and choose a realistic goal with an unreceptive audience.

24.5   Use strategies for effectively organizing a persuasive speech.

Four patterns for organizing a persuasive speech are problem–solution, refutation, cause-and-effect, and the motivated sequence.

THINK ABOUT THESE QUESTIONS

1. **Self Assessment** What specific strategies can you implement to enhance your initial, derived, and final credibility as a public speaker in the minds of your public-speaking classmates?
2. **Ethics Assessment** Does dynamism always contribute to credibility? Should audiences be wary of charismatic speakers?
3. **Critical Assessment** Janice wants to persuade the management of her company to establish a wellness program. Draft outlines for Janice's main ideas according to each of the organizational patterns outlined in this chapter.

SPEAKING ON SPECIAL OCCASIONS

25

OBJECTIVES

25.1 Describe guidelines for effective public-relations speaking.

25.2 Identify occasions and best practices for ceremonial speeches.

25.3 List and explain strategies for creating humor in a speech.

PUBLIC-RELATIONS SPEAKING

25.1 Describe guidelines for effective public-relations speaking.

Public-relations speeches are designed to inform the public and improve relations with them—either in general or because a particular program or situation has raised some questions. If you are called upon to make a public-relations speech, use the following guidelines:

- First, discuss the need or problem that has prompted the speech.
- Go on to explain how the company or organization is working to meet the need or solve the problem, or why it feels there is no problem.
- Anticipate criticism, whether it comes from the audience as a whole or from a minority contingent, and take care not to become unpleasantly defensive.
- Acknowledge and counter potential problems or objections to the policy or program.
- Emphasize the positive aspects of the policy or program. You want to leave the impression that the company or organization has carefully worked through potential pitfalls and drawbacks.

CEREMONIAL SPEAKING

25.2 Identify occasions and best practices for ceremonial speeches.

Ceremonial speeches make up a broad class of speeches delivered on many kinds of occasions.

Introductions

A **speech of introduction** is much like an informative speech. The speaker delivers the introduction to provide information to the audience about the main speaker. You also need to make the speaker feel welcome while revealing some of his or her personal qualities to the audience so that they can feel they know the speaker more intimately.

The ultimate purpose of an introduction, however, is to arouse interest in the speaker and his or her topic. Introducing a speaker is similar to introducing your own speech. You need to get the attention of the audience, build the speaker's credibility, and introduce the speaker's general subject.

There are two cardinal rules of introductory speeches:

- **Be brief.**   The audience has come to hear the main speaker or to honor the guest, not to listen to you.

- **Be accurate.**   Ask the person you are going to introduce to supply you with relevant biographical data beforehand. If someone else provides you with information about the speaker's background, make sure the information is accurate. Be certain that you know how to pronounce the speaker's name and any other names or terms you will need to use.

Keep the needs of your audience in mind at all times. If the person you are introducing truly needs no introduction, do not give one! Just welcome the speaker and step aside. Note that the president of the United States is always introduced simply: "Ladies and gentlemen, the president of the United States."

Toasts

Most people are asked at some time or another to provide a **toast** for some momentous occasion—a wedding, a celebration, a birth, a reunion, or a successful business venture. A toast is a brief salute to such an occasion, usually accompanied by a round of drinks and immediately followed by the raising or clinking together of glasses or goblets.

The modern toast is usually quite short—only a few sentences at most. Some toasts are very personal, as, for example, one given by a best man who is a close friend of both the bride and the groom. In contrast, a toast made by someone who does not know the primary celebrants as intimately may be more generic in nature.

If you are asked to make an impromptu toast, let your audience and the occasion dictate what you say. Sincerity is more important than wit.

Award Presentations

Presenting an award is somewhat like introducing a speaker or a guest: Remember that the audience did not come to hear you, but to see and hear the winner of the award. Making an **award presentation**, a speech accompanying the conferring of an award, is an important responsibility. An award presentation has several distinct components.

REFER TO THE OCCASION   Awards are often given to mark the anniversary of a special event, the completion of a long-range task, the accomplishments of a lifetime, or high achievement in some field.

TALK ABOUT THE HISTORY AND SIGNIFICANCE OF THE AWARD   This section of the speech may be fairly long if the audience knows little about the award; it will be brief if the audience already knows the history and purpose of the award. Whatever the award, a discussion of its significance will add to its meaning for the person who receives it.

NAME THE PERSON   The longest part of this segment is a glowing description of the achievements that elicited the award. If the name of the person getting the award has already been made public, you may refer to him or her by name throughout your description. If you are going to announce the individual's name for the first time, you will probably want to recite the achievements first and leave the person's name for last. Even though some members of the audience may recognize the recipient from your description, you should still save the drama of the actual announcement until the last moment.

Nominations

Nomination speeches are similar to award presentations. They, too, involve noting the occasion and describing the purpose and significance of, in this case, the office to be filled. The person making the nomination should explain clearly why the nominee's skills, talents, and past achievements serve as qualifications for the position. And the actual nomination should come at the end of the speech.

Acceptances

For every award or nomination, there is usually at least a brief **acceptance speech**. If you ever have to give an acceptance speech, it may be impromptu, because you may not know that you have won until the award is presented. A fairly simple formula should help you compose a good acceptance speech on the spur of the moment.

- First, thank the person making the presentation and the organization that he or she represents. It is also gracious to thank a few people who have contributed greatly to your success—but not a long list of everyone you have ever known, down to the family dog.
- Next, comment on what the award means to you. You may also wish to reflect on the larger significance of the award to the people and ideals it honors.
- Finally, try to find some meaning the award may have for your audience—people who respect your accomplishments and who may themselves aspire to similar achievements.

Keynote Addresses

A **keynote address** is usually presented at or near the beginning of a meeting or conference. It sets the theme and tone for other speakers and events. Your challenge as a keynote speaker is to arouse the interest of the audience and motivate them to learn more or work harder. One way is to incorporate examples and illustrations to which your audience can relate. You should also emphasize the importance of the topic or the purpose of the meeting.

Commencement Addresses

To be audience-centered, a **commencement address** must fulfill two important functions. First, the commencement speaker should praise the graduating class. Because the audience includes the families and friends of the graduates, the commencement speaker can gain their goodwill (as well as that of the graduates themselves) by pointing out the significance of the graduates' accomplishments.

A second function of an audience-centered commencement speech is to turn graduates toward the future. Commencement speakers should suggest new goals and try to inspire the graduates to reach for them.

Commemorative Addresses and Tributes

A **commemorative address**, a speech delivered during special ceremonies held to celebrate some past event, is likely to include a tribute to the person or persons involved.

A commemorative speech is, in part, an informative speech. The speaker needs to present some facts about the event or people being celebrated. Then the speaker builds on those facts, urging the audience to let past accomplishments inspire them to achieve new goals.

Eulogies

A **eulogy**—a speech of tribute delivered when someone has died—can be one of the most significant and memorable and also one of the most challenging forms of commemorative address. When you deliver a eulogy, you should mention—indeed, linger on—the unique achievements of the person to whom you are paying tribute and, of course, express a sense of loss.

It is also proper in a eulogy to include personal and even tasteful humorous recollections of the person who has died.

Finally, turn to the living, and encourage them to transcend their sorrow and sense of loss and feel instead gratitude that the dead person had once been alive among them.

QUICK CHECK

Types of Ceremonial Speeches

- Introductions
- Toasts
- Award presentations
- Nominations
- Acceptances
- Keynote addresses
- Commencement addresses
- Commemorative addresses and tributes
- Eulogies

AFTER-DINNER SPEAKING: USING HUMOR EFFECTIVELY

25.3   List and explain strategies for creating humor in a speech.

After-dinner speeches may present information or persuade, but their primary purpose is to entertain. Speakers, actors, and comedians frequently employ the following strategies to make audiences laugh.

Humorous Stories

Humorous stories should be simple. Complicated stories and jokes are rarely perceived by audiences as funny. Successful humorous speakers also need a broad repertoire of jokes, humorous anecdotes, and one-liners. And it is important to know one's anecdotes very well. Only if you know the material can you hope to deliver it with the intonation and timing that will make it funny.

Humorous Verbal Strategies

Either a humorous anecdote or a shorter "one-liner" may rely on one of the following verbal strategies for humorous effect.

PLAY ON WORDS   **Puns** rely on double meanings to create humor. **Spoonerisms** occur when someone switches the initial sounds of words in a single phrase—for example, "sublic peaking" instead of "public speaking." **Malapropism** is the mistaken use of a word that sounds much like the intended word— *destruction* for *instruction*, for example.

HYPERBOLE   **Hyperbole**, or exaggeration, is often funny. In an after-dinner speech on "The Alphabet and Simplified Spelling," Mark Twain claimed,

> Simplified spelling brought about sun-spots, the San Francisco earthquake, and the recent business depression, which we would never have had if spelling had been left all alone.[1]

Of course, spelling could not have caused such catastrophes, but by using hyperbole, Twain makes his point in a humorous way.

UNDERSTATEMENT   The opposite of hyperbole, **understatement** involves downplaying a fact or event.

VERBAL IRONY   A speaker who employs **verbal irony** says just the opposite of what he or she really means. Student Chris O'Keefe opens his speech on reading Shakespeare with the following statement:

HOW TO   Choose Humorous Speech Topics

Your audience "gives attempts at humor their success or failure."[2] The following ideas can help you choose a topic that your audience will agree is funny.

- **Use what makes you laugh.** Chances are that if you have found an experience funny, an audience will, too.
- **Make fun of yourself.** Audiences almost always enjoy hearing self-deprecating humor.
- **Find humor in serious subjects.** Although your speech, as a whole, may be serious, you can often find humor in certain aspects of your topic. In his documentary film *Sicko*, Michael Moore showed a scrolling text of medical conditions that health insurance companies use to deny clients coverage against an outer-space backdrop while playing the *Star Wars* theme music.[3]
- **Avoid inappropriate subjects.** Topics that create a great deal of emotional noise for your audience (such as grief or anger) are not good subjects for humorous speeches.

At a certain point in my life, I came to the realization that I wanted to spend my life's effort to become a great playwright.[4]

Chris reveals the irony of the statement when he continues:

It has been about an hour and a half now and the feeling is still going strong.

WIT   One of the most frequently used verbal strategies for achieving humor is the use of **wit**: relating an incident that takes an unexpected turn at the end. Accepting the 2007 Oscar for Best Actress, Helen Mirren paid tribute to the monarch she had portrayed on screen in *The Queen*:

For 50 years and more, Elizabeth Windsor has maintained her dignity, her sense of duty, and her hairstyle.[5]

The wit occurs in the final phrase "her hairstyle," which catches the audience off-guard since they anticipate another majestic attribute.

Humorous Nonverbal Strategies

After-dinner speakers often create humor through nonverbal cues such as posture, gesture, and voice, which are discussed in detail in Chapters 17 and 18. Well-timed pauses are especially crucial delivery cues for after-dinner speakers to master.

Even if you are a person who is not "naturally" funny, you can use the strategies outlined above to prepare and deliver an after-dinner speech that is lighthearted and clever. Such a speech can still be a success.

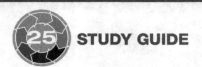 **STUDY GUIDE**

MEET YOUR OBJECTIVES

25.1   Describe guidelines for effective public-relations speaking.
A public-relations speaker describes the problem or program that prompted the speech, anticipating and countering criticisms.

25.2   Identify occasions and best practices for ceremonial speeches.
Chances are that at some time you will be called on to apply your speaking skills to make an introduction, toast, award presentation, nomination, acceptance speech, keynote, commencement or commemorative address, or a eulogy.

25.3   List and explain strategies for creating humor in a speech.
After-dinner speakers entertain through the use of humorous topics and stories, humorous verbal strategies, and humorous nonverbal strategies.

THINK ABOUT THESE QUESTIONS

1. **Self Assessment** You will be introducing a Pulitzer Prize–winning poet before her reading on your campus. How do you follow the cardinal rules of introductory speeches?

2. **Ethics Assessment** Several Web sites offer eulogy-writing services or prewritten generic eulogies. If you were asked to deliver a eulogy, would it be ethical to buy such a speech?

3. **Critical Assessment** A friend has been invited to give an after-dinner speech to a local service group but has no idea what to talk about. What advice can you offer?

SPEAKING IN SMALL GROUPS

OBJECTIVES

26.1 Detail the steps that groups use to solve problems with reflective thinking.

26.2 Explain how to participate effectively in a group.

26.3 Describe common roles and styles of leadership.

26.4 Identify key steps in planning and making a group presentation.

Small group communication is interaction among three to a dozen people who share a common purpose, feel a sense of belonging to the group, and influence one another.[1] Groups typically make better-quality decisions than do individuals because they have more information available, spark creativity among members, and can better recall and more actively process information. Group members are also usually more satisfied with participatory decisions than if someone just told them what to do. However, group members may also feel pressure to conform to the view of the group or of one dominant member. Some members shirk their responsibilities.[2]

SOLVING PROBLEMS IN GROUPS AND TEAMS

26.1 Detail the steps that groups use to solve problems with reflective thinking.

A central purpose of many groups is solving problems—finding ways of overcoming obstacles to achieve a desired goal.

John Dewey, a philosopher and educator, suggested using **reflective thinking**, a series of steps to solve problems:[3]

1. Identify and define the problem.
2. Analyze the problem.
3. Generate possible solutions.
4. Select the best solution.
5. Test and implement the solution.

Although not every problem-solving discussion has to follow these steps, you can use them as a blueprint to relieve uncertainty when groups try to solve problems.

Identify and Define the Problem

Groups work best when they define their problem clearly and early in the problem-solving process. To reach a clear definition, the group should consider the following questions:

- What is the specific problem that concerns us?
- What terms, concepts, or ideas do we need to understand in order to solve the problem?
- Who is harmed by the problem?
- When do the harmful effects occur?

Policy questions can help define a problem and identify a course of action to solve it. Policy questions begin with phrases such as, "What should be done about…?" or "What could be done to improve….?" For example, "What could be done to improve security at U.S. airports?" "What can we do to improve nutrition in school cafeterias?"

Analyze the Problem

Once the group understands the problem and has a well-worded question, the next step is to analyze the problem. **Analysis** is a process of examining the causes, effects, symptoms, history, and other background information that will help a group eventually reach a solution. When analyzing a problem, a group should consider the following questions:

- What is the history of the problem?
- How extensive is the problem?
- What are the causes, effects, and symptoms of the problem?
- Can the problem be subdivided for further definition and analysis?
- What methods do we already have for solving the problem, and what are their limitations?
- What obstacles might prevent a solution?

As part of the process of analyzing the problem, a group should identify **criteria**, standards for identifying an acceptable solution. Criteria not only help you recognize a good solution when you discover one but also help the group stay focused on its goal. Typical criteria for an acceptable solution specify that the solution should be implemented on schedule, should be agreed to by all group members, should be achieved within a given budget, and should remove the obstacles causing the problem.

Generate Possible Solutions

When your group has identified, defined, and analyzed the problem, you will be ready to generate possible solutions using group brainstorming, as described in the How To box on the following page.

Select the Best Solution

Next, the group needs to select the solution that best meets the criteria and solves the problem. At this point, the group may need to modify its criteria or even its definition of the problem.

In evaluating the solution, consider the following questions:

- Which of the suggested solutions deals best with the obstacles?
- Is the solution effective in both the short and the long term?
- What are the advantages and disadvantages?
- Does the solution meet the established criteria?

Brainstorm with a Group

- **Set aside judgment and criticism.** Criticism and faultfinding stifle creativity.
- **Consider anonymous brainstorming.** If group members find withholding judgment difficult, have the individual members write suggestions on paper first and then share the ideas with the group or use an electronic brainstorming app that allows participants to share ideas anonymously.
- **Think of as many possible solutions to the problem as you can.** All ideas are acceptable, even wild and crazy ones. Piggyback off one another's ideas.
- **Record all the ideas that are mentioned.** Use a flipchart, chalkboard, electronic whiteboard, or other device so that all group members can see and respond to all the ideas.
- **After a set time has elapsed, evaluate the ideas.** Use the criteria the group has established. Approach the solutions positively. Do not be quick to dismiss an idea, but do voice any concerns or questions you might have. The group can brainstorm again later if it needs more creative ideas.

- Should the group revise its criteria?
- What is required to implement the solution?
- When can the group implement the solution?
- What result will indicate success?

To achieve **consensus**—all members supporting the final decision—it helps to summarize frequently and keep the group oriented toward its goal. Emphasizing where group members agree, clarifying misunderstandings, writing down known facts for all members to see, and keeping the discussion focused on issues rather than on emotions are also strategies that facilitate group consensus.[4]

Test and Implement the Solution

The group may want to develop a step-by-step plan for implementing the solution, a time frame for implementation, and a list of individuals who will be responsible for carrying out specific tasks.

PARTICIPATING IN SMALL GROUPS

26.2   Explain how to participate effectively in a group.

To be an effective group participant, you have to understand how to manage the problem-solving process. You also need to prepare for meetings, evaluate evidence, effectively summarize the group's progress, listen courteously, and be sensitive to conflict.

Come Prepared for Group Discussions

Prepare for group discussions by researching the issues. Bring your research notes to help the group analyze the problem.

Do Not Suggest Solutions before Analyzing the Problem

Resist the temptation to settle quickly on one solution before your group has systematically examined the causes, effects, history, and symptoms of a problem.

Evaluate Evidence

To make a successful decision, examine and evaluate evidence. Ineffective groups are more likely to reach decisions quickly without considering the validity of evidence (or sometimes without any evidence at all). Such groups usually reach flawed conclusions.

Help Summarize the Group's Progress

It is easy for groups to get off the subject. Frequently summarize what the group has achieved, and point group discussion toward the goal or task at hand. Ask questions about the discussion process rather than about the topic under consideration: "Where are we now?" "Could someone summarize what we have accomplished?" and "Aren't we getting off the subject?"

Listen and Respond Courteously to Others

Understanding what others say is not enough. You also need to respect their points of view. Even if you disagree with someone's ideas, keep your emotions in check and respond courteously. Being closed-minded and defensive usually breeds group conflict.

Help Manage Conflict

In the course of exchanging ideas and opinions about controversial issues, disagreements are bound to occur.[5] You can help prevent conflicts from derailing the problem-solving process by doing the following:

- Keep the discussion focused on issues, not on personalities.
- Rely on facts rather than on personal opinions for evidence.
- Seek ways to compromise; don't assume that there must be a winner and a loser.
- Try to clarify misunderstandings in meaning.
- Be descriptive rather than evaluative and judgmental.
- Keep emotions in check.

LEADING SMALL GROUPS

26.3 Describe common roles and styles of leadership.

To lead is to influence others. Some think of a leader as one individual empowered to delegate work and direct the group. In reality, however, group leadership is often shared.

Leadership Responsibilities

Leaders help groups accomplish their tasks and maintain a healthy social climate. Rarely does one person perform all leadership responsibilities, even if a leader is formally appointed or elected. Most often, individual group members assume some specific leadership task, based on their personalities, skills, sensitivity, and the group's needs.

If you determine that the group needs a clearer focus on the task or more attention to social comfort, be ready to influence the group appropriately to help get the job done in a positive, productive way.

Leadership Styles

Leaders can be described by the patterns of behavior, or leadership styles, they exhibit. The following describe general leadership styles.[6]

- *Authoritarian leaders* assume positions of superiority, giving orders and taking control of the group's activity. Although authoritarian leaders can usually organize group activities with a high degree of efficiency and virtually eliminate uncertainty about who should do what, most problem-solving groups prefer democratic leaders.
- *Democratic leaders* involve group members in the decision-making process, rather than dictate what should be done. Democratic leaders focus more on guiding discussion than on issuing commands.
- *Laissez-faire leaders* allow group members complete freedom in all aspects of the decision-making process. They do little to help the group achieve its goal. This style of "nonleadership" often leaves a group frustrated because it lacks guidance and has to struggle with organizing the work.
- *Transformational leaders* influence others by building a shared vision of the future, inspiring others to achieve, developing high-quality individual relationships with others, and helping people see how what they do is related to a larger framework or system. Transformational leaders are good communicators who support and encourage rather than demean or demand.

What is the most effective leadership style? No single style is effective in every group situation. The best leadership style depends on the nature of the group task, the power of the leader, and the relationship between leader and group members.

GROUP PRESENTATIONS

26.4 Identify key steps in planning and making a group presentation.

After a group has reached a decision, solved a problem, or uncovered new information, group members often present their findings to others. Groups should use the same audience-centered principles as individual speakers. The central and most important step is to analyze the audience that will listen to the presentation. In addition, consider these suggestions for enhancing teamwork:

- Make sure group members understand the task or assignment, and work together to identify a topic.
- Try brainstorming to develop a topic or solve a problem.
- Give group members individual assignments.

Answer Questions after a Group Presentation

Use these tips, as well as the ones in Chapter 19, to help you and your group manage a question-and-answer session:

- **Be prepared for pointed or hostile questions.** First, keep your composure. Second, try to rephrase a negative question. For example, if someone asks, "Why did you make such a mess of things by recommending a budget increase?" you could rephrase by saying, "Why did we recommend a controversial budget increase?"
- **If you don't understand a question, ask for more clarification.**
- **Don't criticize questioners.** If someone asks a question that has just been asked and answered, or asks an irrelevant or poorly worded question, be polite, tactful, and gracious. Calmly provide an answer and move on.
- **Don't let a questioner make a speech.** If it looks as if a questioner is using the question-and-answer period to give an oration, gently ask, "And what is your question?" or "How can we help you?" Such questions should result in a question that you can address and then return the communication process to the control of the group.

- Develop a group outline that reflects the work of your group as an integrated problem-solving team.
- Decide on your presentation format.
- Rehearse the presentation.

The skills needed to give a group presentation are the same audience-centered speaking skills presented throughout this text. In addition, keep the following tips in mind for coordinating efforts among group members.

- **Clarify your purpose.** The first speaker can let listeners know what your speaking goal is and explain why you are presenting the information to them. If your group is responding to a specific question, it may be helpful to visually display the question or purpose of the presentation.
- **Use presentation aids effectively.** Visual aids can help to unify your group presentation. Consider having each group member use the same template and font style to add to the coordinated look and feel of your presentation.
- **Assign someone to serve as coordinator or moderator.** A moderator can provide needed structure to a group presentation by introducing both the topic and the group members, keeping track of time, and ensuring that one or more people don't dominate the discussion or speak too little.
- **Armed with a well-planned outline, present your findings to your audience.** If you are using a symposium format, each group presentation is essentially a mini-speech. A panel or forum presentation is more extemporaneous and may even have an impromptu quality, but your delivery and comments should still be well organized.
- **Be ready to answer questions.** Besides being informed about your topic, you should have thoroughly read any written report the group has distributed.

STUDY GUIDE

MEET YOUR OBJECTIVES

26.1 Detail the steps that groups use to solve problems with reflective thinking.

To solve problems, groups must (1) identify and define the problem, (2) analyze the problem, (3) generate possible solutions, (4) select the best solution, and (5) test and implement the solution.

26.2 Explain how to participate effectively in a group.

Effective group members prepare for meetings, evaluate evidence, effectively summarize the group's progress, listen courteously, and help manage conflict.

26.3 Describe common roles and styles of leadership.

Group members often share leadership responsibility to help groups accomplish tasks and maintain a healthy social climate. Styles of leadership include authoritarian, democratic, laissez-faire, and transformational.

26.4 Identify key steps in planning and making a group presentation.

Group presentations rely on the same principles of audience-centered speaking as individual speeches, but also require a coordinated team effort.

THINK ABOUT THESE QUESTIONS

1. **Self Assessment** Your work team has been assigned to develop a new process for filling orders. What process should the team follow to solve its problem?
2. **Ethics Assessment** One member of Corey's group is not doing a fair share of the work. Is it ethical for other group members to do extra work to make up for the slacker?
3. **Critical Assessment** Karl seems to have taken charge of his group and is giving assignments to members. Although Karl is helping to get a lot accomplished, José resents Karl's overly zealous efforts. Should José keep quiet and just go along with Karl, or speak up and express his concerns about Karl's actions? Why?

Notes

Chapter 1 Speaking in Public

1. Dee-Ann Durbin, "Study: Plenty of Jobs for Graduates in 2000," *Austin American-Statesman* 5 (December 1999), p. A28.
2. Iain Hay, "Justifying and Applying Oral Presentations in Geographical Education," *Journal of Geography in Higher Education* 18, no. 1 1994), pp. 44–45; also see: Morreale and Pearson, "Why Communication Education is Important."

Chapter 2 Improving Your Confidence

1. K. K. Dwyer and M. M. Davidson, "Is Public Speaking Really More Feared Than Death?" *Communication Research Reports* 29, no. 2 (April–June 2012), pp. 99–107.
2. Steven Booth Butterfield, "Instructional Interventions for Reducing Situational Anxiety and Avoidance," *Communication Education* 37 (1988), pp. 214–223; also see Michael Motley, *Overcoming Your Fear of Public Speaking: A Proven Method* (New York: McGraw-Hill, 1995).
3. Joe Ayres and Theodore S. Hopf, "The Long-Term Effect of Visualization in the Classroom: A Brief Research Report," *Communication Education* 39 (1990), pp. 75–78.
4. Survey conducted by R. H. Bruskin and Associates, *Spectra* 9 (Dec. 1973), p. 4; D. Wallechinsky, Irving Wallace, and Amy Wallace, *The People's Almanac Presents the Book of Lists* (New York: Morrow, 1977).
5. John Burk, "Communication Apprehension among Masters of Business Administration Students: Investigating a Gap in Communication Education," *Communication Education* 50 (Jan. 2001), pp. 51–58; Lynne Kelly and James A. Keaten, "Treating Communication Anxiety: Implications of the Communibiological Paradigm," *Communication Education* 49 (Jan. 2000), pp. 45–57; Amber N. Finn, Chris R. Sawyer, and Ralph R. Behnke, "Audience-Perceived Anxiety Patterns of Public Speakers," *Communication Education* 51 (Fall 2003), pp. 470–481.
6. Amber N. Finn, Chris R. Sawyer, and Paul Schrodt, "Examining the Effect of Exposure Therapy on Public Speaking State Anxiety," *Communication Education* 58 (2009), pp. 92–109.
7. Amy M. Bippus and John A. Daly, "What Do People Think Causes Stage Fright? Naïve Attributions About the Reasons for Public-Speaking Anxiety," *Communication Education* 48 (1999), pp. 63–72.
8. Yang Lin and Andrew S. Rancer, "Sex Differences in Intercultural Communication Apprehension, Ethnocentrism, and Intercultural Willingness to Communicate," *Psychological Reports* 92 (2003), pp. 195–200.
9. S. Shimotsu and T. P. Mottet, "The Relationships Among Perfectionism, Communication Apprehension, and Temperament," *Communication Research Reports* 26, 3 (2009), pp. 188–197.
10. Michael J. Beatty, James C. McCroskey, and A. D. Heisel, "Communication Apprehension as Temperamental Expression: A Communibiological Paradigm," *Communication Monographs* 65 (1998), pp. 197–219; Michael J. Beatty and Kristin Marie Valencic, "Context-Based Apprehension Versus Planning Demands: A Communibiological Analysis of Anticipatory Public Speaking Anxiety," *Communication Education* 49 (Jan. 2000), pp. 58–71; Valerie A. MacIntyre, P. D. MacIntyre, and G. Carre, "Heart Rate as a Predictor of Speaking Anxiety," *Communication Research Reports*, 27, no. 4 (2010), pp. 286–297; Michael J. Beatty, A. D. Heisel, R. J. Lewis, M. E. Pence, A. Reinhart, and Y. Tian, "Communication Apprehension and Resting Alpha Range Asymmetry in the Anterior Cortex," *Communication Education* 60, no. 4 (2011), pp. 441–460.
11. Kay B. Harris, Chris R. Sawyer, and Ralph R. Behnke, "Predicting Speech State Anxiety from Trait Anxiety, Reactivity, and Situational Influences," *Communication Quarterly* 54 (2006), pp. 213–226.
12. Desiree C. Duff, Timothy R. Levine, Michael J. Beatty, Jessica Woolbright, and Hee Sun Park, "Testing Public Anxiety Treatments Against a Credible Placebo Control," *Communication Education* 56 (2007), pp. 72–88.
13. Chad Edwards and Suzanne Walker, "Using Public Speaking Learning Communities to Reduce Communication Apprehension," *Texas Speech Communication Journal* 32 (2007), pp. 65–71; also see Chia-Fang (Sandy) Hsu, "The Relationship of Trait Anxiety, Audience Nonverbal Feedback, and Attributions to Public Speaking State Anxiety," *Communication Research Reports* 26, no. 3 (August 2009), pp. 237–246.
14. Finn, Sawyer, and Schrodt, "Examining the Effect of Exposure Therapy on Public Speaking State Anxiety."

Chapter 3 Presenting Your First Speech

1. J. C. Pearson, J. T. Child, and D. H. Kahl, Jr., "Preparation Meeting Opportunity: How Do College Students Prepare for Public Speeches?" *Communication Quarterly*, 54, no. 3 (Aug. 2006), pp. 351–366.
2. Greg Winter, "The Chips Are Down: Frito-Lay Cuts Costs with Smaller Servings," *Austin American-Statesman* 2 (January 2001), p. A6.

Chapter 4 Ethics and Free Speech

1. National Communication Association, "NCA Credo for Communication Ethics," 1999. 27 June 2001.
2. Samuel Walker, *Hate Speech* (Lincoln: U of Nebraska P, 1994), p. 162.
3. "Libel and Slander," *The Ethical Spectacle*. 1 June 1997.
4. "Supreme Court Rules: Cyberspace Will Be Free! ACLU Hails Victory in Internet Censorship Challenge." *American Civil Liberties Union Freedom Network*. 26 June 1997.
5. Associated Press, "Free-Speech, Other Groups File Briefs Opposing Patriot Act." November 4, 2003.
6. Free Speech Debate. FreeSpeechDebate.com.
7. Michele Eodice, "Plagiarism, Pedagogy, and Controversy: A Conversation with Rebecca Moore Howard," *Issues in Writing* 13, no. 1 (Fall/Winter 2002).
8. "Bed Bugs." Centers for Disease Control and Prevention, Web. June 9, 2013 www.cdc.gov/parasites/bedbugs/.

Chapter 5 Listening

1. Laura Ann Janusik, "Building Listening Theory: The Validation of the Conversational Listening Span," *Communication Studies* 58, no. 2 (June 2007), pp. 139–56.
2. Ralph G. Nichols and Leonard A. Stevens, "Six Bad Listening Habits," in *Are You Listening?* (New York: McGraw-Hill, 1957).
3. K. K. Halone and L. L. Pecchioni, "Relational Listening: A Grounded Theoretical Model," *Communication Reports* 14 (2001), pp. 59–71.
4. G. D. Bodie, D. L. Worthington, and C. C. Gearhart, "The Listening Styles Profile-Revised (LSP-R): A Scale Revision and Evidence for Validity," *Communication Quarterly* 16 (2013), pp. 72–90; see Larry L. Barker and Kittie W. Watson, *Listen Up* (New York: St. Martin's Press, 2000); also see M. Imhof, "Who Are We as We Listen? Individual Listening Profiles in Varying Contexts," *International Journal of Listening* 18 (2004), pp. 36–45.
5. For research about the effectiveness of active listening see: H. Weger Jr., G. C. Bell, E. M. Minel, and M. C. Robinson, "The Relative Effectiveness of Active Listening in Initial Interactions," *International Journal of Listening* 28, no. 1 (2014), pp. 13–31.
6. Harold Barrett, *Rhetoric and Civility: Human Development, Narcissism, and the Good Audience* (Albany: SUNY, 1991), p.154.

Chapter 6 Analyzing Your Audience

1. For an excellent discussion of how to adapt to specific audience situations, see Jo Sprague and Douglas Stuart, *The Speaker's Handbook* (Belmont, CA: Wadsworth and Thompson, 2005), p. 345.
2. *Random House Webster's Unabridged Dictionary* (New York: Random House, 1998), p. 1590.
3. Devorah Lieberman, *Public Speaking in the Multicultural Environment* (Boston: Allyn & Bacon, 2000). Also see Edward T. Hall, *The Silent Language* (Greenwich, CT: Fawcett, 1959); and Edward T. Hall, *The -Hidden Dimension* (Garden City, NY: Doubleday, 1966).

Chapter 7 Adapting to Your Audience as You Speak

1. The research summarized here is based on pioneering work by Geert Hofstede and Gert Jan Hofstede, *Cultures and Organizations: Software of the Mind*. Revised and Expanded 2nd Edition (New York: McGraw-Hill, 2005). Also see Edward T. Hall, *Beyond Culture* (New York: Doubleday, 1976).

Chapter 8 Developing Your Speech

1. Alex F. Osborn, *Applied Imagination* (New York: Scribner's, 1962).

Chapter 9   Gathering Supporting Material

1. "Types of Web Sites," Xavier University Library, 2010.
2. Elizabeth Kirk, "Practical Steps in Evaluating Internet Resources," May 7, 2001 http://milton.mse.jhu.edu:8001/research/education/practical.html. Also see: Evaluating Web Sites: A Checklist - University of Maryland Libraries www.lib.umd.edu/binaries/content/assets/public/usereducation/evaluating-web-sites-checklist-form.pdf. Accessed, May 25, 2016
3. Paul Gorski, "A Multicultural Model for Evaluating Educational Web Sites," December 1999 http://curry.edschool.virginia.edu/go/multicultural/net/comps/model.html.

Chapter 10   Supporting Your Speech

1. James Stanfill, "Entomophagy: The Other Other White Meat," *Winning Orations 2009* (Mankato, MN: Interstate Oratorical Association, 2009), p. 24.
2. Michael Blastland and David Spiegelhalter, *The Norm Chronicles: Stories and Numbers about Danger* (London: Profile Books, 2013), p. 47.
3. Daniel Hinderliter, "Collaborative Consumption," *Winning Orations 2012* (Mankato, MN: Interstate Oratorical Association, 2012), p. 140.

Chapter 11   Organizing Your Speech

1. The following information is adapted from Deborah A. Lieberman, *Public Speaking in the Multicultural Environment* (Englewood Cliffs, NJ: Prentice Hall, 1994).
2. Martin Medhurst, "The Text(ure) of the World in Presidential Rhetoric," *Vital Speeches of the Day* (June 2012).
3. Molly A. Lovell, "Hotel Security: The Hidden Crisis," *Winning Orations 1994* (Mankato, MN: Interstate Oratorical Association, 1994), p. 18.

Chapter 14   Developing a Conclusion

1. Lou Gehrig, "Farewell Speech," *Lou Gehrig: The Official Web Site* 23 June 2007.
2. K. Phillip Taylor, "Speech Teachers' Pet Peeves: Student Behaviors That Public Instructors Find Annoying, Irritating, and Unwanted in Student Speeches," *Florida Communication Journal* 33, no. 2 (2005), p. 56.

Chapter 15   Using Words Well

1. David Crystal, "Speaking of Writing and Writing of Speaking," *Longman Dictionaries: Express Yourself with Confidence!* (Pearson Education, 2005), www.pearsonlongman.com, accessed June 28, 2016, p. 2.
2. S. I. Hayakawa and A. R. Hayakawa, *Language in Thought and Action* (New York: Harcourt, Brace, Jovanovich, 1990); Alfred Korzybski, *Science and Sanity* (Lancaster, PA: Science Press, 1941).
3. Michael M. Klepper, *I'd Rather Die Than Give a Speech* (New York: Carol Publishing Group, 1994), p. 45.
4. Michiko Kakutani, "Struggling to Find Words for a Horror Beyond Words," *New York Times*, September 13, 2001, p. E1.
5. John F. Kennedy, "Inaugural Address (January 20, 1961)" in *Speeches in English*, ed. Bower Aly and Lucille F. Aly (New York: Random House, 1968), p. 272.
6. Barack Obama, "Look at the World Through Their Eyes," *Vital Speeches of the Day* (May 2013), pp. 138–142.
7. David Brooks, baccalaureate address at Sewanee: The University of the South. *Sewanee Today* 11 May 2013.

Chapter 16   Methods of Delivery

1. Brody, Marjorie, "Capture an Audience's Attention: Points on Posture, Eye Contact, and More." 1999. www.presentation-pointers.com; Gellis Communications. "Top Tips for Preparing and Delivering a Manuscript Speech." 4 Nov. 2011. www.gellis.com/blog/top-tips-preparing-and-deliveringmanuscript-speech; Stephen Boyd, "The Manuscript Presentation: When and How." Feb. 2013. sboyd.com; David W. Richardson, "Delivering a Manuscript Speech." 2013. www.richspeaking.com/articles/manuscript_speech.html.

Chapter 17 Nonverbal Communication

1. Steven A. Beebe, "Eye Contact: A Nonverbal Determinant of Speaker Credibility," *Speech Teacher* 23 (January 1974), pp. 21–25; Steven A. Beebe, "Effects of *Eye* Contact, Posture, and Vocal Inflection upon Credibility and Comprehension," *Australian Scan Journal of Nonverbal Communication* 7–8 (1979–1980), pp. 57–70; Martin Cobin, "Response to Eye Contact," *Quarterly Journal of Speech* 48 (1963), pp. 415–419.

2. For a comprehensive review of immediacy in an instructional context, see Virginia P. Richmond, Derek R. Lange, and James C. McCroskey, "Teacher Immediacy and the Teacher-Student Relationship," in Timothy P. Mottet, Virginia P. Richmond, and James C. McCroskey, *Handbook of Instructional Communication: Rhetorical and Relational Perspectives* (Boston: Allyn & Bacon, 2006), pp. 167–193.

3. Michael J. Beatty, "Some Effects of Posture on Speaker Credibility," library paper, University of Central Missouri, 1973.

4. Paul Ekman, Wallace V. Friesen, and S. S. Tomkins, "Facial Affect Scoring Technique: A First Validity Study," *Semiotica* 3 (1971), pp. 37-58.

5. Paul Ekman and Wallace Friesen, *Unmasking the Face* (Englewood Cliffs, NJ: Prentice Hall, 1975); D. Keltner and P. Ekman, "Facial Expression of Emotion," in M. Lewis and J. M. Haviland-Jones, eds., *Handbook of Emotions* (New York: Gilford, 2000), pp. 236–249; D. Keltner, P. Ekman, G. S. Gonzaga, and J. Beer, "Facial Expression of Emotion," in R. J. Davidson, K. R. Scherer, and H. H. Goldsmith, eds., *Handbook of Affective Sciences* (New York: Oxford University Press, 2003), pp. 415–432.

Chapter 18 Verbal Communication

1. Adapted from Schilling, Lester. *Voice and Diction for the Speech Arts*, San Marcos: Southwest Texas State University Press, 1979.

2. Gill, Mary M. "Accent and Stereotypes: Their Effect on Perceptions of Teachers and Lecture Comprehension." *Journal of Applied Communication*, vol. 22, 1994, pp. 348–61.

3. These suggestions were made by Sprague, Jo and Douglas Stuart. *The Speaker's Handbook*, Fort Worth, TX: Harcourt Brace Jovanovich, 1992, p. 331, and were based on research by Patricia A. Porter, Margaret Grant, and Mary Draper. *Communicating Effectively in English: Oral Communication for Non-Native Speakers*, Belmont, CA: Wadsworth, 1985.

Chapter 20 Selecting Presentation Aids

1. Emil Bohn and David Jabusch, "The Effect of Four Methods of Instruction on the Use of Visual Aids in Speeches," *The Western Journal of Speech Communication* 46 (Summer 1982), pp. 253–265.

2. J. S. Wilentz, *The Senses of Man* (New York: Crowell, 1968).

3. Michael E. Patterson, Donald F. Dansereau, and Dianna Newbern, "Effects of Communication Aids and Strategies on Cooperative Teaching," *Journal of Educational Psychology* 84 (1992), pp. 453–461.

4. For a good discussion of how to develop and use PowerPoint visuals, see Jerry Weissman, *Presenting to Win: The Art of Telling Your Story* (Upper Saddle River, NJ: Financial Times/Prentice Hall, 2003).

5. A. Buchko, K. Buchko, and J. Meyer, "Perceived Efficacy and the Actual Effectiveness of PowerPoint on the Retention and Recall of Religious Messages in the Weekly Sermon: An Empirical Field Study," *Journal of Communication & Religion* 36, no. 3 (2013), pp. 149–165.

6. Rebecca B. Worley and Marilyn A. Dyrud, "Presentations and the PowerPoint Problem," *Business Communication Quarterly* 67 (March 2004), pp. 78–80; Elizabeth Bumiller, "We Have Met the Enemy and He Is PowerPoint," *New York Times* (April 26, 2010; May 6, 2010) www.nytimes.com.

7. We acknowledge Dan Cavanaugh's excellent supplement *Preparing Visual Aids for Presentations* (Boston: Allyn & Bacon/ Longman, 2001) as a source for many of our tips and suggestions.

Chapter 22 Informative Speaking

1. Joseph L. Chesebro, "Effects of Teacher Clarity and Nonverbal Immediacy on Student Learning, Receiver Apprehension, and Affect," *Communication Education* 52 (Apr. 2003), pp. 135–147; Scott Titsworth, Joseph P. Mazer, Alan K. Goodboy, San Bolkan and Scott A. Myers, "Two Meta-analysis Exploring the Relationship between Teacher Clarity and Student Learning," Communication Education, 64, no. 4 (2015), pp. 385–418.

2. Steven A. Beebe, Timothy P. Mottet, and K. David Roach, *Training and Development: Communicating for Success* (Boston: Pearson, 2013).

3. Katherine E. Rowan, "A New Pedagogy for Explanatory Public Speaking: Why Arrangement Should Not Substitute for Invention," *Communication Education* 44 (1995), pp. 236–250.

4. Michael A. Boerger and Tracy B. Henley, "The Use of Analogy in Giving Instructions," *Psychological Record* 49 (1999), pp. 193–209.

5. Marcie Groover, "Learning to Communicate: The Importance of Speech Education in Public Schools," *In Winning Orations 1984* (Mankato, MN: Interstate Oratorical Association, 1984), p. 7.

6. C. S. Lewis, "On Stories," *Essays Presented to Charles Williams,* C. S. Lewis, ed. (Oxford: Oxford University Press, 1947); also see Walter R. Fisher, *Communication as Narration: Toward a Philosophy of Reason, Value, and Action* (Columbia: University of South Carolina Press, 1987).

7. See Bruce W. A. Whittlesea and Lisa D. Williams, "The Discrepancy-Attribution Hypothesis II: Expectation, Uncertainty, Surprise, and Feelings of Familiarity," *Journal of Experimental Psychology: Learning, Memory, and Cognition* 2 (2001), pp. 14–33; also see Suzanne Hidi, "Interest and Its Contribution as a Mental Resource for Learning," *Review of Educational Research* 60 (1990), pp. 549–571; Mark Sadoski, Ernest T. Goetz, and Maximo Rodriguez, "Engaging Texts: Effects of Concreteness of Comprehensibility, Interest, and Recall in Four Text Types," *Journal of Educational Psychology* 92 (2000), pp. 85–95.

8. George Miller, "The Magical Number Seven, Plus or Minus Two," *Psychological Review* 63 (1956), pp. 81–97.

9. D. K. Cruickshank and J. J. Kennedy, "Teacher Clarity," *Teaching & Teacher Education* 2 (1986), pp. 43–67.

Chapter 23 Understanding Principles of Persuasive Speaking

1. For a discussion of the elaboration likelihood model, see R. Petty and D. Wegener, "The Elaboration Likelihood Model: Current Status and Controversies," in S. Chaiken and Y. Trope, eds., *Dual Process Theories in Social Psychology* (New York: Guilford, 1999), pp. 41–72; also see R. Petty and J. T. Cacioppo, *Communication and Persuasion: Central and Peripheral Routes to Attitude Change* (New York: Springer-Verlag, 1986).

2. Leon Festinger, *A Theory of Cognitive Dissonance* (Evanston, IL: Row, Peterson, 1957).

3. For additional discussion, see Wayne C. Minnick, *The Art of Persuasion* (Boston: Houghton Mifflin, 1967).

4. Abraham H. Maslow, "A Theory of Human Motivation," in *Motivation and Personality* (New York: Harper & Row, 1954), chap. 5.

5. Paul A. Mongeau, "Another Look at Fear-Arousing Persuasive Appeals," in Mike Allen and Raymond W. Preiss, eds., *Persuasion: Advances through Meta-Analysis* (Cresskill, NJ: Hampton Press, 1998), p. 65.

6. K. Witte, "Putting the Fear Back into Fear Appeals: The Extended Parallel Process Model," *Communication Monographs* 59 (1992), pp. 329–347.

7. C. W. Sherif, M. Sherif, and R. E. Nebergall, *Attitudes and Attitude Change: The Social Judgment-Involvement Approach* (Philadelphia: -Saunders, 1965).

Chapter 24 Using Persuasive Strategies

1. Segrin, "The Effects of Nonverbal Behavior on Outcomes of Compliance Gaining Attempts." Also see: Steven A. Beebe, "Eye Contact: A Nonverbal Determinant of Speaker Credibility," *Speech Teacher* 23 (Jan. 1974), pp. 21–25; Steven A. Beebe, "Effects of Eye Contact, Posture and Vocal Inflection upon Credibility and Comprehension," *Australian Scan Journal of Nonverbal Communication* 7–8 (1979–1980), pp. 57–70; John A. Daly and Madeleine H. Redlick, "Handling Questions and Objections Affects Audience Judgments of Speakers," *Communication Education* 65 (April 2016), pp. 164–181.

2. Robin L. Nabi, Emily Moyer-Guse, and Sahara Byrne, "All Joking Aside: A Serious Investigation into the Persuasive Effect of Funny Social Issue Messages," *Communication Monographs* 74 (March 2007), pp. 29–54.

3. For an excellent discussion of the influence of culture on public speaking, see Devorah A. Lieberman, *Public Speaking in the Multicultural Environment* (Englewood Cliffs, NJ: Prentice Hall, 1994), p. 10.

4. Devorah Lieberman and G. Fisher, "International Negotiation," in Larry A. Samovar and Richard E. Porter, eds., *Intercultural Communication: A Reader* (Belmont, CA: Wadsworth, 1991), pp. 193–200.

5. Lieberman and Fisher, "International Negotiation."

6. J. C. Reinard, "The Empirical Study of the Persuasive Effects of Evidence: The Status after Fifty Years of Research," *Human Communication Research* 15 (1988), pp. 37–38.

7. Myron W. Lustig and Jolene Koester, *Intercultural Competence: Interpersonal Communication across Cultures* (Boston: Allyn & Bacon, 2009).

8. K. Rowan, "A New Pedagogy for Explanatory Public Speaking: Why Arrangement Should Not Substitute for Invention," *Communication Education* 44 (1995), pp. 236–250.

9. N. Miller and Donald T. Campbell, "Recency and Primacy in Persuasion as a Function of the Timing of Speeches and Measurements," *Journal of Abnormal and Social Psychology* 59 (1959), pp. 1–9; Adrian Furnham, "The Robustness of the Recency Effect: Studies Using Legal Evidence," *Journal of General Psychology* 113 (1986), pp. 351–357; R. Rosnow, "Whatever Happened to the 'Law of Primacy'?" *Journal of Communication* 16 (1966), pp. 10–31.

10. Douglas Ehninger, Bruce E. Gronbeck, Ray E. McKerrow, and Alan H. Monroe, *Principles and Types of Speech Communication* (Glenview, IL: Scott, Foresman, 1986), p. 15.

Chapter 25   Speaking on Special Occasions

1. Mark Twain, "The Alphabet and Simplified Spelling," address at the dedication of the New York Engineers' Club, December 9, 1907, *Mark Twain's Speeches; with an Introduction by William Dean Howells*, Electronic Text Center, University of Virginia Library, June 4, 2004, etext.lib.Virginia.edu.

2. John C. Meyer, "Humor as a Double-Edged Sword: Four Functions of Humor in Communication," *Communication Theory* 10, no. 3 (August 2000), p. 311.

3. Michael Koresky, "Prognosis: Dire, Michael Moore's 'Sicko'." *indiWIRE* June 22, 2007, www.indiewire.com/movies.

4. Chris O'Keefe, untitled speech, in *Championship Debates and Speeches*, John K. Boaz and James Brey, eds., (Speech Communication Association and American Forensic Association, 1987), p. 99.

5. "Mirren 'Too Busy' to Meet Queen," *BBC News* May 10, 2007.

Chapter 26   Speaking in Small Groups

1. See: Beebe and Masterson, *Communicating in Small Groups*; and in Steven A. Beebe, Susan J. Beebe, and Diana K. Ivy, *Communication Principles for a Lifetime* (Boston: Pearson, 2015), pp. 240–241.

2. For discussions of the advantages and disadvantages of working in small groups, see Norman R. F. Maier, "Assets and Liabilities in Group Problem Solving: The Need for an Integrative Function," *Psychological Review* 74 (1967), pp. 239–249; Michael Argyle, *Cooperation: The Basis of Sociability* (London: Routledge, 1991); J. Surowiecki, *The Wisdom of Crowds* (New York: Anchor, 2005); P. R. Laughlin, E. C. Hatch, J. Silver, and L. Boh, "Groups Perform Better Than the Best Individuals on Letters-to-Numbers Problems: Effects on Group Size," *Journal of Personality and Social Psychology* 90 (2006), p. 644–651. J. S. Mueller, "Why Individuals in Larger Teams Perform Worse," *Organizational Behavior and Human Decision Processes* 117 (2012), p. 111–124; B. R. Staats, K. L. Milkman, and C. R. Fox, "The Team Scaling Fallacy: Underestimating the Declining Efficiency of Larger Teams," *Organizational Behavior and Human Decision Processes* 118 (2012), pp. 132–142; B. M. Waller, L. Hope, N. Burrowes, and E. R. Morrison, "Twelve (Not So) Angry Men: Managing Conversational Group Size Increases Perceived Contribution by Decision Makers," *Group Processes & Intergroup Relations* 14, no. 6 (2011), pp. 835–843.

3. John Dewey, *How We Think* (Boston: Heath, 1910).

4. C. A. VanLear and E. A. Mabry, "Testing Contrasting Interaction Models for Discriminating Between Consensual and Dissentient Decision-Making Groups," *Small Group Research* 30 (1999), pp. 29–58; also see T. J. Saine and D. G. Bock, "A Comparison of the Distributional and Sequential Structures of Interaction in High and Low Consensus Groups," *Central States Speech Journal* 24 (1973), pp. 125–139.

5. For a summary of research about conflict management in small groups, see S. M. Farmer and J. Roth, "Conflict-Handling Behavior in Work Groups: Effects of Group Structure, Decision Processes, and Time," *Small Group Research* 29 (1998), pp. 669–713; also see Beebe and Masterson, *Communicating in Small Groups*.

6. Ralph White and Ronald Lippitt, "Leader Behavior and Member Reaction in Three 'Social Climates'," *in Group Dynamics*, 3rd ed., Darwin Cartwright and Alvin Zander eds. (New York: Harper & Row, 1968), p. 319; Francis J. Yammarino and Alan J. Dubinsky, "Transformational Leadership Theory: Using Levels of Analysis to Determine Boundary Conditions," *Personnel Psychology* 47 (1994), pp. 787–809.

Glossary

acceptance speech   A speech of thanks for an award, nomination, or other honor

accommodation   Sensitivity to the feelings, needs, interests, and backgrounds of other people

ad hominem argument   An attack on irrelevant personal characteristics of the person who is proposing an idea, rather than on the idea itself

after-dinner speech   A humorous presentation, usually delivered in conjunction with a mealtime meeting or banquet

alliteration   The repetition of a consonant sound (usually the first consonant) several times in a phrase, clause, or sentence

analogy   A comparison

analysis   Examination of the causes, effects, and history of a problem in order to understand it better

analytical listener   Someone who prefers messages that are supported with facts and details

andragogy   The art and science of teaching adults

anecdote   An illustration or story

antithesis   Opposition, such as that used in parallel two-part sentences in which the second part contrasts in meaning with the first

appeal to misplaced authority   Use of the testimony of an expert in a given field to endorse an idea or product for which the expert does not have the appropriate credentials or expertise

articulation   The production of clear and distinct speech sounds

attitude   A learned predisposition to respond favorably or unfavorably toward something; likes and dislikes

audience adaptation   The process of ethically using information about an audience in order to adapt one's message so that it is clear and achieves the speaking objective

audience analysis   The process of examining information about those who are expected to listen to a speech

award presentation   A speech that accompanies the conferring of an award

bandwagon fallacy   Reasoning that suggests that because everyone else believes something or is doing something, then it must be valid or correct

bar graph   A graph in which bars of various lengths represent information

belief   An individual's perception of what is true or false

blueprint   The central idea of a speech plus a preview of the main ideas

boom microphone   A microphone that is suspended from a bar and moved to follow the speaker; often used in movies and TV

brainstorming   A creative problem-solving technique used to generate many ideas

brief illustration   An unelaborated example, often only a sentence or two long

cadence   The rhythm of language

causal fallacy   A faulty cause-and-effect connection between two things or events

causal reasoning   Reasoning in which the relationship between two or more events leads you to conclude that one or more of the events caused the others

cause-and-effect organization   Organization that focuses on a situation and its causes or a situation and its effects

central idea   A one-sentence statement of what a speech is about

channels   The visual and auditory means by which a message is transmitted from sender to receiver

charisma   Characteristic of a talented, charming, attractive speaker

chart   A display that summarizes information by using words, numbers, or images

chronological organization   Organization by time or sequence

citation manager   Web-based software package for collecting, organizing, and formatting citation information

clip art   Images or pictures stored in a computer file or in printed form that can be used in a presentation aid

closed-ended questions   Questions that offer alternatives from which to choose, such as true/false, agree/disagree, or multiple-choice

closure   The quality of a conclusion that makes a speech "sound finished"

code   A verbal or nonverbal symbol for an idea or image

cognitive dissonance   The sense of mental discomfort that prompts a person to change when new information conflicts with previously organized thought patterns

commemorative address   A speech delivered during ceremonies held in memory of some past event or the person(s) involved

commencement address   A speech delivered at a graduation or commencement ceremony

common ground   Similarities between a speaker and audience members in attitudes, values, beliefs, or behaviors

competent   Being informed, skilled, or knowledgeable about one's subject

complexity   Arrangement of ideas from the simple to the more complex

conclusion   The logical outcome of a deductive argument, which stems from the major premise and the minor premise

connotation   The meaning listeners associate with a word, based on their experience

consensus   The support and commitment of all group members to the decision of the group

context   The environment or situation in which a speech occurs

credibility   An audience's perception of a speaker as competent, trustworthy, knowledgeable, and dynamic

crisis rhetoric   Language used by speakers during momentous or overwhelming times

criteria   Standards for identifying an acceptable solution to a problem

critical listener   Someone who prefers to evaluate messages

critical listening   Evaluating the quality of information, ideas, and arguments presented by a speaker

critical thinking   Making judgments about the conclusions presented in what you see, hear, and read

culture   A learned system of knowledge, behavior, attitudes, beliefs, values, and norms shared by a group of people

declamation   The delivery of an already famous speech

decode   To translate verbal or nonverbal symbols into ideas and images

deductive reasoning   Reasoning that moves from a general statement of principle to a specific, certain conclusion

definition   A statement about what a term means or how it is applied in a specific instance

demographics   Statistical information about the age, race, gender, sexual orientation, educational level, and religious views of an audience

denotation   The literal meaning of a word

derived credibility   The perception of a speaker's credibility that is formed during a speech

description   A word picture of something

dialect   A consistent style of pronouncing words that is common to an ethnic group or geographic region

direct persuasion route   Persuasion that occurs when audience members critically examine evidence and arguments

domain   Category in which a Web site is located on the Internet, indicated by the last three letters of the site's URL

dynamism   An aspect of a speaker's credibility that reflects whether the speaker is perceived as energetic

either–or fallacy   The oversimplification of an issue into a choice between only two outcomes or possibilities

elaborate   From the standpoint of the elaboration likelihood model (ELM) of persuasion, to think about information, ideas, and issues related to the content of a message

elaboration likelihood model (ELM) of persuasion   The theory that people can be persuaded by logic, evidence, and reasoning, or through a more peripheral route that may depend on the credibility of the speaker, the sheer number of arguments presented, or emotional appeals

elocution   The expression of emotion through posture, movement, gesture, facial expression, and voice

empowerment   Having resources, information, and attitudes that lead to action to achieve a desired goal

encode   To translate ideas and images into verbal or nonverbal symbols

ethical speech   Speech that is responsible, honest, and tolerant

ethics   The beliefs, values, and moral principles by which people determine what is right or wrong

ethnic vernacular   A variety of English that includes words and phrases used by a specific ethnic group

ethnicity The portion of a person's cultural background that includes such factors as nationality, religion, language, and ancestral heritage, which are shared by a group of people who also share a common geographic origin

ethnocentrism The assumption that one's own cultural perspectives and methods are superior to those of other cultures

ethos The term Aristotle used to refer to a speaker's credibility

eulogy A speech of tribute delivered when someone has died

evidence The facts, examples, opinions, and statistics that a speaker uses to support a conclusion

examples Illustrations used to dramatize or clarify a fact

expert testimony An opinion offered by someone who is an authority on a subject

explanation A statement that clarifies how something is done or why it exists in its present form or existed in its past form

extemporaneous speaking Speaking from a written or memorized speech outline without having memorized the exact wording of the speech

extended illustration A detailed example that resembles a story

external noise Physical sounds that interfere with communication

fact Something that has been directly observed to be true or can be proven to be true by verifiable evidence

fallacy False reasoning that occurs when someone attempts to persuade without adequate evidence or with arguments that are irrelevant or inappropriate

fear appeal Seeking to motivate or persuade by threatening harm or danger unless action is taken to reduce the harm or danger

feedback Verbal and nonverbal responses provided by an audience to a speaker

figurative analogy A comparison between two essentially dissimilar things that share some common feature on which the comparison depends

figurative language Words that deviate from their ordinary, expected meaning to make a description or comparison unique, vivid, and memorable

final summary A restatement of the main ideas of a speech, occurring near the end of the speech

First Amendment The amendment to the U.S. Constitution guaranteeing free speech; the first of the ten amendments to the U.S. Constitution known collectively as the Bill of Rights

fonts Particular styles of typefaces

free speech Legally protected speech or speech acts

gender The culturally constructed and psychologically based perception of one's self as feminine or masculine

general purpose The overarching goal of a speech—to inform, persuade, or entertain

generalization An all-encompassing statement

graph A pictorial representation of statistical data

hard evidence Factual examples and statistics

hasty generalization A conclusion reached without adequate evidence

hyperbole Exaggeration

hypothetical illustration An example that might happen but that has not actually occurred

illustration A story or anecdote that provides an example of an idea, issue, or problem a speaker is discussing

immediacy Nonverbal expressions of closeness to and liking for an audience, made through such means as physical approach or eye contact

impromptu speaking Delivering a speech without advance preparation

indirect persuasion route Persuasion that occurs as a result of factors peripheral to a speaker's logic and argument, such as the speaker's charisma or emotional appeals

inductive reasoning Reasoning that uses specific instances or examples to reach a general, probable conclusion

inference A conclusion based on partial information or an evaluation that has not been directly observed

inflection The variation in the pitch of the voice

initial credibility The impression of a speaker's credibility that listeners have before the speaker starts a speech

initial preview   A statement in the introduction of a speech about what the main ideas of the speech will be

internal noise   Physiological or psychological interference with communication

internal preview   A statement in the body of a speech that introduces and outlines ideas that will be developed as the speech progresses

internal summary   A restatement in the body of a speech of the ideas that have been developed so far

invention   The development or discovery of ideas and insights

inversion   Reversal of the normal word order of a phrase or sentence

jargon   The specialized language of a profession or interest group

keynote address   A speech that sets the theme and tone for a meeting or conference

lavaliere microphone   A microphone that can be clipped to an article of clothing or worn on a cord around the neck

lay testimony   An opinion or description offered by a non-expert who has firsthand experience

line graph   A graph that uses lines or curves to show relationships between two or more variables

listening styles   Preferred ways of making sense out of spoken messages

literal analogy   A comparison between two similar things

literary quotation   An opinion or description by a writer who speaks in a memorable and often poetic way

logos   Literally, "the word"; the term Aristotle used to refer to logic—the formal system of using rules to reach a conclusion

main ideas   The key points of a speech

major premise   A general statement that is the first element of a syllogism

malapropism   The mistaken use of a word that sounds much like the intended word

manuscript speaking   Reading a speech from a written text

memorized speaking   Delivering a speech word for word from memory without using notes

message   The content of a speech and the mode of its delivery

metaphor   An implied comparison between two things or concepts

minor premise   A specific statement about an example that is linked to the major premise; the second element of a syllogism

model   A small object that represents a larger object

motivation   The internal force that drives people to achieve their goals

myth   A shared belief based on the underlying values, cultural heritage, and faith of a group of people

nomination speech   A speech that officially names someone as a candidate for an office or a position

non sequitur   Latin for "it does not follow"; an idea or conclusion that does not logically relate to or follow from the previous idea or conclusion

nonverbal transition   A facial expression, vocal cue, or physical movement indicating that a speaker is moving from one idea to the next

omission   Leaving out a word or phrase that the listener expects to hear

online databases   Subscription-based electronic resources that may offer access to abstracts and/or the full texts of entries, as well as bibliographic data

onomatopoeia   When a word is pronounced like its meaning

open-ended questions   Questions that allow for unrestricted answers by not limiting answers to choices or alternatives

opinion   Testimony or a quotation that expresses someone's attitudes, beliefs, or values

oral citation   The spoken presentation of source information, including the author, title, and year of publication

parallelism   Use of the same grammatical pattern for two or more phrases, clauses, or sentences

patchwriting   Failing to give credit for phrases taken from another source

pathos   The term used by Aristotle to refer to appeals to human emotion

personal illustration   An anecdote drawn from the speaker's experience

personification   The attribution of human qualities to inanimate things or ideas

persuasion   The process of changing or reinforcing a listener's attitudes, beliefs, values, or behavior

picture graph   A graph that uses images or pictures to symbolize data

pie graph   A circular graph divided into wedges that show each part's percentage of the whole

pitch   How high or low a voice sounds

plagiarizing   Presenting someone else's words or ideas as though they were one's own

prejudice   Preconceived opinions, attitudes, and beliefs about a person, place, thing, or message

preliminary bibliography   A list of potential resources to be used in the preparation of a speech

preparation outline   A detailed outline of a speech that includes the central idea, main ideas, and supporting material; and that may also include the specific purpose, introduction, conclusion, and references

presentation aid   Any image, object, or sound that reinforces your point visually or aurally so that your audience can better understand it

preview   A statement of what is to come

primacy   Arrangement of ideas from the most to the least important

problem-solution organization   Organization focused on a problem and its various solutions or on a solution and the problems it would solve

pronunciation   The proper use of sounds to form words clearly and accurately

proposition   A statement that summarizes the ideas a speaker wants an audience to agree with

proposition of fact   A proposition focusing on whether something is true or false or whether it did or did not happen

proposition of policy   A proposition advocating a change in a policy, procedure, or behavior

proposition of value   A proposition calling for the listener to judge the worth or importance of something

psychological audience analysis   Examining the attitudes, beliefs, values, and other psychological information about an audience in order to develop a clear and effective message

public speaking   The process of presenting a spoken message to an audience

public-relations speeches   Speeches designed to inform the public, to strengthen alliances with them, and in some cases to recommend policy

pun   The use of double meanings to create humor

race   A group of people with a common cultural history, nationality, or geographical location, as well as genetically transmitted physical attributes

reasoning   The process of drawing a conclusion from evidence

receiver   A listener or an audience member

recency   Arrangement of ideas from the least to the most important

red herring fallacy   Irrelevant facts or information used to distract someone from the issue under discussion

reflective thinking   A method of structuring a problem-solving discussion that involves (1) identifying and defining the problem, (2) analyzing the problem, (3) generating possible solutions, (4) selecting the best solution, and (5) testing and implementing the solution

regionalisms   Words or phrases used uniquely by speakers in one part of a country

relational-oriented listener   Someone who is comfortable listening to others express feelings and emotions

relationship   An ongoing connection you have with another person

reluctant testimony   A statement by someone who has reversed his or her position on a given issue

repetition   Use of a key word or phrase more than once for emphasis

rhetorical criticism   The process of using a method or standards to evaluate the effectiveness and appropriateness of messages

rhetorical question   A question intended to provoke thought rather than elicit an answer

self-actualization need   The need to achieve one's highest potential

sex   A person's biological status as male or female, as reflected in his or her anatomy and reproductive system

signposts   Cues about the relationships between a speaker's ideas

simile   A comparison between two things that uses the word *like* or *as*

situational audience analysis   Examination of the time and place of a speech, the audience size, and the speaking occasion in order to develop a clear and effective message

small group communication   Interaction among three to twelve people who share a common purpose, feel a sense of belonging to the group, and influence one another

social judgment theory   A theory that categorizes listener responses to a persuasive message according to the latitude of acceptance, the latitude of rejection, or the latitude of noncommitment

socioeconomic status   A person's perceived importance and influence based on income, occupation, and education level

soft evidence   Supporting material based mainly on opinion or inference; includes hypothetical illustrations, descriptions, explanations, definitions, and analogies

source   The public speaker

spatial organization   Organization based on location or direction

speaking notes   A brief outline used when a speech is delivered

specific purpose   A concise statement of the desired audience response, indicating what you want your listeners to remember, feel, or do when you finish speaking

speech act   A behavior, such as flag burning, that is viewed by law as nonverbal communication and is subject to the same protections and limitations as verbal speech

speech to inform   A speech that teaches others new information, ideas, concepts, principles, or processes to enhance their knowledge or understanding about something

spoonerism   A phrase in which the initial sounds of words are switched

stacks   The collection of books in a library

Standard American English (SAE)   The English taught by schools and used in the media, business, and government in the United States

standard outline form   Numbered and lettered headings and subheadings arranged hierarchically to indicate the relationships among parts of a speech

stationary microphone   A microphone attached to a podium, sitting on a desk, or standing on the floor

statistics   Numerical data that summarize facts or samples

summary   A recap of what has been said

suspension   Withholding a key word or phrase until the end of a sentence

syllogism   A three-part argument that consists of a major premise, a minor premise, and a conclusion

target audience   A specific segment of an audience that you most want to influence

task-oriented listener   Someone who prefers information that is well organized, brief, and precise

terminal credibility   The final impression listeners have of a speaker's credibility after a speech concludes

toast   A brief salute to a momentous occasion

topical organization   Arrangement of the natural divisions in a central idea according to recency, primacy, complexity, or the speaker's discretion

transition   A verbal or nonverbal signal indicating that a speaker has finished discussing one idea and is moving to another

trustworthiness   An aspect of a speaker's credibility that reflects whether the speaker is perceived as being believable and honest

understatement   A statement downplaying a fact or event

value   An enduring concept of good and bad, right and wrong

verbal irony   A statement that expresses the exact opposite of the intended meaning

verbal transition   A word or phrase that indicates the relationship between two ideas

vertical search engine   A Web site that indexes World Wide Web information in a specific field

visual rhetoric   The use of images as an integrated element in the total communication effort a speaker makes to achieve a speaking goal

volume   The softness or loudness of a speaker's voice

wit   Verbal means of relating an incident or a statement so that it concludes in an unexpected way

word picture   A vivid description that appeals to the senses

working memory theory of listening   A theory that suggests that listeners find it difficult to concentrate and remember when their short-term working memories are full

written citation   The print presentation of source information including the author, title, and year of publication, usually formatted according to a conventional style guide

Credits

p. 1: Dee-Ann Durbin, "Study: Plenty of Jobs for Graduates in 2000," *Austin American Statesman* 5 (December 1999), p. A28. p. 28: National Communication Association, "NCA Credo for Communication Ethics," 1999. 27 June 2001. www.natcom.org/conferences/Ethics/ethicsconfcredo99.htm. p. 29: *United States Constitution*. p. 29: Samuel Walker, *Hate Speech* (Lincoln: University of Nebraska Press, 1994), p. 162. p. 29: "Supreme Court Rules: Cyberspace Will Be Free! ACLU Hails Victory in Internet Censorship Challenge," *American Civil Liberties Union Freedom Network,* (26 June 1997), 1 June 1998 www.aclu.org/technologyand-liberty/aclu-hails-supreme-court-victory-internet-censorship-challenge. p. 33: "Bed Bugs," Centers for Disease Control and Prevention, (13 January 2013). Web. 9 June 2013. p. 101: Martin Medhurst, "The Text(ure) of the World in Presidential Rhetoric," *Vital Speeches of the Day* (June 2012). p. 126: David Crystal, "Speaking of Writing and Writing of Speaking," *Longman Dictionaries: Express Yourself with Confidence!* (Pearson Education, 2005). p. 131: Michael M. Klepper, *I'd Rather Die Than Give a Speech* (New York: Carol Publishing Group, 1994), p. 45. p. 132: Michiko Kakutani, "Struggling to Find Words for a Horror Beyond Words," *New York Times* (13 Sept. 2001), p. E1. p. 133: John F. Kennedy, Inaugural Address (20 Jan. 1961), *Speeches in English*, ed. Bower Aly and Lucille F. Aly (New York: Random House, 1968), p. 272. p. 133: Barack Obama, "Look at the World Through Their Eyes," *Vital Speeches of the Day* (May 2013), pp. 138–142. p. 187: Marcie Groover, "Learning to Communicate: The Importance of Speech Education in Public Schools," *Winning Orations 1984* (Mankato, MN: Interstate Oratorical Association, 1984), p. 7. p. 201: Maslow, Abraham H.; Frager, Robert D.; Fadiman, James, *Motivation and Personality*, 3rd ed., © 1987. Reprinted and electronically reproduced by permission of Pearson Education, Upper Saddle River, New Jersey. p. 231: Mark Twain, "The Alphabet and Simplified Spelling," address at the dedication of the New York Engineers' Club, December 9, 1907, *Mark Twain's Speeches; with an Introduction by William Dean Howells*, Electronic Text Center, University of Virginia Library, (4 June 2004) etext.lib.Virginia.edu. p. 232: John C. Meyer, "Humor as a Double-Edged Sword: Four Functions of Humor in Communication," *Communication Theory* 10(3) (August 2000), p. 311. p. 232: Chris O'Keefe, untitled speech, in John K. Boaz and James Brey, eds., 1987 *Championship Debates and Speeches* (Speech Communication Association and American Forensic Association, 1987), p. 99. p. 237: "Mirren 'Too Busy' to Meet Queen," *BBC News* (10 May 2007). p. 240: John Dewey, *How We Think* (Boston: Heath, 1910).

Index

Tips and materials
for success in your
Public Speaking course!

THE FOLLOWING SECTIONS INCLUDES:

√ **Supplemental information** to help you be
successful on assignments. Read it carefully.

> Questionnaire on Public Speaking
>
> Criteria for Evaluating Speeches
>
> Attention Getting Devices
>
> Presenting Oral Citations
>
> Constructing an Outline
>
> Constructing a Bibliography-MLA Style

√ **Informative Speech Assignments**

> The Demonstration Speech
>
> The Cultural Artifact Speech
>
> The Informative Speech

√ **Persuasive Speech Assignments**

> The "Critical Review" Speech
>
> The Tribute/Eulogy Speech
>
> The Speech to Convince-"Proposition to Proof"
>
> The Problem-Solution Persuasive Speech

HOW DO I FEEL WHEN SPEAKING IN FRONT OF PEOPLE???

Name_____ **Class**_____**Due**_____

PROCEDURE: Complete each of the statements below as openly and honestly as possible. You may be asked to share your statements with others in small groups.

1. When I am speaking in front of strangers I

2. When I speak to a group, the <u>hardest</u> thing for me to do is

3. When I speak to a group, the <u>easiest</u> thing for me to do is

4. If I could change one thing about the way I speak publicly it would be

5. What I want to learn how to do/learn how to control when I speak is

6. A strength(s) that I possess right now that can help me be successful in this class is

7. Communication is/is not important to me because

8. People who can successfully speak in front of groups are (list as many specific things as possible)

A4

CRITERIA FOR EVALUATING SPEECHES

The *average speech* (grade C range) should meet the following criteria:

- Conform to the kind of speech assigned. (Demo, informative, persuasion, etc.)
- Be ready for presentation on the assigned date.
- Conform to the time limit.
- Fulfill any special requirements of the assignment—such as preparing an outline with a sources cited page, using visual aids, minimum research requirements, use of note card(s) or outlines, etc.
- Have a clear specific purpose and preview.
- Have an identifiable introduction, body, conclusion, and use of transitions.
- Show reasonable directness and competence in delivery.
- Be free of serious errors in grammar, pronunciation, and word usage.

The *above average speech* (grade B range) should meet the above criteria plus:

- Deal with a challenging topic.
- Fulfill all major functions of a speech introduction and conclusion.
- Display clear organization of main points and supporting materials.
- Support main points with evidence that meets the tests of accuracy, relevance, objectivity, and sufficiency.
- Exhibit proficient use of connectives—transitions, internal previews, internal summaries, and signposts.
- Be delivered skillfully enough so as not to distract attention from the speaker's message—at least 75% eye contact.

The *superior speech* (grade A range) should meet all the above criteria plus:

- Constitute a genuine contribution by the speaker to the knowledge or beliefs of the audience.
- Sustain positive interest, feeling, and/or commitment among the audience.
- Contain elements of vividness and special interest in the use of language.
- Be delivered in a fluent, polished manner that strengthens the impact of the speaker's message.

The *below average speech* (grade D or F range) is seriously deficient in the criteria required for the C speech.

ATTENTION GETTING DEVICES

In addition to the attention getters listed in Chapter 6, the following devices can be effective methods for use in your introduction. The key to effective attention getters is that they must relate to the topic. If you cannot make the link do not use them.

TELL A STORY

Use Illustrations or Anecdotes - found in your research or from your own personal experience, stories engage interest and provide visual context for your topic.

USE A QUESTION

Rhetorical questions are those that do not require a direct answer, but instead encourage the audience to think about how each would answer the question. These are a commonly used device, especially in simple speeches, but should be used sparingly with more complicated topics.

BEGIN WITH A MEMORABLE QUOTATION

Well-worded or well-known quotations can be very effective openers. However, you must cite the author and link the quotation to the topic.

USE HUMOR

The key to using to humor is be certain it will be funny. Feel confident before selecting something humorous. Also, the humor must relate to your topic.

USE REFERENCES TO HISTORICAL OR CURRENT EVENTS

The key to the effectiveness of this attention getter is audience analysis. The audience should be familiar with the event you have selected. Otherwise, you must spend valuable time explaining the details of the event. Never assume that a short reference to an event will make sense to the audience - check out their knowledge beforehand.

AROUSE CURIOSITY OR SUSPENSE

This can be effective as an attention getter if it truly surprises and gains the attention of the audience without offending them. Be careful with this one.

USE AN AUDIO OR VIDEO CLIP

This can be an effective device to gain attention as it engages to the two primary methods through which people learn – through visual and auditory methods.

ORAL SOURCE CITATIONS

Citations must ALWAYS include:

The name of the publication or person you interviewed
The date of publication, or date of your interview

Citations SHOULD include if available:

The credentials of the person who is cited
How information was collected (a study of 50 people...)
The author of the article or book, if relevant

Citation Language Suggestions:

"According to the <u>publication</u> of <u>date</u>..."
"As reported in the <u>publication</u> of <u>date</u>..."
"On <u>date</u>, the <u>publication</u> reported that..."
"The <u>publication</u> of <u>date</u> states that..."
<u>Title/Name of Person</u> told the <u>publication</u> of <u>date</u> that..."
"In a personal interview on <u>date</u>, with <u>title/name of person</u>..."

**For Internet Sources you should report the date based on the following:
1. Published date is used first, if available
2. If published date is not available, last "updated" date is used
3. If there is not "updated" date, then accessed date is used.

SOURCE CITATION VERBS

Verbs carry so much information. Often beginners don't remember this and they just repeat words like "according to" and "states" to introduce their source citations. For clarity and interest, try to use variety when selecting verbs. Examples:

Adds, agitated, agrees, argues, ascertained, asserted, called for claimed, confirmed, considered, contended, contests, debates, described, detected, determined, differs, discovered, discussed, disputes, encountered, established, estimated, explained, figured, found, further supports, held, hit, informed us that, learned, located, met, noted, noticed, observed, perceived, pleaded, pointed out that, pondered, proudly observed, reported, requested, rescued, retrieved, revealed, reviewed, said, suggested, summed it up best, surveyed, talked about, uncovered, unearthed, viewed, warned us that, wrote.

CONSTRUCTING AN OUTLINE

The following explains the format and order for constructing an effective outline. Before beginning review the guidelines for outlining in Chapter 6.

Here is the standard format for a public speaking outline:

Specific Purpose Statement: According to Fujishin "state exactly what you want to do with your audience and what you want to tell them."

Introduction:

    Attention Step: Write your attention step out in full sentences.

    Clarification Statement: Write your thesis out in full sentences. (on the informative and persuasive speech the thesis step should include a statement of why your topic is significant and/or relevant)

    Preview: Write the preview of your two or three main points out in full sentences.

Body:

I.   A Roman numeral represents a statement of a major point and should be written in a short, declarative sentence.

    A.   A capital letter represents a main subdivision of a major point and should be written in a short, declarative sentence.

        1.   A small numeral represents support material for the main point and should be in key words only!

            a. A small letter represents support to the material directly above it and should be in key words only.

    B.   A capital letter represents a main subdivision of a major point and should be written in a short, declarative sentence.

        1.   A small numeral represents support material for the main point and should be in key words only!

            a. A small letter represents support to the material directly above it and should be in key words only.

Transition: This should be written out in full sentences and summarize the previous point as well as preview the next point.

Constructing An Outline (cont.)

II. Again, main point = short, full, declarative sentence

    A.   Sub point = short, full sentence

          1. Supporting material = key words

             a. sub supporting material = key words

    B.   Sub point = short, full sentence

          1. Supporting material = key words

             a. sub supporting material = key words

Conclusion:

Review: A review of your main points should be in full sentences.
Concluding statements: Should restate the thesis, should tie back to your
attention-getter and should include a "clincher" that brings a strong closure to the
speech. These concluding statements should be written out in full sentences

CREATING A BIBLIOGRAPHY OR SOURCE CITED LIST
Courtesy of the Orange Coast College Library
MLA Style Guide

Rules for MLA Works Cited

* List all sources in a Works Cited Sheet in alphabetical order by author's last name or, if no author, by title, but ignore leading articles (A, An, or The). If no author, lead with the title.
* Capitalize all significant words in the title including in the subtitle.
* Italicize all titles of books, periodicals, films and video recordings, databases, and web sites.
* If the date is not listed, use n.d.; if the page is not listed, use n. page.; if no publisher, use N. p.
* Put the medium (print, web, DVD) at the end or, if electronic or web, before the access date.
* Only include the URL of a web source if the reader will not be able to otherwise locate the source.
* Use correct punctuation (periods, commas, semi-colons) and end each citation with a period.
* Indent the second and any subsequent line five spaces.

BOOKS:

Basic Form -- Author/Editor Name/Corporate Name (last name, first name). *Title of the Book* (italicized). Edition (if not first edition). Publisher location: Publisher, Publication year. Publication Medium (Print).

Examples --

Wilson, Frank R. *The Hand: How Its Use Shapes the Brain.* New York: Pantheon, 1998. Print.

Eggins, Susanne, and Diane Slade. *Analyzing Casual Conversation.* London: Cassell, 1997. Print.

Quirk, Randolph, et al. *A Comprehensive Grammar.* 4th ed. London: Longman, 1985. Print.

ESSAYS/CHAPTERS/CRITICISM IN BOOKS WITH OR WITHOUT EDITOR:

Basic Form -- Author of Essay Name. "Title of Essay." *Title of the Book.* Ed. and Editor
Name. Publisher location: Publisher, Publication date. Page Number(s). Publication Medium (Print).

Examples --

Wiley, Stein. "Gangs Present a Serious Threat." *Gangs: Opposing Viewpoints.* Ed. Laura Engendort. San Diego: Greenhaven Press, 2001. 45-50. Print.

Winters, Yvor. *The Post-Symbolist Methods* (Allen Swallo, 1967): reprinted in *Contemporary Literary Criticism*. Vol. 85. Ed. Christopher Giroux. Detroit: Gale, 1995. 223-26. Print.

"Stem Cell Research." *Encyclopedia Britannica*. 2007 ed. Print.

BOOKS FROM ELECTRONIC RESOURCES:

Basic Form -- Author Name. *Title of the Book*. Publisher location: Publisher, Publication date. *Electronic Resource Title*. Date. Publication Medium (Web). Date of access.

Examples –

Zeinert, Karen. *Those Courageous Women of the Civil War*. Brookfield, CN: Millbrook Press, 1968. *NetLibrary e-Books*. 2009. Web. 9 Sept. 2009.

MAGAZINE AND NEWSPAPER ARTICLES:

Basic Form -- Author Name. "Title of Article." *Title of Periodical* Date of issue: page (or section and page). Publication Medium (Print).

Examples --

Mehta, Pratap Bhanu. "Exploding Myths." *New Republic* 6 June 1998: 17-19.

Lohr, Steve. "The Day Time Stopped." *New York Times* 3 Apr. 1998: C1+ Print.

SCHOLARLY ARTICLES (INCLUDING IN AN ANTHOLOGY OR LITERARY CRITICISM):

Basic Form -- Author Name. "Title of Article." *Title of Periodical* Volume.Issue (Date of issue): page-page. Publication Medium (Print).

Examples --

Lajolo, Marisa. "The Female Reader on Trial." Brasil 14.1 (1995): 61-81. Print.

Morrison, Jago. "Narration in McEwan's Fiction." *Critique* 42.3 (spring 2001): 253-68. Reprinted in *Contemporary Literary Criticism*. Ed. Janet Witalee. Detroit: Gale, 2003. 212-20. Print.

ARTICLES RETRIEVED FROM ELECTRONIC RESOURCES:

Basic Form -- Author Name. "Title of Article." *Title of Periodical* (or *Web Site*) Volume.Issue (if scholarly) Date of issue: page-page (or section and page if newspaper). *Database Name* (italicized). Publication Medium (Web). Date of access.

Examples --

Davidson, Paul. "Globalization." *Journal of Economics* 24 (2002): 475+. *Academic OneFile*. Web. 9 Sept. 2009.

Richardson, Lynda. "Minority Students In Special Education." *New York Times* 6 Apr. 1994: A1+.

Lexis-Nexis Academic. Web. 9 Sept. 2009.

DVDS, VIDEOCASSETTES, AND FILMS:

Basic Forms -- *Title* (italicized). Dir. followed by director's name. Perf. followed by performers. Other relevant roles followed by names. Original copyright year. Distributor, Year. Publication Medium (DVD, VHS, Film).

If you are citing the contribution of a particular individual (director, performer, writer), begin with his/her name.

Examples --

Amadeus. Dir. Milos Forman. Perf. F. Murray Abraham, Tom Hulce, and Elizabeth Berridge. 1985. Warner Home Video, 1997. DVD.

Logan, John, writ. *The Time Machine*. Dir. Simon Wells. 2002. DreamWorks/Warner Bros., 2002. Video casssette.

WEB PAGES AND SITES:

Basic Form -- Author (if any). "Title of page" (if part of a larger site). *Title of Web Site* (italicized). Publisher or sponsor of website (or N.p.), Date of publication or update (or n. d.). Publication Medium (Web). Date of access. <URL if necessary or required by your instructor>.

Examples –

Barlow, Amy. "Jane Austen Redux." *JaneAustenforever.com*. N.p., 15 Apr. 2004. Web. 9 Sept. 2009.

"Swine Flu." *Centers for Disease Control and Prevention*. USA.gov, 30 Mar. 2009. Web. 9 Sept. 2009.

Sinclair, Peter. *Climate Denial Crock of the Week*. Crock, 20 Apr. 2009. *YouTube.com*. Web. 5 June 2009.

From: *MLA Handbook for Writers of Research Papers*. 7th ed. New York: MLA, 2009.

INFORMATIVE
STYLE
SPEECHES

THE FOLLOWING SECTIONS INCLUDES:

√ **Informative Style Speech Assignments**

THE DEMONSTRATION SPEECH
THE CULTURAL ARTIFACT SPEECH
THE INFORMATIVE SPEECH

THE DEMONSTRATION SPEECH

GOALS • To demonstrate a process to your audience.
- • To organize material into a simple pattern.
- • To use short, clear sentences.
- • To use examples to clarify.
- • To use descriptive language.
- • To research information as well as information from your own experiences.
- • To practice out loud until comfortable.
- • To maintain a confident and relaxed posture.
- • To speak in a clear, relaxed manner.
- • To maintain direct eye contact with individual audience members.
- • To excite your audience about this process.

TIME: **POINTS:**

TOPIC- You will be demonstrating information to your audience on a topic you have selected. You should pick a topic that is relevant and interesting to your audience, is interesting to you, that, possibly, you have experience in and one that you feel you can make exciting and interesting. Avoid topics that are so simplistic that we do not learn anything new from listening to you. Your job will be to demonstrate or teach about your topic, therefore, organization and preparation are critical to the success of this speech. Please remember the keyword for this speech is "SIMPLICITY." There is still plenty of latitude in this assignment for creativity once you have satisfied the basic requirements.

RESEARCH AND PREPARATION - This assignment is deceptively simple looking. It does require analysis and organization. Finding information to supplement your own knowledge of how to do something should not be difficult. You may want to support your own ideas with at least one outside source.

Once you have decided on the organization, you need to decide on how much information can be covered in the time allowed for this assignment. You may have to reduce the information to a single aspect of the process or a single process. Make decisions about what forms of support would be most effective. Make decisions about how much you know, how much the audience knows and what is the most interesting information for the audience. You should be able to combine your analysis of the research into a single statement of purpose. Be able to state your specific purpose in a single sentence that includes the thesis statement and the main points of the speech. If you can do this you have probably done a successful analysis of the research.

Finally, there are some key analytical decisions you will want to make about the material, your audience and yourself. How much does your audience already know about the subject? How much do you know? What will be the most interesting information for the audience? What are you the most comfortable talking about? You should be able to combine all of the analysis of the research into a single statement of purpose. Be able to say what your goal is in a single sentence that includes the main idea and sub points of your speech. If you can do this in one clear sentence you have probably done a successful analysis of the research. <u>Identify your purpose at the top of your preparation outline.</u>

ORGANIZATION OF MAIN POINTS- You will choose one of the following patterns of arrangement to outline your main points as explained in Chapters 3 and 5. Pay careful attention to how these patterns help you organize your research:

Chronological, Spatial and Topical Patterns

The goal here is to be clear. Use simple patterns of organization. Make sure your audience understands the main ideas. The overall pattern should include an introduction, body and a conclusion. The introduction will have to be brief but it should at the minimum have some short attention step and a specific preview of the main ideas in the speech - see "Attention Getting Devices" in Supplemental Information. The conclusion should briefly summarize the key points. The body of the speech should be a simple pattern (see above) of 2-3 main ideas supported with specific examples, techniques, or visual aids. If you have a subject that has many steps involved you have two options:
1) Limit the subject to a part of the overall topic and then develop 2-3 sections of this portion or
2) "Group" the steps into common areas that will fit into 2-3 main ideas.
Overall, the goal of this organizational pattern should be simplicity.

LANGUAGE – Your purpose should be to explain - not to persuade that what you are saying is right. Work for clarity and interest. Use your own words. Spend time trying to develop the best words to get your idea across. Clarity is achieved with short, simple sentences at main ideas, good organization and the use of previews, transitions and reviews. Interest is achieved by supporting the simple main ideas with vivid descriptions and the use of personal pronouns. Remember, the language you use may be different from what you planned to say - that's okay, for if you have practiced you will still come across well.

DELIVERY- Delivery should be extemporaneous. Again, **do not write out your speech!!** Trust me on this one. Also, do not memorize your speech - it's another recipe for disaster!! If you feel these rules do not apply to you, then see me privately. Most important here is **PRACTICE!!!** Practice out loud alone and in front of others. Practice sounding lifelike, not like a "public speaker." Be yourself, but be a little more organized and direct than you normally are. Also, practice with your body. Practice standing in a relaxed and confident posture and using relaxed gestures and movements. Work to eliminate obviously nervous gestures and habits. Define the space and the amount of movement you feel confident using. If you are using visual aids, practice with them to get used to the feel and build your confidence. The key is behavior. Organize your movements. You can be as nervous as you want, but if the audience "sees" a confident, relaxed speaker, that is what they will believe you are!!

This may all seem fairly intimidating, but giving a speech requires you to think on more than one level. It demands that you coordinate both the analytical and behavioral aspects of your brain at the same time. This is a new set of behaviors for most of us. The key is in doing. Try doing these new actions and your brain will begin to accept this new pattern of behavior. The results may not seem spectacular at first but the eventual power you are able to achieve through the use of your brain in this fashion is an incredible reward for the work you put in. Good luck on your first effort.

SPECIFIC PURPOSE STATEMENT: To demonstrate to an audience how to hang wallpaper.

Introduction:

Attention Getter: About 10 years ago, my husband and I decided to do some redecorating. It was a rude awakening as I am sure most of you know, that contractors charge at least an arm and a leg to do this kind of work around a home. We realized that we needed some alternative choices, so instead of hiring out to do all the work, we divided what needed to be done into a couple of areas: what my husband and I could do ourselves and what we had to hire out to have done. This was more within our budget.

Clarification: I never expected I would become so enamored with what I learned to do: wallpapering and it is easy and rewarding.

Preview: First I want to roll out some reasons that you need to consider learning this process, then I will hang the process of wallpapering for you, and then we'll smooth out these steps to see the results.

Body:

I. Hanging wallpaper is an easy and rewarding experience.
   A. It's much simpler than you think.
      1. easy to learn
   B. It's very rewarding.
      1. Contractors
      2. You have the control

Transition: Now that you have my philosophy and motivation for this project, let's discuss the process.

II. The actual process breaks down into organizing materials and paper hanging.
   A. The 1st step is to assemble the tools.
      1. tape measure, a 4' level, and razor blades.
      2. a bucket of paste, a paint roller
      3. 4" broad knife, a smoothing brush, a seam roller, and a sponge.
   B. There are 4 steps in the hanging process.
      1. measure wall and roll your paper
      2. paste and cut your paper.
      3. hang expanded sheet.

4. finish up.
   a. trim the top and bottom.
   b. roll the edges of the paper.

Transition: I hope that the job of hanging wallpaper sounds easier than you might have anticipated. Now let's discuss the finishing touches.
Wallpaper Demo. Prep. Outline (cont.)

III. Complete three panels and examine them.
   A. Look for excess paste.
      1. smooth and remove
   B. Look for uniformity.
      1. color
      2. patterns

Conclusion:

Review: So now you have a very basic understanding of why hanging paper is worth investigating as well as how to go about doing it.
Restatement of thesis: It is a rewarding experience and something I take great pride in having accomplished. I know I can plan to make changes in any room of my house. Just think about how much $$$ you will save and how creative and beautiful your space will be. You will discover that you have an artist's touch after all.

DEMONSTRATION SPEECH ON WALLPAPER HANGING
KEYWORD OUTLINE - CARROLL, FRICKER, MONAHAN

SPECIFIC PURPOSE STATEMENT: To demonstrate to an audience how to hang wallpaper.

Introduction:
Attention Getter: 10 years ago, redecorating. rude awakening --contractors charge - what could do what we had to hire out. budget.
Clarification: so enamored easy and rewarding.
Preview: roll out reasons, hang the process, smooth out steps

Body:

I. easy and rewarding experience.
  A. simpler .
      1. easy to learn
  B. rewarding.
      1. Contractors
      2. control

Transition: my philosophy and motivation, the process.

II. actual process organizing materials and paper hanging.
  A. assemble the tools.
      1. tape measure, a 4' level, and razor blades.
      2. a bucket of paste, a paint roller
      3. 4" broad knife, a smoothing brush, a seam roller, and a sponge.
  B. 4 steps
      1. measure wall and roll your paper
      2. paste and cut your paper.
      3. hang expanded sheet.
      4. finish up.
          a. trim the top and bottom.
          b. roll the edges of the paper.

Transition: sounds easier, finishing touches.

III. three panels, examine them.
  A. excess paste.
      1. smooth and remove
  B. uniformity.
      1. color
      2. patterns

Conclusion:
  Review: worth investigating, how to do it.
  Conclude: rewarding experience, great pride, make changes in any room . how much $$$ you will save and how creative and beautiful. discover artist's touch after all.

TOPIC SELECTIONS FOR THE DEMONSTRATION SPEECH

Name_____Class_____Due_____

FIRST CHOICE:
Topic:_____

Why is it important/interesting to this audience?

_____

_____

What are your 2-3 main ideas?

1.

2.

3.

SECOND CHOICE:
Topic:_____

Why is it important/interesting to this audience?

_____

_____

What are your 2-3 main ideas?

1.

2.

3.

THIRD CHOICE:
Topic:_____

Why is it important/interesting to this audience?

_____

_____

What are your 2-3 main ideas?

1.

2.

3.

ANXIETY REDUCING CHECK LIST

Name_____   Speech_____

1. **Preparation Outline:** I have:
   Narrowed main points to assignment requirement   _____
   Identified specific purpose statement on outline   _____
   Checked for outline structure   _____

2. **Speaking Outline/Note Cards:** I have:
   Checked for **key words only**   _____
   Narrowed to pages to assignment requirement   _____
   Practiced from this outline   _____

3. **Practice:** I have
   Practiced my speech out loud   _____
      Approx. number of times: _____
      Approx. amount of time: _____
   Timed my speech and edited where necessary   _____

4. **Nonverbal behavior:** When I practice
   I am in control of my breathing   _____
   I take several deep breaths while waiting
      my turn to speak   _____
   I "center" my awareness of my breathing   _____
   I slow the rate of breathing   _____
   I "image" a calm, relaxed and confident speaker   _____
   I am comfortable and stable in my speaking stance   _____
   My legs are relaxed and stable, knees not locked   _____
   I am able to gesture to emphasize meanings and ideas   _____
      Gestures are above the waist   _____
      Move toward center of my body and out   _____
      Display open palm, relaxed fingers   _____
   I have practiced with my speaking outline   _____
   I have practiced audience contact   _____
   I focus on individuals rather than groups   _____
   I speak to each person 3-5 seconds or until the end
      of an idea or concept   _____
   I shift easily between outline and audience   _____

5. **Vocal Dimensions:** When I practice
      I am louder than I am in normal conversations   _____
      I emphasize the meaning of words an concepts
         through variation in pitch   _____
      I am speaking at a conversational rate   _____
      I use pauses where necessary and effective   _____
      My voice sounds relaxed and friendly. It expresses
         a desire to communicate.   _____

POST-SPEECH SELF-EVAULATION

Name _____Day/Time of class_____Assignment#_____

Evaluate your performance. Were you (circle one)

Very Satisfied   Somewhat Satisfied   Dissatisfied   Very Dissatisfied

1.   Do you think you successfully met your specific purpose? Why or why not?

2.   How did you feel about your ability to give this speech before you gave it?

3.   How did you feel about your ability to give this speech while you were giving it?

4.   How do you feel about your use of your use of outlines? Did the preparation outline help you feel "prepared?" Did the key word outline help you while you spoke? Why or why not?

5.   How do you feel about your use of research and supporting material. Did you gather enough research to be able to clearly explain your main points? Did you utilize a variety of support devices? If so, which ones? Did the research you use stimulate interest in the audience?

6.   How do you feel about your breath control. Did you take several deep breaths while you were waiting for your turn to speak? Were you able to "center" your awareness of breathing? Did you slow your rate of breathing?

7. How do you feel about your comfort/confidence level on this first speech. Were you comfortable and stable in your speaking stance, legs relaxed and knees unlocked? Were you able to "image" a calm, relaxed, comfortable speaker?

8. How do you feel about your use of gestures. Did you use gestures to emphasize meanings and ideas? Were your gestures above the waist? Did they move toward the center of the body and out? Did you display an open palm, relaxed fingers?

9. How do you feel about your use of audience contact. Did you focus on individuals or groups? Did you speak to each person for 3-5 seconds or until the end of a concept or idea? Did you shift easily between outline and audience? Did you utilize visual aides, if any, to clarify ideas for the audience?

10. How do you feel about your use of style of delivery. Did you speak at a conversational rate? Were you louder than you are in normal conversation? Did you emphasize the meaning in concepts through variation in pitch? Did your voice sound relaxed and friendly? Did it express a desire to communicate?

What specifically do you want to work on to improve your speech and performance? In the space below set three goals for your next speech-use full sentences:

Goal #1

Goal #2

Goal #3

Answer the following additional questions for Speech 2, 3, 4 and so on.

1. Discuss the goals that you set in your last evaluation that you feel you've met successfully. State each goal and describe why you feel sucessful:

2. What helped you be successful in helping you meet these goals? List each goal and describe in detail what methods you used to achieve this success:

3. Discuss the goals that you set in the last evaluation that you failed to achieve. List each goal and evaluate what barriers and challenges you encountered:

4. What methods will you try in order to achieve mastery of the goals listed in #3? Per each goal describe the techniques and methods you will utilize to overcome your challenges:

VIDEO EVALUATION

NAME_____**ASSIGNMENT**_____**TOPIC**_____

Some reminders before you watch your video. Keep your viewing of your speech in perspective. Remember that this is not a professional tape. We use older equipment that provides a poorer image and less clear sound so resist the temptation to compare yourself to a professionally lit and produced performance. Additionally, the image you of see of yourself fails to capture the true dynamics of the live speaking situation. Also, keep in mind that you are not a professional speaker. You are a beginner. You should evaluate your performance against what you think is a realistic and fair standard for you, not for a professional.

Overall evaluation: Circle the one that comes closest:

Very satisfied with my performance
Somewhat satisfied
Somewhat dissatisfied
Very dissatisfied with my performance

Vocal Dimension:
After hearing the tape I decided I like the following things I did with my voice (i.e. rate, pitch, volume, etc.):

_____

_____

_____

After hearing the tape I decided I disliked the following things I did with my voice:

_____

_____

_____

Nonverbal Dimension:
After seeing the tape I decided I like the following nonverbal aspects of my delivery (i.e. stance, gestures, audience contact, etc.):

_____

_____

_____

After seeing the tape I decided I disliked the following nonverbal aspects:

_____

_____

_____

THE CULTURAL ARTIFACT SPEECH - CARROLL, FRICKER, MONAHAN

GOALS
- To about the cultural significance of an object or symbol.
- To organize material into 2-3 clear and related main points.
- To use examples to clarify.
- To use descriptive language.
- To research information as well as information from your own experiences.
- To maintain a confident and relaxed posture.
- To speak in a clear, relaxed manner.
- To maintain direct eye contact with individual audience members.

TIME: **POINTS**:

TOPIC- Most of your research should come from your personal background. You need to choose a physical item that is readily available to you. This item should have both personal and cultural significance. The item should represent a culture, a sub-culture or a co-culture. The history of the item you are discussing should come as second nature to you. Most Jewish people can recite the story behind the menorah without pause, many African-Americans can share the story of Kwanzaa, deaf people will readily share the history of American Sign Language and Muslims can quickly tell you the significance of their prayer mats. The item you choose should be as much a part of your identity as it is a part of your culture. You will need to share the cultural significance of your item as well as its personal importance. You will also need to decide whether you speech should include a demonstration of the use of the item. In the past students have chosen to include a few of the following demonstrations: how to braid cornrows, how to bet on dreadle, how to drape a sari, how to do a Basque dance and how to perform a Japanese Tea Ceremony. If you use outside information, be sure to cite the source.

RESEARCH & PREPARATION: This assignment is deceptively simple looking. It does require analysis and organization. Refer to the chapters on content, organization and visual aides (if you intend to do anything visually) to help you prepare this speech. Once you have decided on the organization, you need to decide on how much information can be covered in the time allowed for the assignment. Make decisions about what forms of support would be most effective. Make decisions about how much you know, how much the audience knows and what is the most interesting information for the audience. You should be able to combine your analysis of the research into a single statement of purpose. Be able to state your specific purpose in a single sentence that includes the thesis statement and the main points of the speech. If you can do this you have probably done a successful analysis of the research. Identify your purpose at the top of your preparation outline.

ORGANIZATION OF MAIN POINTS: See organization for Demonstration Speech..

FORMS OF SUPPORT: See the section on forms of support in the text. The ones most commonly used for this type of speech are examples, narrations, descriptions, analogies (comparisons), definitions and specific instances. You can also use statistics and testimonies.

DELIVERY- See Delivery for Demonstration Speech.

CULTURAL ARTIFACT SPEECH
PREPARATION OUTLINE - CARROLL, FRICKER, MONAHAN

Specific Purpose: To teach the audience about the Polynesian Hei Matau.

Attention getter: Strength, determination, peace, prosperity, safety, and good health. When I visited Kauai over the summer I did a lot of surfing. The first place we surfed was Pakallas, a perfect left. What I didn't know, until we got out, was that it was a shark breeding ground. "Oops!" I noticed Todd had a Polynesian Fish Hook around his neck. He said it was for good luck. That day I bought one because I knew that we would be going back to surf Pakallas a number of times.

Purpose statement: Today I am going to tell you about the Polynesian Fish Hook or hei matau (hey-may-tow.) The hei matau is a fish hook symbol hung on a necklace that has special significance to the Polynesian culture.

Preview: I am going to tell you about the different types of hei matau then about some of the old and modern tools used to make them and lastly the meaning of the hei matau.

Body

I.   There are different types of hei matau depending on the type of fishing being done.

      A.   When trolling for Bonito or Tuna you use this type of hei matau
          1.   Mother of pearl shell (8)
          2.   Bone hook (2:273)

      B.   Another type of hook is used for fishing at greater depths or bottom fishing
          1.   wood (8)
          2.   Angular bend (8)
          3.   Sinker attached (8)
          4.   Designed to release (8)

      C.   The shark hook is very heavy duty
          1.   hard woods (8)
          2.   curved shank (8)
          3.   roots of ngangie tree (8)
          4.   Largest 20.5 in. (2:274)

Transition: Now that I have told about a few of the types of hei matau I will now tell you about some of the tools used both old and new to make them.

II.   A large variety of tools have been used throughout the ages to make the hei matau

      A.   Some very old tools were very effective at the job.
          1.   Pump drill (4)
          2.   Chisel and mallet (3)

3. Hardwood lava rock (3)
4. Lash or cord (3)
5. Bone-Whale (3)

B. Newer tools have made construction of the hei matau easier.
    1. Fretsaw (7)
    2. Wood Rasp (3)
    3. Files (5)
    4. Gravers (6)
    5. Wet dry sandpaper (3)

Transition: Those are some of the tools used both old and new to make the hei matau now let's learn about the meaning of the hei matau.

II. The hei matau has a rich cultural significance.

    A. The hei matau may be worn by priests as talismans during ceremonial practices.
        1. Fishing season (3), (5)
        2. Opening closed water (5)
        3. More ornate (5)

    B. There is also a mythological side to the hei matau
        1. Maui the great mariner (2:46, 86)
        2. Fishing w/brothers (1:46)
        3 Cast out his hei matau (1:12
        4. Great fish (2:47, 48)
        5. New Zealand (2:48)

    C. It is worn by everyday people to bring them the good fortune of the hei matau
        1. Surfers (3)
        2. Almost the whole cast and crew of Lord of the Rings
        3. Tourist (3)

Review: Today I told about the hei matau, three different types, the tools both old and new, and the meaning of the hei matau.

Conclusion: Strength, determination, peace, prosperity, safety, and good health, if you are having difficulty attaining these things in your life. It may not hurt to get yourself a hei matau what have you got to loose.

Works Cited

1. Best, Elsdon, <u>The Maori As He Was,</u> Wellington, New Zealand: A.R. Shearer, Gov, Printer, 1924.

2. Dansey, Harry, <u>The Maori in Colour,</u> Rutland, Vermont: Charles E. Tuttle Co. 1963

3. "Fish Hook Carvings." Aotearoe, Accessed March 13, 2007, www.aotearoa.cinz/bones/maui.htm.

4. "Hooks," Primitive Ways, Accessed, March 13, 2007, www.primitiveways.com.

5. Indiana University Art Museum, Raymond & Laura Wieglus Collection, 18th Century, www.indiana.edu/d~iuam/iuam_home/php, accessed March12, 2007.

6. "Pump Drills," Grobet USA, Accessed March 13, 2007, www.robetusa.com.

7. "The Fret Saw," Techology Student, Accessed March 13, 2007, www.tachnologystudent.com/equipl/fretsaw/htm.

8. "The Maroi-Volume II", New Zealand Electronict Text Centre, Accessed March 13, 2007, www.nzetc.ort/htm

CULTURAL ARTIFACT - CARROLL, FRICKER, MONAHAN
KEYWORD OUTLINE

Attention getter: Strength, determination, peace, prosperity, safety, good health. Kauai surfing, Pakallas. shark breeding ground Polynesian fish hook. bought one

Purpose statement: Polynesian fish hook or hei matau

Preview: types of hei mata, old and modern tools used to make, meaning
Body

I.   types of hei matau
     A.   trolling
         1.   Mother of pearl shell
         2.   Bone hook
     B.   depths or bottom fishing
         1.   wood
         2.   Angular bend
         3.   Sinker attached
         4.   Designed to release
     C.   ]heavy duty
         1.   hard woos
         2.   curved shank
         3.   roots of ngangie tree
         4.   Largest 20.5 in.

Transition: types tools

II.   variety of tools
     A.   old tools
         1.   Pump drill
         2.   Chisel and mallet
         3.   Hardwood lava rock
         4.   Lash or cord
         5.   Bone-Whale

     B. Newer tools
         1.   Fretsaw
         2.   Wood Rasp
         3.   Files
         4.   Gravers
         5.   Wet dry sandpaper

Transition: tools used, meaning.

II. cultural significance.
    A. priests, talisman
        1. Fishing season
        2. Opening closed water
        3. More ornate
    B. mythological side
        1. Maui the great mariner
        2. Fishing w/brothers
        3   Cast out his hei matau
        4. Great fish
        5. New Zealand
    C. everyday people, good fortune
        1. Surfers
        2. Almost the whole cast and crew of Lord of the Rings
        3. Tourist.

Review: different types, the tools, meaning of the hei matau.

Conclusion: Strength, determination, peace, prosperity, safety, and good health. Difficulty, hei matau

TOPIC FOR THE CULTURAL ARTIFACT SPEECH-CARROLL, FRICKER, MONAHAN

Name_____Day/Time of class_____Due_____

FIRST CHOICE: Avoid general, broad topics – narrow this down
    Topic:_____

    Why is it important to this audience?

    _____

    _____

    What 2-3 main points might your audience find interesting?

    1.

    2.

    3.

SECOND CHOICE: Avoid general, broad topics – narrow this down
    Topic:_____

    Why is it important to this audience?

    _____

    _____

    What 2-3 main points might your audience find interesting?

    1.

    2.

    3.

THIRD CHOICE: Avoid general, broad topics – narrow this down
    Topic:_____

    Why is it important to this audience?

    _____

    _____

    What 2-3 main points might your audience find interesting?

    1.

    2.

    3.

Cultural Artifact Topics – Felicia Coco
This format is described in more detail in the syllabus.

a. **Artifact Description** what the artifact is and where it is from before you elaborate.

_____

_____

    i. **Description:** You want to show us the artifact and explain what it is.

    _____

    _____

    ii. **History**: A brief history of the artifact.

    _____

    _____

b. **Cultural Representation** - How does the artifact represent/symbolize the culture?

_____

_____

    i. **Culture:** How the artifact relates to the culture

    _____

    _____

    ii. **Use:** How is it used or displayed?

    _____

    _____

c. **Significance** - What significance the <u>culture</u> has to you and society?

_____

_____

    i. **Myself:** Why is this important to you?

    _____

    _____

    ii. **Society:** Why should people learn more about this culture?

    _____

    _____

ANXIETY REDUCING CHECK LIST

Name_____   Speech_____

1. **Preparation Outline:** I have:
   Narrowed main points to assignment requirement   _____
   Identified specific purpose statement on outline   _____
   Checked for outline structure   _____

2. **Speaking Outline/Note Cards:** I have:
   Checked for **key words only**   _____
   Narrowed to pages to assignment requirement   _____
   Practiced from this outline   _____

3. **Practice:** I have
   Practiced my speech out loud
      Approx. number of times: _____
      Approx. amount of time: _____
   Timed my speech and edited where necessary   _____

4. **Nonverbal behavior:** When I practice
   I am in control of my breathing   _____
   I take several deep breaths while waiting
      my turn to speak   _____
   I "center" my awareness of my breathing   _____
   I slow the rate of breathing   _____
   I "image" a calm, relaxed and confident speaker   _____
   I am comfortable and stable in my speaking stance   _____
   My legs are relaxed and stable, knees not locked   _____
   I am able to gesture to emphasize meanings and ideas   _____
      Gestures are above the waist   _____
      Move toward center of my body and out   _____
      Display open palm, relaxed fingers   _____
   I have practiced with my speaking outline   _____
   I have practiced audience contact   _____
   I focus on individuals rather than groups   _____
   I speak to each person 3-5 seconds or until the end
      of an idea or concept   _____
   I shift easily between outline and audience   _____

5. **Vocal Dimensions:** When I practice
      I am louder than I am in normal conversations   _____
      I emphasize the meaning of words an concepts
         through variation in pitch   _____
      I am speaking at a conversational rate   _____
      I use pauses where necessary and effective   _____
      My voice sounds relaxed and friendly. It expresses
         a desire to communicate.   _____

POST-SPEECH SELF-EVAULATION

Name _____Day/Time of class_____Assignment#_____

Evaluate your performance. Were you (circle one)

Very Satisfied   Somewhat Satisfied   Dissatisfied   Very Dissatisfied

1.   Do you think you successfully met your specific purpose? Why or why not?

2.   How did you feel about your ability to give this speech before you gave it?

3.   How did you feel about your ability to give this speech while you were giving it?

4.   How do you feel about your use of your use of outlines? Did the preparation outline help you feel "prepared?" Did the key word outline help you while you spoke? Why or why not?

5.   How do you feel about your use of research and supporting material. Did you gather enough research to be able to clearly explain your main points? Did you utilize a variety of support devices? If so, which ones? Did the research you use stimulate interest in the audience?

6.   How do you feel about your breath control. Did you take several deep breaths while you were waiting for your turn to speak? Were you able to "center" your awareness of breathing? Did you slow your rate of breathing?

7.	How do you feel about your comfort/confidence level on this first speech. Were you comfortable and stable in your speaking stance, legs relaxed and knees unlocked? Were you able to "image" a calm, relaxed, comfortable speaker?

8.	How do you feel about your use of gestures. Did you use gestures to emphasize meanings and ideas? Were your gestures above the waist? Did they move toward the center of the body and out? Did you display an open palm, relaxed fingers?

9.	How do you feel about your use of audience contact. Did you focus on individuals or groups? Did you speak to each person for 3-5 seconds or until the end of a concept or idea? Did you shift easily between outline and audience? Did you utilize visual aides, if any, to clarify ideas for the audience?

10.	How do you feel about your use of style of delivery. Did you speak at a conversational rate? Were you louder than you are in normal conversation? Did you emphasize the meaning in concepts through variation in pitch? Did your voice sound relaxed and friendly? Did it express a desire to communicate?

What specifically do you want to work on to improve your speech and performance? In the space below set three goals for your next speech-use full sentences:

	Goal #1

	Goal #2

	Goal #3

Answer the following additional questions for Speech 2, 3, 4 and so on.

1. Discuss the goals that you set in your last evaluation that you feel you've met successfully. State each goal and describe why you feel sucessful:

2. What helped you be successful in helping you meet these goals? List each goal and describe in detail what methods you used to achieve this success:

3. Discuss the goals that you set in the last evaluation that you failed to achieve. List each goal and evaluate what barriers and challenges you encountered:

4. What methods will you try in order to achieve mastery of the goals listed in #3? Per each goal describe the techniques and methods you will utilize to overcome your challenges:

VIDEO EVALUATION

NAME_____ASSIGNMENT_____TOPIC_____

Some reminders before you watch your video. Keep your viewing of your speech in perspective. Remember that this is not a professional tape. We use older equipment that provides a poorer image and less clear sound so resist the temptation to compare yourself to a professionally lit and produced performance. Additionally, the image you of see of yourself fails to capture the true dynamics of the live speaking situation. Also, keep in mind that you are not a professional speaker. You are a beginner. You should evaluate your performance against what you think is a realistic and fair standard for you, not for a professional.

Overall evaluation: Circle the one that comes closest:

Very satisfied with my performance
Somewhat satisfied
Somewhat dissatisfied
Very dissatisfied with my performance

Vocal Dimension:
After hearing the tape I decided I like the following things I did with my voice (i.e. rate, pitch, volume, etc.):

_____
_____
_____

After hearing the tape I decided I disliked the following things I did with my voice:

_____
_____
_____

Nonverbal Dimension:
After seeing the tape I decided I like the following nonverbal aspects of my delivery (i.e. stance, gestures, audience contact, etc.):

_____
_____
_____

After seeing the tape I decided I disliked the following nonverbal aspects:

_____
_____
_____

INFORMATIVE SPEECH

GOALS •   To inform your students audience about a significant topic.
- •   To organize material into 2-3 clear and related main points.
- •   To become familiar with specific research techniques.
- •   To develop information within a specific organizational pattern.
- •   To utilize examples, statistics and opinions as support materials.
- •   To skillfully use visual aids.
- •   To use oral source citations.
- •   To demonstrate an increased confident delivery style and clear preparedness.
- •   To use descriptive language.
- •   To maintain direct eye contact with individual audience members.
- •   To excite your audience about this information.

TIME: **Points:**

TOPIC-   You must select a subject that is significant and relevant to your audience. Pick something that they can relate to, that has some relationship to their lives and that you can find current, new research information on. Your speech should be timely and "news" to your audience.

Instead of thinking "how to" begin to think "what," "who," or "where" as topic areas. Topics for this speech might include things like new technology (what) or a particular type of art like tattoos (what). A "who" speech may look at a particular person like Madonna or Hillary Clinton. Finally, a "where" version of this speech might focus on Ibeza off the coast of Spain or a tour of the best sites on the Internet. There may still be some demo involved but it is more likely that the informative skills of defining, describing, and explaining will be developed to increase the awareness and understanding of your audience.

RESEARCH - Research is required for this speech – you must use research to be credible to your students/audience.
1.   Use at least 5-6 published sources (books, magazines, etc.) Your sources should be from the last 3 years.
2.   Include a bibliography with at least 5 sources written in MLA style.
3.   Sources must be documented on the preparation outline. Use parenthesis at the end of a line with the source number from your bibliography and the page the information came from; i.e. (2:25) at the end of a line would indicate the second source in your bibliography, page 25. This format should also be used for Internet sources.

        When to Document:
- •   When the information doesn't come from you.
- •   When you change sources.
- •   When your audience might question the source of the information (numbers, dates, opinions from others, etc.)
- •   When you choose to cite the information orally.

4.   Oral citations may be required in this speech. See "Presenting Oral Citations" in Supplemental Information

Informative Speech (cont.)

PREPARATION: Like the Demonstration Speech, you should be able to combine your analysis of the research into a single statement of purpose. Be able to state your specific purpose in a single sentence that includes the thesis statement and the main points of the speech. If you can do this you have probably done a successful analysis of the research.

ORGANIZATION OF MAIN POINTS: Use no more than 2-3 main points. You will choose one of the following patterns to outline your main points: Chronological, Spatial, or Topical.

FORMS OF SUPPORT: You should use at least three types of supporting material in this speech, for example you might use statistics, examples, and or opinions. *****Visual Aids** may be required for this speech.

PREPARATION OUTLINE - a preparation outline is required. The preparation outline must have a specific purpose statement and be structured in three parts: Introduction, Body and Conclusion. Within these sections use the following guidelines:

1. Introduction: The attention-getter, thesis and preview should be written out in full sentences.
2. Body: Roman Numerals (I, II, III, etc.) represent the topic sentence of your main point and should be written out in full, short sentences. Capital letters (A, B, C. etc) represent subdivisions of main points and should be in full, short sentences. Small numerals, lower case letters and all other lower levels should be in key words only (see outline guide sheet)! All transitions should be written out in full sentences.
3. Conclusion: The review and conclusion should be written out in full sentences.
4. Identify specific purpose, and pattern at top of outline.

LANGUAGE - Again, your goal should be language that is both clear and interesting. A carefully worded specific purpose should include the speaker's intent and main ideas. Good speakers use concrete words, vivid, imagery, and personal pronouns to facilitate audience understanding. Main ideas should be written as short, simple, declarative sentences. Use precise words like "two" or "four" rather than vague language like "several" or "various." These ideas should be supported with vivid examples and lively descriptions. Don't be afraid to use words like "we", "us," and "our" during your speech. These words lessen the distance between you and your audience. Transitions should be written out between main ideas and should summarize the previous point as well as preview the next main idea. Each main idea should include at least one oral citation.

DELIVERY- Delivery should be extemporaneous. Again, **do not write out your speech and do not memorize your speech**. Be yourself, but be a little more organized and direct than you normally are. Practice relaxed posture, gestures and movements. Practice with any visual aids until you feel comfortable and confident. You can be as nervous as you want, but if the audience "sees" a confident, relaxed speaker, that is what they will believe you are!! This is a more complex speech with additional speaking techniques. For example, the introduction and oral citations should be practiced independently from the rest of the speech so you can say them with confidence and ease.

INFORMATIVE SPEECH ON ORCAS
SAMPLE #1 OF THE KEYWORD OUTLINE

Introduction:

Attention Step: visit great amusement parks, Sea World, the Shamu exhibit. tricks and friendly   label him as a Killer whale. until a video that showed me the true nature of the Killer whale.

Clarification Step: the true nature dispersed, deadly . Many people believe cold regions farther from the truth. Share information to know the truth about them

Preview: First, general physical general locations in the world, am going to let dangerous hunting techniques and eating habits that

.

Body:

I.   certain characteristics

      A.   unique coloration
          1.   extremely distinctive
          2.   disruptive coloration
      B.   size
          1.   small
          a.   A male 22 ft. in length and weigh 8,000 -12, 000 lbs.
          b.   A female 19 ft.length &weigh between 3000 - 8,000 lbs.
      C.   48-52 teeth, large, conical
          1.   teeth ripping

Transition: difference whales & killer whale, locations find Killer whales.

II.   "Next to humans, Killer whales are the most widely distributed mammal."

      A.   inhabit all oceans.
          1.   Artic, Antarctic, coastal areas of the U.S.
          2.   tropical areas
             a. Columbia River
      B.   Migration
          1.   seasonal
          2.   travel in pods
             a.   family members
             b.   two types of pods:
             c.   resident pod, transient pod

Transition: Killer whale looks like, where found, called Killer whales discuss eating habits.

III.   Good hunters

        A.   fish, mammals, whales.
           1.   Fish, squid, etc.
        B.   cooperative hunting,
           1.   techniques and situations typical
               a.   Beaching
                   1)   only species
               b.   Surrounding cooperatively
                    capture and kill it.
                   1)   30 killer whales assaulted and killed a
                        60ft. blue whale
           2.   two whales, great white shark

Conclusion:

Review: physical characteristics, their distribution, deadly but effective
              food behaviors.

Concluding: useful, the wolf of the sea.

SAMPLE #1 OF THE MAIN OUTLINE - INFORMATIVE SPEECH ON ORCAS

SPECIFIC PURPOSE STATMENT: To inform the audience about what Orcas (a.k.a. Killer whales) are truly like with respect to their general physical characteristics, their distribution around the world, and their food habits.

Introduction:

Attention Step: During my life I have been able to visit many of California's great amusement parks, but the one that seemed to always interest me was Sea World, especially the Shamu exhibit. You see, as a kid I remember going to Sea World and watching Shamu do all of his tricks and act so friendly to all that came near him. In my opinion he couldn't hurt a fly, and that is why I was so puzzled and confused to why they would label him as a Killer whale. This confusion lasted for many years until I got a hold of a video that showed me the true nature of the Killer whale.

Clarification Step: You see many people don't understand the true nature of Killer whales and how widely they are dispersed, as well as how deadly they really are. Many people believe Killer whales to be those friendly, loving, fish-eating mammals that spend most of their time in the cold regions of the poles. But this could not be farther from the truth. Today, I am going to share with you some very interesting information about Killer whales in order for you to know the truth about them

Preview: First, I am going to give you some general physical characteristics that Killer whale's have, then I am going to give you an idea of their general locations in the world, and finally I am going to let you in on some of the most dangerous hunting techniques and eating habits that Killer whales possess.

Body:
    I.   All animals possess certain characteristics that separate them from other animals, and Killer whales are no different.

        A.   Killer whales have a unique coloration that helps distinguish them from other whales in the ocean.
            1.   distinctive **(2:1)**
            2   disruptive coloration **(4:1)**
        B.   Size is another physical characteristic that helps distinguish a killer whale from other whales
            1.   small for whales:
                a.   male 22 ft & weigh 8,000 - 12, 000 lbs. **(4:2)**
                b.   female 19 ft. &weigh 3000 - 8,000 lbs. **(4:2)**
        C.   Killer whales, according to the National Marine Mammal Laboratory, "have about 48 to 52 teeth that are large and conical in shape."**(2:1)**
            1.   teeth ripping **(4:1)**

Transition: Now that we can tell the difference between other whales and a killer whale, lets move on to some of the locations to where you might find Killer whales.

    II.   According to Sea World, "next to humans, Killer whales are the most widely distributed mammal." **(4:1)**

        A.   Killer whales inhabit all oceans.
            1.   Artic, Antarctic, coastal areas of the U.S
            2.   tropical areas
                a.   Columbia River
        B.   Migration is a key part of the Killer whales life.
            1.   Migration seasonal
            2.   travel in pods **(5:2)**
                a.   pods-family members **(3)**
                b.   two types of pods:
                    1)   resident pod (stable over time)
                    2)   transient pod (dynamic in structure and are constantly changing)

Transition: Now that we know what the Killer whale looks like and where it can be found, lets take a look into why they are called Killer whales in the first place and discus their eating habits.

    III.   Killer whales are very good hunters and will eat almost anything that they can get.

        A.   Some of the things that have been found in the stomachs of Killer whales are a variety of fish, mammals, and other whales.
            1. Fish, squid, etc.
        B.   According to the National Marine Mammal Laboratory, "Killer whales are very successful hunters due to their cooperative hunting, where all members within the pod participate." **(2:1)**
            1.   techniques and situations typical.
                a.   Beaching
                    1)   perfected this technique **(1)**
                b.   prey -cooperatively capture and kill it.
                    2)   30 assaulted, killed a 60ft. blue whale **(4:2)**
            2.   two whales, great white shark

Conclusion:
    Review: Tonight we discussed the truth about Killer whales with respect to their physical characteristics, their distribution around the world, and their deadly but effective food behaviors.
    Conclude: I hope that the information in which I have given you was something that can be useful to you, your friends and your family and that the next time you see a Killer whale you will see it for what it truly can be, the wolf of the sea.

Sources Cited

1. Attenborough, David. The Trials of Life: Hunting and Escaping. Time Life Video & Turner. 1991.

2. Drumm, Laura. "Killer Whales." National Marine Mammal Laboratory, US Department of Commerce. www.nmml.afsc.noaa.gov/education/cetaceans/killer1.html (6 January, 2003)

3. Killer Whales: The Wolves of the Sea., National Geographic Video. NGS, 1993.

4. Sea World. "Killer Whales." Busch Animal Information Database. www.seaworld.org/infobooks/Killer Whale.html (2002).

5. Zimmerman, Steven T. "Orca." ADF&G Wildlife Notebook Series. http://www.state.ak.us/locl/akpages/FISH.GAME/notebook/marine/orca.htm (03/29/2002).

TOPIC SELECTIONS FOR THE INFORMATIVE SPEECH

Name_____Day/Time of class_____Due_____

FIRST CHOICE- Avoid general, broad topics – narrow this down

Topic:_____

Why is this topic important to this audience?

_____

_____

What 2-3 main points might your audience find interesting?

1.

2.

3.

SECOND CHOICE: Avoid general, broad topics – narrow this down

Topic:_____

Why is this topic important to this audience?

_____

_____

What 2-3 main points might your audience find interesting?

1.

2.

3.

THIRD CHOICE: Avoid general, broad topics – narrow this down

Topic:_____

Why is this topic important to this audience?

_____

_____

What 2-3 main points might your audience find interesting?

1.

2.

3.

ANXIETY REDUCING CHECK LIST

Name_____   Speech_____

1. **Preparation Outline:** I have:
Narrowed main points to assignment requirement _____
Identified specific purpose statement on outline   _____
Checked for outline structure   _____

2. **Speaking Outline/Note Cards:** I have:
Checked for **key words only**   _____
Narrowed to pages to assignment requirement   _____
Practiced from this outline   _____

3. **Practice:** I have
Practiced my speech out loud   _____
   Approx. number of times: _____
   Approx. amount of time: _____
Timed my speech and edited where necessary   _____

4. **Nonverbal behavior:** When I practice
I am in control of my breathing   _____
I take several deep breaths while waiting
   my turn to speak   _____
I "center" my awareness of my breathing   _____
I slow the rate of breathing   _____
I "image" a calm, relaxed and confident speaker   _____
I am comfortable and stable in my speaking stance   _____
My legs are relaxed and stable, knees not locked   _____
I am able to gesture to emphasize meanings and ideas   _____
   Gestures are above the waist   _____
   Move toward center of my body and out   _____
   Display open palm, relaxed fingers   _____
I have practiced with my speaking outline   _____
I have practiced audience contact   _____
I focus on individuals rather than groups   _____
I speak to each person 3-5 seconds or until the end
   of an idea or concept   _____
I shift easily between outline and audience   _____

5. **Vocal Dimensions:** When I practice
I am louder than I am in normal conversations _____
I emphasize the meaning of words an concepts
   through variation in pitch   _____
I am speaking at a conversational rate   _____
I use pauses where necessary and effective   _____
My voice sounds relaxed and friendly. It expresses
   a desire to communicate.   _____

POST-SPEECH SELF-EVAULATION

Name _____Day/Time of class_____Assignment#_____

Evaluate your performance. Were you (circle one)

Very Satisfied   **Somewhat Satisfied**   **Dissatisfied**   **Very Dissatisfied**

1.   Do you think you successfully met your specific purpose? Why or why not?

2.   How did you feel about your ability to give this speech before you gave it?

3.   How did you feel about your ability to give this speech while you were giving it?

4.   How do you feel about your use of your use of outlines? Did the preparation outline help you feel "prepared?" Did the key word outline help you while you spoke? Why or why not?

5.   How do you feel about your use of research and supporting material. Did you gather enough research to be able to clearly explain your main points? Did you utilize a variety of support devices? If so, which ones? Did the research you use stimulate interest in the audience?

6.   How do you feel about your breath control. Did you take several deep breaths while you were waiting for your turn to speak? Were you able to "center" your awareness of breathing? Did you slow your rate of breathing?

7. How do you feel about your comfort/confidence level on this first speech. Were you comfortable and stable in your speaking stance, legs relaxed and knees unlocked? Were you able to "image" a calm, relaxed, comfortable speaker?

8. How do you feel about your use of gestures. Did you use gestures to emphasize meanings and ideas? Were your gestures above the waist? Did they move toward the center of the body and out? Did you display an open palm, relaxed fingers?

9. How do you feel about your use of audience contact. Did you focus on individuals or groups? Did you speak to each person for 3-5 seconds or until the end of a concept or idea? Did you shift easily between outline and audience? Did you utilize visual aides, if any, to clarify ideas for the audience?

10. How do you feel about your use of style of delivery. Did you speak at a conversational rate? Were you louder than you are in normal conversation? Did you emphasize the meaning in concepts through variation in pitch? Did your voice sound relaxed and friendly? Did it express a desire to communicate?

What specifically do you want to work on to improve your speech and performance? In the space below set three goals for your next speech-use full sentences:

Goal #1

Goal #2

Goal #3

Answer the following additional questions for Speech 2, 3, 4 and so on.

1. Discuss the goals that you set in your last evaluation that you feel you've met successfully. State each goal and describe why you feel sucessful:

2. What helped you be successful in helping you meet these goals? List each goal and describe in detail what methods you used to achieve this success:

3. Discuss the goals that you set in the last evaluation that you failed to achieve. List each goal and evaluate what barriers and challenges you encountered:

4. What methods will you try in order to achieve mastery of the goals listed in #3? Per each goal describe the techniques and methods you will utilize to overcome your challenges:

VIDEO EVALUATION

NAME_____ASSIGNMENT_____TOPIC_____

Some reminders before you watch your video. Keep your viewing of your speech in perspective. Remember that this is not a professional tape. We use older equipment that provides a poorer image and less clear sound so resist the temptation to compare yourself to a professionally lit and produced performance. Additionally, the image you of see of yourself fails to capture the true dynamics of the live speaking situation. Also, keep in mind that you are not a professional speaker. You are a beginner. You should evaluate your performance against what you think is a realistic and fair standard for you, not for a professional.

Overall evaluation: Circle the one that comes closest:

Very satisfied with my performance
Somewhat satisfied
Somewhat dissatisfied
Very dissatisfied with my performance

Vocal Dimension:
After hearing the tape I decided I like the following things I did with my voice (i.e. rate, pitch, volume, etc.):

_____
_____
_____

After hearing the tape I decided I disliked the following things I did with my voice:

_____
_____
_____

Nonverbal Dimension:
After seeing the tape I decided I like the following nonverbal aspects of my delivery (i.e. stance, gestures, audience contact, etc.):

_____
_____
_____

After seeing the tape I decided I disliked the following nonverbal aspects:

_____
_____
_____

PERSUASIVE STYLE SPEECHES

THE FOLLOWING SECTIONS INCLUDES:

√ **Persuasive Speech Assignments**

THE CRITICAL REVIEW SPEECH

THE TRIBUTE-EULOGY SPEECH

THE SPEECH TO CONVINCE-PROPOSITION TO PROOF

THE PROBLEM-SOLUTION PERSUASIVE SPEECH

THE SOCIAL ACTION SPEECH

CRITICAL REVIEW SPEECH

GOALS:•   To persuasively express your opinion.
- To convince your audience that your choice is the best choice.
- To use the "Proposition to Proof" organization of main points.
- To use and support the reasons for your opinion.
- To use claims.
- To speak in an energized persuasive manner.
- To maintain direct eye contact with individual audience members
- To use gestures and body movement to emphasize language

TIME: **POINTS:**

TOPIC: The following is an opportunity to persuade the audience about some form of entertainment you think is good or bad and why. You may, for example, choose a book, movie, music, concert, play, restaurant, theme park, etc. You must back up the position you take with "reasons" why the form of entertainment is good or bad. These reasons must be supported by examples—they are required for this choice of assignment. Other forms of support from outside sources may be used as well to support your point of view, e.g., testimony or statistics, descriptions and illustrations. If you use any outside source material, include a bibliography. Make sure the sources you use are credible.

ORGANIZATION: The introduction needs to include an attention step, a clarification step, and a preview. The <u>clarification step</u> must include a thesis statement in the form of a simple claim - "One of the all-time greatest basketball teams are the current National Champions, the Los Angeles Lakers." The intro also needs a <u>preview of the reasons</u> you will use to support the claim. No more than 3 main points should be used. Often only two reasons are developed. This is often called the "proposition to proof" style. Each main point establishes an "argument," or a proposition; e.g. "The Laker's are the greatest basketball team in history." Your main points are the claims that support this proposition. Your supporting material (evidence) is used to prove each main point. So, you start with a proposition, have 2-3 claims to support it and evidence to prove your claims are correct.

LANGUAGE: Pay attention to language by using simple, persuasive sentences. The key is clarity. Avoid wordiness and vagueness. Find concrete and specific language to describe your argument and examples. Pay attention to the parts of the introduction to help facilitate the audience's understanding. Think about the supporting material and make it interesting. Personalize the language—remember you are speaking for the "ear", not for the "eye". Descriptive language may be critical to your claims and supporting material. Try to develop language that creates a "see, feel, smell, touch and taste" experience. Use metaphor to explain the unfamiliar. Use the language of the audience.

DELIVERY: Work to build on the positive behaviors from your last speech. Try to correct any behaviors that have been noted and incorporate these into your practice sessions. Don't assume you don't have to practice because the speech is short! Work for direct audience contact, verbal fluency and a confident attitude. Remember, you will be advocating something so work to have a good grasp of the information. I expect you to demonstrate that you have rehearsed and are a bit more comfortable for this time around. I want to see eye contact with individual members of the audience as well. Also, work on verbal fluency.

CRITICAL REVIEW SPEECH ON THE CHECKERBOARD LOUNGE
PREPARATION OUTLINE

Specific Purpose: To persuade the audience that the Checkerboard Lounge is the best blues club in Chicago.

Introduction

Attention Step: Most people have a hobby. Mine includes travel, fun late nights, and the best music in the world. I collect blues clubs by visiting them in the various cities I go to as part of my job. One of the best places in the world to hear live blues is Chicago. (play excerpt from CD) That's Buddy Guy, blues legend. I enjoy his club in Chicago, but it's not the best.

Clarification: (claim) The best blues club in Chicago is The Checkerboard Lounge.

Preview: Today I'll give you 2 reasons why this is true. First, the fact that it's the best adventure, and second, it's incredible sense of authenticity.

Body:

I.   The Checkerboard Lounge is a great club because of where it is and what happens.
    A. It's on the South Side of Chicago.
        1. Cab driver story
        2. Security parking
    B. The music plays all night long.
        1. First show, 9.30
        2. Second show, midnight
        3. Third show, 2AM
        4. Jam

Transition: Not only is the club a true blues adventure, it is also probably one of the most authentic clubs in the USA.

II.   Location, atmosphere, and music make the Checkerboard superior.
    A. The South side is the home of urban blues.
        1. Muddy Waters, Howlin' Wolf, Willy Dixon, Buddy Guy
    B. The atmosphere is blues friendly.
        1. Small, dark, smoky, racially mixed
    C. The music is real.
        1. Magic Slim & the Teardrops (sample)
        2.

Conclusion:

Review: Christine Bird, author of <u>The Jazz and Blues Lovers Guide to the</u> <u>U.S.</u> lists the Checkerboard Lounge as her personal favorite in Chicago. I agree. Whenever I'm in town, that's where I go. It's an adventure, and it's authentic.

Conclude: It's one of the best clubs I have ever collected.

CRITICAL REVIEW SPEECH ON THE CHECKERBOARD LOUNGE
KEYWORD OUTLINE

Purpose: To persuade the audience that the Checkerboard Lounge is the best blues club in Chicago.

Introduction:

Attention Step: hobby. travel, fun late nights, best music in the world. collect blues clubs in various cities . best places /Chicago. (play excerpt from CD) Buddy Guy. not the best.

Clarification: (claim) The best /The Checkerboard Lounge.

Preview: 2 reasons. best adventure, and second, authenticity.

Body:
    I.   where it is and what happens.
            A.   South Side.
                    1.   Cab
                    2.   Security parking
            B.   all night long.
                    1.   9.30
                    2.   midnight
                    3.   2AM
                    4.   Jam
Transition: true blues adventure, most authentic clubs

    II.   Location, atmosphere, and music.
            A.   urban blues.
                    1.   Muddy Waters, Howlin' Wolf, Willy Dixon, Buddy Guy
                    2.   blues friendly.
                    3.   Small, dark, smoky, racially mixed
            B.   Real.
                    1.   Magic Slim & the Teardrops (sample)

Conclusion: Christine Bird. Where I go. Adventure/authentic/best club coll

CRITICAL REVIEW SPEECH ON THE "300"
PREPARATION OUTLINE

Specific Purpose: To persuade the audience that the movie "300" is the best movie they will ever see.

Introduction:

Attention Step: Catching people's attention. That's what entertainment is all about. A little while ago I went to the theaters and sat through a movie that made me want to pass out. My girlfriend was complaining about the movie and we started to argue about it. If anything I needed something to get her to stop nagging at me and to have a good time as well.

Clarification Step: We left that movie to go see the best movie of all time "300". Wikipedia reported that it broke box office records in it's first week and it is the third best R-rated opening movie ever.

Preview: Today I'll share with you two reasons why this movie is so great. First, the fact that it has the most magnificent storyline, and second, it's full of intense and phenomenal action packed scenes.

Body:

I. "300" is a fantastic movie, because of the truth about it and the overall idea.
   A. It has a war of impossible odds for the Spartans
      1. 300 against million
      2. Fantastical creatures
      3. Wave after wave

   B. It is a movie bringing a 2487 year old news story to life
      1. Spartans vs Persians
      2. Grade school
      3. Fantasize

Transition: Not only is the movie great for it's story, it is also incredible for its action packed scenes.

II. Quanitity and quality make of the action make "300" unbelievably amazing.
   A. There are waves after waves of intense battle scenes
      1. Soldiers
      2. Immortals
      3. Monsters

B.   The graphic battle sequences are amazing
        1.   Well choreographed
        2.   Strategy

Conclusion:

Review: I have shared with you that 300 is the best movie ever made, because of its great story and astounding action scenes.

Conclude: When the movie was over everyone in the theater applauded and when we left all my girlfriend and I did was rave about how great the movie was. All my friends who had seen it would talk about it all the time with me. I guarantee 300 is better than any movie you have ever seen and will ever see!

CRITICAL REVIEW SPEECH ON THE "300"
KEYWORD OUTLINE

Introduction:

Attention Step: attention. Entertainment. Movie...pass out. My girlfriend complaining..stop nagging.

Clarification Step: best movie "300". Wikipedia broke box office records.

Preview: two reasons. First, magnificent storyline, second, intense, phenomenal action packed scenes.

Body:

I. Truth, overall idea.
    A.   Spartans
          1.   300 against million
          2.   Fantastical creatures
          3.   Wave after wave

    B.   2487 year old news story
          1.   Spartans vs Persians
          2.   Grade school
          3.   Fantasize

Transition: great story, action packed scenes.

II. Quanitity, quality actionamazing.
    A.   intense battle scenes
          1.   Soldiers
          2.   Immortals
          3.   Monsters

    B.   graphic battle sequences
          1.   Well choreographed
          2.   Strategy

Conclusion:

Review: great story, astounding action scenes.

Conclude: theater applauded, rave great movie. friends talk all time. 300 better-ever see!

A77

TOPIC SELECTIONS FOR THE CRITICAL REVIEW SPEECH

Name_____Day/Time of class_____Due_____

FIRST CHOICE: Narrow your topic!

_____

What do you want to persuade the audience to believe about your topic?

_____

_____

What are your 2-3 main positions do you to take for or against this topic?

1.

2.

3.

SECOND CHOICE: Narrow your topic!

_____

What do you want to persuade the audience to believe about your topic?

_____

_____

What are your 2-3 main positions do you to take for or against this topic?

1.

2.

3.

THIRD CHOICE: Narrow your topic!

_____

What do you want to persuade the audience to believe about your topic?

_____

_____

What are your 2-3 main positions do you to take for or against this topic?

1.

2.

3.

ANXIETY REDUCING CHECK LIST

Name_____   Speech_____

1. **<u>Preparation Outline</u>:** I have:
   Narrowed main points to assignment requirement
   Identified specific purpose statement on outline   _____
   Checked for outline structure   _____

2. **<u>Speaking Outline/Note Cards</u>:** I have:
   Checked for **key words only**   _____
   Narrowed to pages to assignment requirement   _____
   Practiced from this outline   _____

3. **<u>Practice</u>:** I have
   Practiced my speech out loud
      Approx. number of times: _____
      Approx. amount of time: _____
   Timed my speech and edited where necessary   _____

4. **<u>Nonverbal behavior</u>:** When I practice
   I am in control of my breathing   _____
   I take several deep breaths while waiting
      my turn to speak   _____
   I "center" my awareness of my breathing   _____
   I slow the rate of breathing   _____
   I "image" a calm, relaxed and confident speaker   _____
   I am comfortable and stable in my speaking stance   _____
   My legs are relaxed and stable, knees not locked   _____
   I am able to gesture to emphasize meanings and ideas _____
      Gestures are above the waist   _____
      Move toward center of my body and out   _____
      Display open palm, relaxed fingers   _____
   I have practiced with my speaking outline   _____
   I have practiced audience contact   _____
   I focus on individuals rather than groups   _____
   I speak to each person 3-5 seconds or until the end
      of an idea or concept   _____
   I shift easily between outline and audience   _____
5. **<u>Vocal Dimensions</u>:** When I practice
      I am louder than I am in normal conversations   _____
      I emphasize the meaning of words an concepts
         through variation in pitch   _____
      I am speaking at a conversational rate   _____
      I use pauses where necessary and effective   _____
      My voice sounds relaxed and friendly. It expresses
         a desire to communicate.   _____

A80

POST-SPEECH SELF-EVAULATION

Name _____ Day/Time of class_____ Assignment#_____

Evaluate your performance. Were you (circle one)

Very Satisfied   Somewhat Satisfied   Dissatisfied   Very Dissatisfied

1.   Do you think you successfully met your specific purpose? Why or why not?

2.   How did you feel about your ability to give this speech before you gave it?

3.   How did you feel about your ability to give this speech while you were giving it?

4.   How do you feel about your use of your use of outlines? Did the preparation
      outline help you feel "prepared?" Did the key word outline help you while you
      spoke? Why or why not?

5.   How do you feel about your use of research and supporting material. Did you
      gather enough research to be able to clearly explain your main points? Did you
      utilize a variety of support devices? If so, which ones? Did the research you use
      stimulate interest in the audience?

6.   How do you feel about your breath control. Did you take several deep breaths
      while you were waiting for your turn to speak? Were you able to "center" your
      awareness of breathing? Did you slow your rate of breathing?

7.	How do you feel about your comfort/confidence level on this first speech. Were you comfortable and stable in your speaking stance, legs relaxed and knees unlocked? Were you able to "image" a calm, relaxed, comfortable speaker?

8.	How do you feel about your use of gestures. Did you use gestures to emphasize meanings and ideas? Were your gestures above the waist? Did they move toward the center of the body and out? Did you display an open palm, relaxed fingers?

9.	How do you feel about your use of audience contact. Did you focus on individuals or groups? Did you speak to each person for 3-5 seconds or until the end of a concept or idea? Did you shift easily between outline and audience? Did you utilize visual aides, if any, to clarify ideas for the audience?

10.	How do you feel about your use of style of delivery. Did you speak at a conversational rate? Were you louder than you are in normal conversation? Did you emphasize the meaning in concepts through variation in pitch? Did your voice sound relaxed and friendly? Did it express a desire to communicate?

What specifically do you want to work on to improve your speech and performance? In the space below set three goals for your next speech-use full sentences:

Goal #1

Goal #2

Goal #3

Answer the following additional questions for Speech 2, 3, 4 and so on.

1.   Discuss the goals that you set in your last evaluation that you feel you've met successfully. State each goal and describe why you feel sucessful:

2.   What helped you be successful in helping you meet these goals? List each goal and describe in detail what methods you used to achieve this success:

3.   Discuss the goals that you set in the last evaluation that you failed to achieve. List each goal and evaluate what barriers and challenges you encountered:

4.   What methods will you try in order to achieve mastery of the goals listed in #3? Per each goal describe the techniques and methods you will utilize to overcome your challenges:

VIDEO EVALUATION

NAME_____ASSIGNMENT_____TOPIC_____

Some reminders before you watch your video. Keep your viewing of your speech in perspective. Remember that this is not a professional tape. We use older equipment that provides a poorer image and less clear sound so resist the temptation to compare yourself to a professionally lit and produced performance. Additionally, the image you of see of yourself fails to capture the true dynamics of the live speaking situation. Also, keep in mind that you are not a professional speaker. You are a beginner. You should evaluate your performance against what you think is a realistic and fair standard for you, not for a professional.

Overall evaluation: Circle the one that comes closest:

    Very satisfied with my performance
    Somewhat satisfied
    Somewhat dissatisfied
    Very dissatisfied with my performance

Vocal Dimension:
After hearing the tape I decided I like the following things I did with my voice (i.e. rate, pitch, volume, etc.):

_____

_____

_____

After hearing the tape I decided I disliked the following things I did with my voice:

_____

_____

_____

Nonverbal Dimension:
After seeing the tape I decided I like the following nonverbal aspects of my delivery (i.e. stance, gestures, audience contact, etc.):

_____

_____

_____

After seeing the tape I decided I disliked the following nonverbal aspects:

_____

_____

_____

TRIBUTE/EULOGY" SPEECH

GOALS
- To present a strong topic that you "feel" something for
- To concisely organize material and to use vivid and captivating language
- To express your emotions in an open and, yet, controlled manner
- To maintain a confident and relaxed posture
- To speak in a clear, relaxed manner
- To maintain direct eye contact with individual audience members
- To use gestures and body movement to extend your message

TIME: **POINTS**:

TOPIC- The research for this topic does not require going to the library. What is required is a strong topic that you have an emotional connection to. You will choose a person who has made a significant impact on your life and you will pay a tribute to that person. This person may be living or dead. You may want to talk to others who know or knew the person to collect stories to choose from when developing your tribute or eulogy. If the person is living you may want to talk to the person about stories s/he is able to share with you. One or two of these stories will become the support for your speech. In this speech you argue that someone has been significant to you and that what they taught you was of value.

ORGANIZATION: You will follow the format but you may want to de-formalize the language to make this speech more personal. In situations where a tribute is required you usually have been introduced and the audience already has their attention on you. However, you want to use good structure so we always know where you are. Additionally, let us know early who the person is/was and what your relationship to the person is/was. You should announce a simple thesis that tells us in one sentence how the person has affected you life. The "body" should include of one or two brief stories (examples) that demonstrate some important quality about the person. This proof you are offering about the person is called "narrative proof." The extended examples and stories you utilize should show us why you chose this person. The conclusion should be an informal review and restatement of the importance of this person in your life. Use no more than 2-3 main points. **DON'T USE THE CHRONOLOGICAL PATTERN!**

LANGUAGE - The language you use is a key element to the success of this assignment. Keep the ideas simple. Write brief meaningful sentences at the level of main ideas. Choose descriptive words carefully when trying to isolate the qualities you wish to include. On the other hand, try to make your supporting stories as descriptive and vivid as possible. Because the type of proof you are using is "narrative" in nature the type and quality of language you choose will involve descriptive story telling. Include details that will provide a solid sense of physical description of the person and place. Don't be afraid to make people laugh or cry. You can also use quotations, famous sayings or other language devices to explain or set up the story elements. This will connect your stories to a particular value and will help to provide a sense of continuity throughout. sp

DELIVERY- The delivery should be very direct and personal. Extemporaneous style continues to be used here! Because you are sharing something that is close to your heart, practice is essential. Practice out loud until you feel very comfortable sharing this information.

EULOGY SPEECH ON BUD FRICKER- PREPARATION OUTLINE

Purpose : To acquaint the audience with my dad, and let them know how he helped me to become a better father.

Introduction:

Attention step: AT EASE! Loud, commanding, and a bit scary. That was one side of my dad. He was a Master Sergeant in the Army when I was growing up. At times we didn't know if we were his kids or his soldiers. We had inspections, curfews, and we were sometimes restricted to our rooms. That was just part of the duty.

But there was a another side of my dad that people rarely saw. He was a warm and loving father who would do almost anything for his kids. Today I'd like to tell you how he made me a better father by sharing a few stories about him with you.

Body:

I.   My dad always went out of his way to do special father-son and father daughter things for us, like going fishing.
   A.   The "freezing to death fishing trip is a good example.
      1.   5:30 morning, frigid cold
      2.   San Francisco, Golden Gate bridge
      3.   A military pier
      4.   veins in dad's face breaking
   B.   We had absolutely the wrong type of fishing gear
      1.   line "rope" size
      2.   hand lines, no poles
      3.   Caught one ugly fish in two hours
   C.   It was the best day ever
      a.   two of us
      b.   guy stuff
      c.   peeing off the dock

Transition: This was the first of many good fishing days. Some with all the right equipment, lots of fish, and perfect weather. But this one was the first. It was only one of the times that Dad taught me to go out of my way to help my kids.

II. The "cave-man costume" helped to make me a star.
    A. Without dad's help the costume would have never worked.
        1. found the leather
        2. found and cooked giant bone for club
    B. Dad let me do most of the work
        1. wig selection
        2. mask
        3. performance elements
    C. The support was there if I needed it.
        1. had won on my own.
        2. I did

Conclusion: Review: Taking a son fishing on a freezing day with the wrong equipment and stepping aside so a kid can do something on his own is not all there is to being a good father. There is much, much more. **Conclude:** Now that my Dad is gone, I'm learning on my own, but there is so much I know because he was here. Thanks, Dad.

EULOGY SPEECH ON BUD FRICKER
KEYWORD OUTLINE

Purpose : To acquaint the audience with my dad, and let them know how he helped me to become a better father.

Introduction:

Attention step: AT EASE! Loud, commanding, scary. one side. Master Sergeant. kids or his soldiers. inspections, curfews, restricted. part of the duty.
another side. warm and loving father, anything for his kids. made me a better father

Body:

I.   father-son and father daughter, going fishing.

        A.   "freezing to death fishing trip
            1.   5:30 morning, frigid cold
            2.   San Francisco, Golden Gate bridge
            3.   A military pier
            4.   veins in dad's face breaking
        B.   wrong type of fishing gear
            1.   line "rope" size
            2.   hand lines, no poles
            3.   Caught one ugly fish in two hours
        C.   best day ever
            a.   two of us
            b.   guy stuff
            c.   peeing off the dock

Transition: many good fishing days. right equipment, lots of fish, and perfect weather. one was the first. taught me to go out of my way to help my kids.

II.   "cave-man costume" - a star.
        A.   never worked.
            1.   found the leather
            2.   found and cooked giant bone for club

B.   let me do most of the work
    1.   wig selection
    2.   mask
    3.   performance elements
C.   support was there
    1.   had won on my own.
    2.   I did

Conclusion:
Review: son fishing on a freezing day, wrong equipment; stepping aside-on his own is not all there is to being a good father. Much more
Conclude: Dad is gone, learning on my own, much I know because he was here.
Thanks, Dad.

TRIBUTE SPEECH ON PEG TAYLOR
PREPARATION OUTLINE -

Specific Purpose: To pay tribute to Peg Taylor, Orange Coast College Director of Speech and Debate Team

Introduction

Attention-Getter: Almost everyone has daydreams of winning some big award, yet every now and then we meet someone who would far rather see others get public credit for his/her own deeds. I admire this kind of humility. Tonight, we honor just such as person. I feel that awards of this nature are somewhat defined by the people who win them. This year, The Jack Howe Award goes to someone who will help add her own unique meaning to the trophy.

Thesis: The person winning this award means so much to me - it is my personal pleasure to tell you more about this person.

Preview: I've known this person for many years. I was her student, I competed against her and most recently I coached with her. Let me tell you about these experiences.

Body

I. My association with this person goes back 17 years
   A. As her student she taught me about pride.
      1. Not boastful
      2. Work

   B. Pride in preparation and self-improvement
      1. "I'm proud of you."
      2. "We're proud of you too."

Transition: I moved on from being her student to, for many years, being one of her competitors

II. For 9 years I was at another school competing against her.
   A. Legendary efficiency
      1. Tab rooms
      2. Pencils
      3. Coffee

   B. We honor her efficiency today

Transition: From spending many years competing against her, in the last few years I have found myself working with her.

III. For 4 years I have been privileged to be her co-worker.
   A. I never stop learning from her.
      1. Growth,
      2. joy
      3. healing

        B. Growth transcends winning and losing
           1. enriches this award
           2. her name

Conclusion:

Review: From being a student, a fellow professional to a co-worker this person has taught me so much - pride, efficiency and growth.

Conclude: I join the entire organization as we present the Jack Howe Award for Continuing Excellence to Peg Taylor of Orange Coast College

TRIBUTE SPEECH ON PEG TAYLOR
KEYWORD OUTLINE

Introduction

Attention-Getter: Awards defined by the people. Jack Howe Award goes to - unique meaning
Thesis: my personal pleasure
Preview: known many years. student, competed against, coached with her

Body

I. 17 years.

    A. Student - pride.
       1. Not boastful
       2. Work

    B. preparation/self-improvement
       1. "you."
       2. "you too."

Transition: from being her student to one of her competitors

II. 9 years- another school

    A. Legendary efficiency
       1. Tab rooms
       2. Pencils
       3. Coffee

    B. efficiency today

Transition: competing against her to working with her.

III. 4 years- her co-worker.

    A. learning from her.
       1. Growth,
       2. joy
       3. healing

    B. Growth-winning and losing
       1. enriches this award
       2. her name

Conclusion:

Review: student, fellow professional, co-worker - pride, efficiency and growth.
Conclude: Organization - Jack H. Award for Continuing Excellence - Peg Taylor of 0CC

TOPIC SELECTIONS FOR THE TRIBUTE/EULOGY SPEECH

Name_____Day/Time of class_____Due_____

FIRST CHOICE: Narrow to a specific person
    Topic:_____

What makes this person important/interesting to this audience?

_____

_____

What are your 2-3 main points you will make about this person?

1.

2.

3.

SECOND CHOICE: Narrow to a specific person
    Topic:_____

What makes this person important/interesting to this audience?

_____

_____

What are your 2-3 main points you will make about this person?

1.

2.

3.

THIRD CHOICE: Narrow to a specific person
    Topic:_____

What makes this person important/interesting to this audience?

_____

_____

What are your 2-3 main ideas?

1.

2.

3.

ANXIETY REDUCING CHECK LIST

Name_____   Speech_____

1. **Preparation Outline**: I have:
   Narrowed main points to assignment requirement   _____
   Identified specific purpose statement on outline   _____
   Checked for outline structure   _____

2. **Speaking Outline/Note Cards**: I have:
   Checked for **key words only**   _____
   Narrowed to pages to assignment requirement   _____
   Practiced from this outline   _____

3. **Practice**: I have
   Practiced my speech out loud   _____
     Approx. number of times: _____
     Approx. amount of time: _____
   Timed my speech and edited where necessary   _____

4. **Nonverbal behavior**: When I practice
   I am in control of my breathing   _____
   I take several deep breaths while waiting
     my turn to speak   _____
   I "center" my awareness of my breathing   _____
   I slow the rate of breathing   _____
   I "image" a calm, relaxed and confident speaker   _____
   I am comfortable and stable in my speaking stance   _____
   My legs are relaxed and stable, knees not locked   _____
   I am able to gesture to emphasize meanings and ideas   _____
     Gestures are above the waist   _____
     Move toward center of my body and out   _____
     Display open palm, relaxed fingers   _____
   I have practiced with my speaking outline   _____
   I have practiced audience contact   _____
   I focus on individuals rather than groups   _____
   I speak to each person 3-5 seconds or until the end
     of an idea or concept   _____
   I shift easily between outline and audience   _____

5. **Vocal Dimensions**: When I practice
   I am louder than I am in normal conversations   _____
   I emphasize the meaning of words an concepts
     through variation in pitch   _____
   I am speaking at a conversational rate   _____
   I use pauses where necessary and effective   _____
   My voice sounds relaxed and friendly. It expresses
     a desire to communicate.   _____

POST-SPEECH SELF-EVAULATION

Name _____Day/Time of class_____Assignment#_____

Evaluate your performance. Were you (circle one)

Very Satisfied   **Somewhat Satisfied**   **Dissatisfied**   **Very Dissatisfied**

1.   Do you think you successfully met your specific purpose? Why or why not?

2.   How did you feel about your ability to give this speech before you gave it?

3.   How did you feel about your ability to give this speech while you were giving it?

4.   How do you feel about your use of your use of outlines? Did the preparation
      outline help you feel "prepared?" Did the key word outline help you while you
      spoke? Why or why not?

5.   How do you feel about your use of research and supporting material. Did you
      gather enough research to be able to clearly explain your main points? Did you
      utilize a variety of support devices? If so, which ones? Did the research you use
      stimulate interest in the audience?

6.   How do you feel about your breath control. Did you take several deep breaths
      while you were waiting for your turn to speak? Were you able to "center" your
      awareness of breathing? Did you slow your rate of breathing?

A102

7.   How do you feel about your comfort/confidence level on this first speech. Were you comfortable and stable in your speaking stance, legs relaxed and knees unlocked? Were you able to "image" a calm, relaxed, comfortable speaker?

8.   How do you feel about your use of gestures. Did you use gestures to emphasize meanings and ideas? Were your gestures above the waist? Did they move toward the center of the body and out? Did you display an open palm, relaxed fingers?

9.   How do you feel about your use of audience contact. Did you focus on individuals or groups? Did you speak to each person for 3-5 seconds or until the end of a concept or idea? Did you shift easily between outline and audience? Did you utilize visual aides, if any, to clarify ideas for the audience?

10.   How do you feel about your use of style of delivery. Did you speak at a conversational rate? Were you louder than you are in normal conversation? Did you emphasize the meaning in concepts through variation in pitch? Did your voice sound relaxed and friendly? Did it express a desire to communicate?

What specifically do you want to work on to improve your speech and performance? In the space below set three goals for your next speech-use full sentences:

    Goal #1

    Goal #2

    Goal #3

Answer the following additional questions for Speech 2, 3, 4 and so on.

1.   Discuss the goals that you set in your last evaluation that you feel you've met successfully. State each goal and describe why you feel sucessful:

2.   What helped you be successful in helping you meet these goals? List each goal and describe in detail what methods you used to achieve this success:

3.   Discuss the goals that you set in the last evaluation that you failed to achieve. List each goal and evaluate what barriers and challenges you encountered:

4.   What methods will you try in order to achieve mastery of the goals listed in #3? Per each goal describe the techniques and methods you will utilize to overcome your challenges:

VIDEO EVALUATION

NAME_____**ASSIGNMENT**_____**TOPIC**_____

Some reminders before you watch your video. Keep your viewing of your speech in perspective. Remember that this is not a professional tape. We use older equipment that provides a poorer image and less clear sound so resist the temptation to compare yourself to a professionally lit and produced performance. Additionally, the image you of see of yourself fails to capture the true dynamics of the live speaking situation. Also, keep in mind that you are not a professional speaker. You are a beginner. You should evaluate your performance against what you think is a realistic and fair standard for you, not for a professional.

Overall evaluation: Circle the one that comes closest:

Very satisfied with my performance
Somewhat satisfied
Somewhat dissatisfied
Very dissatisfied with my performance

Vocal Dimension:
After hearing the tape I decided I like the following things I did with my voice (i.e. rate, pitch, volume, etc.):

_____
_____
_____

After hearing the tape I decided I disliked the following things I did with my voice:

_____
_____
_____

Nonverbal Dimension:
After seeing the tape I decided I like the following nonverbal aspects of my delivery (i.e. stance, gestures, audience contact, etc.):

_____
_____
_____

After seeing the tape I decided I disliked the following nonverbal aspects:

_____
_____
_____

SPEECH TO CONVINCE-PROPOSITION TO PROOF

Goals:
- To convince us that something you believe is the best way to believe.
- To develop credible arguments
- To use good evidence and good sources.
- To continue to use support material.
- To continue to develop good strong delivery skills.

TIME: **POINTS:**

TOPIC AND AUDIENCE: Select a topic that addresses a problem the students you will be teaching are facing. In selecting the topic you must also determine the audience. For example, you might do a persuasive speech on the necessity for sex education in grade school and present it to the local school board. Or you might address the level of violence on your high school campus and try to convince the PTSA group that anger management courses must be taught. Or you might address drug use with a group of students.

Research: This speech requires that you do more research than on previous speeches. You will need to utilize at least seven current sources beyond your own knowledge. These sources might be found in magazines, interviews, television programs, the internet, pamphlets, or almost any other form of information that carries a copyright. You may want to call special interest groups and ask them to send or fax you information to support your position. Be sure to review the chapter on research. While you should start with your own knowledge, running an "infotrac search" or other form of electronic search (Lexis Nexis in our library) will be essential.

Sources: Sources should be current (within the last 2 years.) Sources older than this may be used, but at least five "current" sources should be used. Oral citations are required in this speech (a minimum of five). These citations help build your credibility so be sure your information comes from unbiased, qualified sources. Original research is also better than secondary.

A bibliography with at least 7 sources is required. Follow the bibliography guide in section one and the standards for the Informative Speech.

Support Material: Look for supporting evidence including examples, statistics, illustrations and testimonies. Look for a variety of support material.

Organization: No more than 3 main points should be used. The style of this speech is called the "proposition to proof" style. Each main point establishes an "argument," or a proposition; e.g. "The death penalty is wrong and should be abolished." Your main points are the claims that support this proposition. Your supporting material (evidence) is used to prove each main point. So, you start with a proposition, have 2-3 claims to support it and evidence to prove your claims are correct.

Language: The language of persuasion is more assertive than the language of informing. At the heart of this assertive process is the writing of your claims. A claim should be a brief sentence stating a position. It is not a question. It states a position you feel you can support with your evidence. It is direct and strong - do not get wimpy here! You can make claims throughout your speech, but the key claims are the main points. Keep the language of your preview, transition and summary strong. Look for interesting and compelling ways of telling your position. This may be reflected in the vividness of your examples or the use of metaphors, analogies and quotations.

Delivery: The delivery continues to be extemporaneous. The delivery style contributes to the strength of your argument. Audiences are likely to buy proof from those they see as involved and committed advocates. We accept proof more readily from those we perceive as dynamic. Work to become familiar with the material and to express it in an animated and believable manner. Work for more audience contact and less contact with your outline. Work for

SPEECH TO CONVINCE ON INDIAN GAMING
PREPARATION OUTLINE

Look at this for format – problem-solution content would not be appropriate for this assignment

Specific Purpose: To prove that Indian Gaming is undesirable

Introduction

Attn. Getter: Plastic garbage bags serve as roofs, faucets along the dirt road serve as showers. The Kickapoo tribe of Eagle Bend Texas lives in poverty. A quarter of the population is unemployed, more than half is illiterate and much to the embarrassment of the tribal elders, the single crop in the tribal garden is marijuana. The Kickapoos feel they have a way out of their problems. That way is bingo. The situation of the Kickapoos, described by David Segal in his article "Dances With Sharks" from the Washington Monthly of 1992, is unfortunately all too common. Since congress passed the Indian Gaming Act of 1988, hundreds of tribes have started Indian gambling operations. **(3:81)**

Clarification Step: Unfortunately for the Kickapoos, gambling is probably not the answer to the tribes problems. While Indian gambling has worked fro some tribes, the opposite for most is true. Today, I'd like to convince you that Indian Gaming is undesirable.

Preview: First, I'll show you that in too many cases Indian Gaming has been infiltrated by organized crime. Next, I'll demonstrate that the average Indian does not benefit from Indian gaming.

I.   Indian gaming is undesirable because it is infiltrated by undesirable characters.

    A.   Indian gaming is infiltrated by organized crime.
        1.   Robert Allen Warrior "many Native Americans worry that casino gambling brings corruption, organized crime and social deterioration." **(4:189)**
        2.   Inadequate government oversight invites organized crime infiltration (1:98)
            a.   Rocco Zangari/Cabazons **(3:85)**
            b.   Banks - no loans/Indians = mafia loans

    B.   Indian gaming is infiltrated by disorganized crime.
        1.   Greedy mgmt. companies
            a.   Wayne Newton/Seneca-Cayugas **(3:85)**
            b.   Cash = rig books

Transition: organized crimes is taking advantage of the Indians, but that's not the only reason Indian gaming is undesirable. The true tragedy is the fact that Indian Gaming does not benefit the average Indian.

II.   Indian Gaming is a losing proposition for the average Indian.

    A.   The average Indian doesn't get the money.
        1.   Wm. Safire, pol. analyst, '92 NY Times "Redskin Revenge" "Casino gambling will help the average Indian as much as the NY State Lottery has provided great new facilities for the average school child." **(2:A16)**

    B.   Gambling has increased existing social problems.
        1.   Unemployment, drugs, alcohol **(3:84)**
        2.   Fraticide
        a.   Mohawk war = 2 deaths **(2:A17)**

Conclusion:

Review: It is clear that Indian Gambling doesn't work. Organized and disorganized crime scoops up the profits while the average Indian doesn't gain any benefit.

Conclude: The story of Indian gaming is pretty ugly. Organized crime, tribal warfare, greedy management companies and cheated Indians. It is a story that has been told far too often in our society. Indian gaming is undesirable. And it's a bet the Kickapoos, along with all the other tribes, shouldn't make.

BIBLIOGRAPHY

1.   Poplin, James R., "Organized Crime May Infiltrate Indian Casinos," U.S. News and World Report, July   16, 1992, p. 98

2.   Safire, William, "Redskins' Revenge," The New York Times, January 6, 1992, p. A17.

3.   Segal, David, "Dances With Sharks," The Washington Monthly, March 1992, p. 80.

4.   Warrior, Robert, "Indian Gaming is a Bad Bet," The Atlantic Monthly, April 1992, p. 189.

A111

SPEECH TO CONVINCE ON INDIAN GAMING
KEYWORD OUTLINE

Attn. Getter: garbage bags, faucets . Kickapoo - poverty. quarter/population-unemployed, half - illiterate, single crop - marijuana. Way is bingo. David Segal in his article "Dances With Sharks" from the Washington Monthly of 1992 too common. Gaming Act of 1988 - Indian gambling operations.

Clarification Step: gambling not answer......Indian Gaming is undesirable.

Preview: 1st, Indian Gaming infiltrated by organized crime. Then, average Indian does not benefit

I.   infiltrated by undesirable characters.

    A.   infiltrated - organized crime.
        1.   Robert Allen Warrior "many Native Americans worry that casino gambling brings corruption, organized crime and social deterioration." (4.189)
        2.   Inadequate government oversight invites organized crime infiltration (1:98)
            a.   Rocco Zangari/Cabazons
            b.   Banks - no loans/Indians = mafia loans

    B.   Infiltrated - disorganized crime.
        1.   Greedy mgmt. companies
            a.   Wayne Newton/Seneca-Cayugas
            b.   Cash = rig books

Transition: organized crimes taking advantage of the Indians -Indian Gaming does not benefit the average Indian.

II.   Losing proposition for the average Indian.

    A.   Doesn't get the money.
        1.   Wm. Safire, pol. analyst, '92 NY Times "Redskin Revenge" "Casino gambling will help the average Indian as much as the NY State Lottery has provided great new facilities for the average school child." (2"A16)

    B.   Increased existing social problems.
        1.   Unemployment, drugs, alcohol
        2.   Fraticide
            a.   Mohawk war = 2 deaths

Conclusion:
    Review: Gambling doesn't work. Organized, disorganized = profits, average Indian - no benefit.
    Conclude: Pretty ugly. Organized crime, tribal warfare, greedy management companies, cheated Indians. Indian gaming undesirable. And it's a bet - shouldn't make.

TOPIC SELECTIONS FOR THE SPEECH TO CONVINCE

Name_____Day/Time of class_____Due_____

FIRST CHOICE: Be very, very narrow in your topic selection

_____

What position do you want the audience to hold after hearing your speech?

_____

_____

What are your 2-3 main arguments for or against this topic?

1.

2.

3.

SECOND CHOICE: Be very, very narrow in your topic selection

_____

What position do you want the audience to hold after hearing your speech?

_____

_____

What are your 2-3 main arguments for or against this topic?

1.

2.

3.

THIRD CHOICE: Be very, very narrow in your topic selection

_____

What position do you want the audience to hold after hearing your speech?

_____

_____

What are your 2-3 main arguments for or against this topic?

1.

2.

3.

ANXIETY REDUCING CHECK LIST

Name_____   Speech_____

1. **Preparation Outline:** I have:
   Narrowed main points to assignment requirement   _____
   Identified specific purpose statement on outline   _____
   Checked for outline structure   _____

2. **Speaking Outline/Note Cards:** I have:
   Checked for **key words only**   _____
   Narrowed to pages to assignment requirement   _____
   Practiced from this outline   _____

3. **Practice:** I have
   Practiced my speech out loud   _____
       Approx. number of times: _____
       Approx. amount of time: _____
   Timed my speech and edited where necessary   _____

4. **Nonverbal behavior:** When I practice
   I am in control of my breathing   _____
   I take several deep breaths while waiting
       my turn to speak   _____
   I "center" my awareness of my breathing   _____
   I slow the rate of breathing   _____
   I "image" a calm, relaxed and confident speaker   _____
   I am comfortable and stable in my speaking stance   _____
   My legs are relaxed and stable, knees not locked   _____
   I am able to gesture to emphasize meanings and ideas   _____
       Gestures are above the waist   _____
       Move toward center of my body and out   _____
       Display open palm, relaxed fingers   _____
   I have practiced with my speaking outline   _____
   I have practiced audience contact   _____
   I focus on individuals rather than groups   _____
   I speak to each person 3-5 seconds or until the end
       of an idea or concept   _____
   I shift easily between outline and audience   _____

5. **Vocal Dimensions:** When I practice
       I am louder than I am in normal conversations   _____
       I emphasize the meaning of words an concepts
         through variation in pitch   _____
       I am speaking at a conversational rate   _____
       I use pauses where necessary and effective   _____
       My voice sounds relaxed and friendly. It expresses
         a desire to communicate.   _____

POST-SPEECH SELF-EVAULATION

Name _____Day/Time of class_____Assignment#_____

Evaluate your performance. Were you (circle one)

Very Satisfied   **Somewhat Satisfied**   **Dissatisfied**   **Very Dissatisfied**

1.   Do you think you successfully met your specific purpose? Why or why not?

2.   How did you feel about your ability to give this speech before you gave it?

3.   How did you feel about your ability to give this speech while you were giving it?

4.   How do you feel about your use of your use of outlines? Did the preparation outline help you feel "prepared?" Did the key word outline help you while you spoke? Why or why not?

5.   How do you feel about your use of research and supporting material. Did you gather enough research to be able to clearly explain your main points? Did you utilize a variety of support devices? If so, which ones? Did the research you use stimulate interest in the audience?

6.   How do you feel about your breath control. Did you take several deep breaths while you were waiting for your turn to speak? Were you able to "center" your awareness of breathing? Did you slow your rate of breathing?

7.   How do you feel about your comfort/confidence level on this first speech. Were you comfortable and stable in your speaking stance, legs relaxed and knees unlocked? Were you able to "image" a calm, relaxed, comfortable speaker?

8.   How do you feel about your use of gestures. Did you use gestures to emphasize meanings and ideas? Were your gestures above the waist? Did they move toward the center of the body and out? Did you display an open palm, relaxed fingers?

9.   How do you feel about your use of audience contact. Did you focus on individuals or groups? Did you speak to each person for 3-5 seconds or until the end of a concept or idea? Did you shift easily between outline and audience? Did you utilize visual aides, if any, to clarify ideas for the audience?

10.   How do you feel about your use of style of delivery. Did you speak at a conversational rate? Were you louder than you are in normal conversation? Did you emphasize the meaning in concepts through variation in pitch? Did your voice sound relaxed and friendly? Did it express a desire to communicate?

What specifically do you want to work on to improve your speech and performance? In the space below set three goals for your next speech-use full sentences:

Goal #1

Goal #2

Goal #3

Answer the following additional questions for Speech 2, 3, 4 and so on.

1. Discuss the goals that you set in your last evaluation that you feel you've met successfully. State each goal and describe why you feel sucessful:

2. What helped you be successful in helping you meet these goals? List each goal and describe in detail what methods you used to achieve this success:

3. Discuss the goals that you set in the last evaluation that you failed to achieve. List each goal and evaluate what barriers and challenges you encountered:

4. What methods will you try in order to achieve mastery of the goals listed in #3? Per each goal describe the techniques and methods you will utilize to overcome your challenges:

VIDEO EVALUATION

NAME_____ASSIGNMENT_____TOPIC_____

Some reminders before you watch your video. Keep your viewing of your speech in perspective. Remember that this is not a professional tape. We use older equipment that provides a poorer image and less clear sound so resist the temptation to compare yourself to a professionally lit and produced performance. Additionally, the image you of see of yourself fails to capture the true dynamics of the live speaking situation. Also, keep in mind that you are not a professional speaker. You are a beginner. You should evaluate your performance against what you think is a realistic and fair standard for you, not for a professional.

Overall evaluation: Circle the one that comes closest:

     Very satisfied with my performance
     Somewhat satisfied
     Somewhat dissatisfied
     Very dissatisfied with my performance

Vocal Dimension:
After hearing the tape I decided I like the following things I did with my voice (i.e. rate, pitch, volume, etc.):

_____

_____

_____

After hearing the tape I decided I disliked the following things I did with my voice:

_____

_____

_____

Nonverbal Dimension:
After seeing the tape I decided I like the following nonverbal aspects of my delivery (i.e. stance, gestures, audience contact, etc.):

_____

_____

_____

After seeing the tape I decided I disliked the following nonverbal aspects:

_____

_____

_____

PROBLEM-SOLUTION PERSUASIVE SPEECH-Carroll, Fricker, Monahan

GOALS:
- To persuade a particular audience--your peers in the class.
- To inspire your audience to action.
- To change the way people think and also what people do.
- To use in-depth analysis in the development of your argument.
- To use a variety of support to prove your point.
- To use an energized and passionate speaking style.
- To make sustained and direct eye contact with individual audience members.
-

TIME: **POINTS:**

TOPIC: This speech asks you to argue the existence of a specific problem, to suggest societal changes and to involve your audience in actions to solve this problem. This speech is similar to the "critical review" and/or the "tribute/eulogy" in that you take and support a position. There are however, some significant differences. This speech is longer, the topics are more controversial and significant, and you will be supporting the ideas with evidence and developing arguments within a very specific organizational pattern, the problem/solution format. Overall, the argument and the use of proof will be stronger than in the "critical review" and the delivery will demonstrate a stronger sense of advocacy and involvement.

ORGANIZATION: Success in this speech will largely be based on your ability to develop your argument in the problem/solution organizational pattern. You need to be sure to correctly develop not only the broad areas of problem and solution, but to also develop the main ideas in each major point in the correct order and format. Problem/Solution is the only format acceptable for the body of the speech. Write out the introduction, the conclusion. Outline the body with full sentences at Roman numerals and capital letters. Key words, phrases, fragments can be used below this level. Develop three specific arguments in the problem area and two specific arguments in the solution (See Preparation Guide Below for the outlining directions.)

RESEARCH: Once you have decided on a topic area doing on *Infotrac* search or other type of magazine and periodical search is essential. Pay particular attention to dates and to the kinds of supporting materials you discover. Because these topics are current controversies it is important that your information be current. Things change rapidly in our society and information from the 1980's, 90's and anything before the last few years is probably just not current enough. It is also essential that your speech have "real people" examples, statistics, oral citations from credible sources and logical explanations supporting your side. Look for these types of supporting material in the current sources you find.

Finally, there is a ton of information available online and on the Internet. Web sites, gophers, home pages, list-serves and frequently asked questions (FAQ's) are easily accessed. "American Rhetoric" is an excellent site. In addition, you should use search engines like Google, Dogpile and others to supplement your research.

Problem-Solution Persuasive (cont.)

SOURCES OF SUPPORT: At least 6-8 published sources should be cited. No more than 50% can be online sources. A bibliography should be attached, MLA style. Documentation needs to be on the outline. The speaker should utilize oral citation of supporting material. A variety of sources should be utilized to provide ethical, emotional, and logical proof - see Chapter Nine for "Aristotle's Three Persuasive Proofs."

LANGUAGE: A carefully worded specific purpose should include the speaker's intent and main ideas. Particular attention should be paid to the policy claim (specific purpose) and to the language in main points and transitions. This speech should reflect your best use of oral style to meet the goals of clarity, interest and proof. Main ideas should be written as short, simple, declarative sentences. Transitions should be written out between main ideas and should summarize the previous point as well as preview the next main idea.

Each main idea should include at least one oral citation. Speakers should use personal pronouns, concrete words, and vivid imagery to facilitate audience understanding. Try to maximize language use to provide ethical, emotional, and logical proof.

DELIVERY: Extemporaneous. Practice, practice, out loud. Develop familiarity with the ideas, claims, and citations within the speech. Eye contact should be focused on individuals and small groups of individuals, NOT the note cards. Vocal aspects should emphasize the importance of the ideas. Gestures and movement should appear comfortable and not random. Delivery standards should be the highest of any of your speeches. Be sure to allow yourself plenty of time to practice prior to your speaking day.

THE PREPARATION GUIDE FOR THE PROBLEM-SOLUTION OUTLINE

Introduction: (consists of 2 parts, first an attention step, then a clarification step, including a clear preview.)

Attention Step: Usually an example or a couple of brief examples that demonstrate the nature of the problem. Include a source cite after giving the example(s).

Clarification Step: May include several elements: a brief statement from a qualified source that there is a serious problem, a brief statement about the seriousness of the problem from a qualified source. This statement may act as a thesis. You will also want include any direct connection you have to the problem. This could enhance your credibility. Include your persuasive proposition at this point.

Preview: A preview that specifies the major points in your speech.

Body: (While other forms may be acceptable, the body usually has two Major points. The first argument develops the problem (size, harms, causes), and the second argument develops a solution. These points are necessarily unbalanced. The problem will form 2/3rd of the body and the solution will form 1/3rd.)

I. _____ is a serious problem.
  A. The problem is large. (It is necessary to overcome the presumption that we don't have to act to solve the problem. Several types of statistical arguments may be used to demonstrate the scope of the problem and to demonstrate a need to attend to the problem before it affects your audience. Sources should be drawn from a variety of qualified sources to increase credibility)
     1. Estimates from reliable sources
     2. Problem is increasing
     3. A trend is apparent
     4. Ratio (number of people in a given area, in this class, etc.)
     5. Frequency of problem (# of times per year, hour, during this speech, etc.)
     6. Localization
        (Remember, you don't have to use all of these. Just establish size.)

Transition Statement
  B. The problem is harmful. (It is not enough to show the problem is large. You also need to demonstrate the loss of things we consider to be good. This will also demonstrate to your audience that they should act to prevent these harms from happening to them or to people they value. Most of the proof here should be supported with examples. This is where you become the storyteller to develop pathos.)
     1. Examples demonstrating physical harms
     2. Examples demonstrating psychological harms
     3. Examples demonstrating monetary harms
     4. Examples demonstrating social harms
     5. Examples demonstrating environmental harms
     (Again, you do not need all of these, but you DO need to humanize the statistics and show us what we stand to lose if we fail to act.)

A126

Problem-Solution Speech (cont.)

Transition Statement

C. We are failing to solve the problem. (This point is necessary due to our belief that we do not need to act because someone else is taking care of it. We need to demonstrate that the problem will not go away unless we act. This section also allows us to examine what may be the causes of the problem or to examine barriers to overcoming the problem.)

    1. Our failure to solve is rooted in poor laws. (some, not all.)
       a. no laws apply
       b. laws have not caught up with technology
       c. laws are weak
       d. laws are not enforced
       e. laws form patchwork of jurisdiction
       f. laws act as a disincentive
       g. laws allow for self-regulation
       h. laws have been co-opted by special interests
       i. laws need updating
    2. Our failure to solve is rooted in poor attitudes.
       a. ignorance
       b. apathy
       c. evil

Transition Statement: (This is a good time to do an internal summary to prepare the audience for the solution.)

II. We can solve the problem of _____.

A. A change in policy will work.
    1. Change laws
    2. Change educational process
    3. Demonstrate workability through examples
B. Policy change will only work if we change our attitudes and act individually.
    1. personal steps to take to solve the problem
    2. recommendation of ways we can change our attitudes and the attitudes of others

Conclusion: This needs to include a few elements: a specific review of your major points, a restatement of your thesis as well as going back to the intro example to demonstrate change. Close with a strong clincher.

PROBLEM-SOLUTION SPEECH ON ELDERLY DRIVERS
PREPARATION OUTLINE

Specific Proposition Statement: Significant actions need to be implemented to increase the safety of our elderly drivers.

Introduction:

Attention Step: Does anyone know who Russell Weller is? He is an 86 year-old man who ran down 10 people and injured another 45 in a Santa Monica farmers market in June of 2003. When questioned by police about the incident Weller replied that he had mistaken the gas pedal for the break.

Clarification Step: Incidents such as this occur more often than anyone thinks and have sparked a large debate about elderly driving. According to The American Medical Association "By the year 2030, the number of older Americans is expected to double to 70 million. An increasing portion of this population will be licensed to drive, and these license holders will drive increasingly higher mileage. If we fail to adequately address the safety needs of older drivers, the number of traffic fatalities in this population could triple in upcoming years". **(1:1)**

Preview: Today, I will de discussing the growing number of elderly drivers, the harmful nature of elderly drivers, why we are failing to solve this problem with elderly drivers, and finally how we can solve the problem with elderly drivers.

Body:

I. A rapidly increasing elderly population with lack luster driving renewal policies is a serious problem.

    A. "Motor vehicle injuries are the leading cause of death (65 and older)".
       1. According to smartmotoist.com a study was done by the NHSTA in 1997 stating that "Older people made up 9 percent of the population but accounted for 14 percent of all traffic fatalities and 17 percent pedestrian fatalities". **(9:1)**
       2. According to an article written by Neal Pierce with the Washington Post "Fatalities among drivers aged 70 or older jumped 27 percent from 1991 to 2001". **(10:1)**
       3. According to the AMA "Per mile driven, the fatality rate for drivers 85 years and older is nine times higher than the rate for drivers 25 to 69 years old".**(2:1)**
       4. According to an article written by the AARP "By 2030, nearly every fifth person in the united states will be 65 and over". **(8:1)**

Transition: Traffic fatalities and pedestrian fatalities are not only harmful to the elderly but to our society as a whole.

    B. Elderly drivers tend to have higher risk in traffic fatalities and pedestrian fatalities.
       1. Russell Weller killed 10, injured 45

Problem-Solution Elderly Drivers Prep. Outline (cont.)
2.   According to an article from MSNBC WICHITA, Kansas "A Maize police
officer remains n critical condition after a head on crash with an 88 year old
driver traveling the wrong way on K-96". woman died head on **(7:1)**

Transition: Incidents such as Russell Weller's or the 88 year old woman from Kansas
could have been avoided. Here are some reasons why these incidents occurred.

C.   We are failing to solve this problem for 3 reasons.
1.   lack of laws for elderly driver's renewal
a.   "There are relatively few states that have retesting requirements
for license renewal that are aimed strictly at older age groups.
Only two states, Illinois and New Hampshire require a road test
(at age 75). Three states require only drivers who have reached
a certain age to have a vision test before license renewal. The
most common types of age based conditions involve states that
either prohibit mail renewal by elderly drivers (five states) or
make older drivers renew their licenses at a more frequent
intervals than other drivers (11 states)". **(6:1)**
2.   senior advocacy groups oppose regulations
a.   "Senior-advocacy groups have pushed state lawmakers to defeat
age-based driving bills in both Florida and Texas". **(4:1)**
3.   elderly drivers reluctance to turn in licenses

Transition: It's evident that elderly driving has become a major societal issue that
demands action to insure the safety of all. Unfortunately there are still some who oppose
stricter regulations. Let's look at a few ways to make a difference.

II. We can improve the safety of everyone on and off the road.

A. First, we can support legislation.
1.   stricter testing
2.   Require physicians to report
3.   "Support Formula Grant programs for the elderly". **(8:3)**
4.   public transportation.
B.   Second, we need to be more involved in our elderly loved ones lives.
1.   Be aware of state
2.   Communicate
3.   know when take keys away. **(3:1)**
4.   Improve vehicle safety standards

Conclusion:
   Review: Today we have discussed the rapid growth in our elderly population, statistics on fatalities among our elderly involved in accidents, the affects of having elderly drivers behind the wheel, why we are failing to solve this problem presently and finally how we can solve this problem as a society and personally.
   Conclude: It is very important to take action in this matter to insure the safety of our loved ones presently and in the future.

BIBIOGRAPHY

"AMA Focuses on the Problems of Older Drivers." American Medical Association. 31 Jul. 2003: 1 Http://www.seniorjournal.com/news/aging/3-07-31drivers.htm

Bolas, Lori. "Older Driver Safety." *American Medical Association.* 29 Mar. 2004: 1 Http://www.ama-asn.org/ama/pub/category/print/8925.thml

"Elderly Drivers- Is Your Loved One Driving Safely"? *Aging Solutions.* 20 Apr. 2004: 3 <Http://www.againg-parents-and-elder-care.com>

"Elderlry Driving" 2001: 1 <Http:// www.avsands.com states>

Fabrizo, Richard. "When should the elderly give up the keys?" *PortsMouth Herald* 20 Jul 2003: 2 <Http://wwwseacoastlne.com>

Fazzalaro, James J. "Driver Licensing Testing and Older Drivers." OLR Research Report 15 Mar. 2002: 1 <Http:// http://prdbasis.cga.state.ct.us>

Hertneky, Dana. "Elderly Driver". *MSNBC News.* 23 Sept 2002: 1 <Http:www.mnbccom/local/ksnw/m327199.asp?>

Need For better Transportation". *AARP* 25 Jul 2002: 1& 3 Http://www.aarp.org/articles/a2004-03-26-transportation.html

"Older Drivers" *Smart Motorist.* 18 Apr. 2004: 1 Http://www.smartmotorist.com/eld/eldhtm

Peirce, Neal. "Elderly Driver Crashes: Where Are Our Opinions." *The Washington Post.* 15 Apr. 2004: 1 Http://www.postwritersgroup.com/archives/peir0811.htm

PROBLEM-SOLUTION SPEECH ON ELDERLY DRIVERS
KEYWORD OUTLINE

Introduction:

Attention Step: Russell Weller? 86 year-old, 10 people killed, injured 45 June of 2003. police-Weller mistaken the gas pedal for the break.

Clarification Step: large debate about elderly driving. According to The American Medical Association "By the year 2030, the number of older Americans is expected to double to 70 million. An increasing portion of this population will be licensed to drive, and these license holders will drive increasingly higher mileage. If we fail to adequately address the safety needs of older drivers, the number of traffic fatalities in this population could triple in upcoming years".

Preview: Today, growing number of elderly drivers, harmful nature, why failing to solve, finally solve the problem with elderly drivers.

Body:

I.   Rapidly elderly population
    A.   "leading cause of death (65 and older)".
        1.   According to smartmotoist.com a study was done by the NHSTA in 1997 stating that "Older people made up 9 percent of the population but accounted for 14 percent of all traffic fatalities and 17 percent pedestrian fatalities".
        2.   According to an article written by Neal Pierce with the Washington Post "Fatalities among drivers aged 70 or older jumped 27 percent from 1991 to 2001".
        3.   According to the AMA "Per mile driven, the fatality rate for drivers 85 years and older is nine times higher than the rate for drivers 25 to 69 years old"
        4.   According to an article written by the AARP "By 2030, nearly every fifth person in the united states will be 65 and over".

Transition: Traffic fatalities and pedestrian fatalities,to our society
    B.   higher risk traffic fatalities, pedestrian fatalities.
        1.   Russell Weller killed 10, injured 45
        2.   According to an article from MSNBC WICHITA, Kansas "A Maize police officer remains n critical condition after a head on crash with an 88 year old driver traveling the wrong way on K-96". woman died head on

Transition: Russell Weller's or 88 year old woman, reasons why

Problem-Solution Elderly Drivers Keyword Outline (cont.)

      C.   Failing to solve 3 reasons.
           1.   lack of laws for renewal
                 a.   "There are relatively few states that have retesting requirements for license renewal that are aimed strictly at older age groups. Only two states, Illinois and New Hampshire require a road test (at age 75). Three states require only drivers who have reached a certain age to have a vision test before license renewal. The most common types of age based conditions involve states that either prohibit mail renewal by elderly drivers (five states) or make older drivers renew their licenses at a more frequent intervals than other drivers (11 states)".
           2.   senior advocacy groups oppose
                 a.   "Senior-advocacy groups have pushed state lawmakers to defeat age-based driving bills in both Florida and Texas".
           3.   elderly drivers reluctance

Transition: major societal issue, some oppose stricter regulations. make a difference.

II.   Improve safety

     A. support legislation.
           1.   stricter testing
           2.   physicians to report
           3.   "Support Formula Grant programs for the elderly".
           4.   public transportation.
     B.   be more involved.
           1.   Be aware
           2.   Communicate
           3.   take keys away.
           4.   vehicle safety standards

Conclusion:
    Review: discussed rapid growth, statistics on fatalities, affects of elderly drivers behind wheel, failing to solve, can solve as society and personally.
    Conclude: take action, insure the safety of loved ones

TOPIC SELECTIONS FOR THE PROBLEM-SOLUTION SPEECH

Name_____Day/Time of class_____Due_____

FIRST CHOICE: The specific problem I want to solve is:

_____

What are the main causes of the problem?

What societal solution(s) would you recommend?

How, specifically, can audience members help solve the problem?

SECOND CHOICE: The specific problem I want to solve is:

_____

What are the main causes of the problem?

What societal solution(s) would you recommend?

How, specifically, can audience members help solve the problem?

THIRD CHOICE: The specific problem I want to solve is:

_____

What are the main causes of the problem?

What societal solution(s) would you recommend?

How, specifically, can audience members help solve the problem?

MONROE'S MOTIVATED SEQUENCE - TOPIC IDEAS

First Choice Topic

_____

Need

_____

_____

_____

Satisfaction

_____

_____

_____

Action

_____

_____

_____

Second Choice Topic

_____

Need

_____

_____

_____

Satisfaction

_____

_____

_____

Action

_____

_____

_____

A137

ANXIETY REDUCING CHECK LIST

Name_____   Speech_____

1. **Preparation Outline:** I have:
   Narrowed main points to assignment requirement   _____
   Identified specific purpose statement on outline   _____
   Checked for outline structure   _____

2. **Speaking Outline/Note Cards:** I have:
   Checked for **key words only**   _____
   Narrowed to pages to assignment requirement   _____
   Practiced from this outline   _____

3. **Practice:** I have
   Practiced my speech out loud
       Approx. number of times: _____
       Approx. amount of time: _____
   Timed my speech and edited where necessary   _____

4. **Nonverbal behavior:** When I practice
   I am in control of my breathing   _____
   I take several deep breaths while waiting
       my turn to speak   _____
   I "center" my awareness of my breathing   _____
   I slow the rate of breathing   _____
   I "image" a calm, relaxed and confident speaker   _____
   I am comfortable and stable in my speaking stance   _____
   My legs are relaxed and stable, knees not locked   _____
   I am able to gesture to emphasize meanings and ideas   _____
       Gestures are above the waist   _____
       Move toward center of my body and out   _____
       Display open palm, relaxed fingers   _____
   I have practiced with my speaking outline   _____
   I have practiced audience contact   _____
   I focus on individuals rather than groups   _____
   I speak to each person 3-5 seconds or until the end
       of an idea or concept   _____
   I shift easily between outline and audience   _____

5. **Vocal Dimensions:** When I practice
       I am louder than I am in normal conversations   _____
       I emphasize the meaning of words an concepts
           through variation in pitch   _____
       I am speaking at a conversational rate   _____
       I use pauses where necessary and effective   _____
       My voice sounds relaxed and friendly. It expresses
           a desire to communicate.   _____

POST-SPEECH SELF-EVAULATION

Name _____Day/Time of class_____Assignment#_____

Evaluate your performance. Were you (circle one)

Very Satisfied   Somewhat Satisfied   Dissatisfied   Very Dissatisfied

1. Do you think you successfully met your specific purpose? Why or why not?

2. How did you feel about your ability to give this speech before you gave it?

3. How did you feel about your ability to give this speech while you were giving it?

4. How do you feel about your use of your use of outlines? Did the preparation outline help you feel "prepared?" Did the key word outline help you while you spoke? Why or why not?

5. How do you feel about your use of research and supporting material. Did you gather enough research to be able to clearly explain your main points? Did you utilize a variety of support devices? If so, which ones? Did the research you use stimulate interest in the audience?

6. How do you feel about your breath control. Did you take several deep breaths while you were waiting for your turn to speak? Were you able to "center" your awareness of breathing? Did you slow your rate of breathing?

7.   How do you feel about your comfort/confidence level on this first speech. Were you comfortable and stable in your speaking stance, legs relaxed and knees unlocked? Were you able to "image" a calm, relaxed, comfortable speaker?

8.   How do you feel about your use of gestures. Did you use gestures to emphasize meanings and ideas? Were your gestures above the waist? Did they move toward the center of the body and out? Did you display an open palm, relaxed fingers?

9.   How do you feel about your use of audience contact. Did you focus on individuals or groups? Did you speak to each person for 3-5 seconds or until the end of a concept or idea? Did you shift easily between outline and audience? Did you utilize visual aides, if any, to clarify ideas for the audience?

10.   How do you feel about your use of style of delivery. Did you speak at a conversational rate? Were you louder than you are in normal conversation? Did you emphasize the meaning in concepts through variation in pitch? Did your voice sound relaxed and friendly? Did it express a desire to communicate?

What specifically do you want to work on to improve your speech and performance? In the space below set three goals for your next speech-use full sentences:

Goal #1

Goal #2

Goal #3

Answer the following additional questions for Speech 2, 3, 4 and so on.

1. Discuss the goals that you set in your last evaluation that you feel you've met successfully. State each goal and describe why you feel sucessful:

2. What helped you be successful in helping you meet these goals? List each goal and describe in detail what methods you used to achieve this success:

3. Discuss the goals that you set in the last evaluation that you failed to achieve. List each goal and evaluate what barriers and challenges you encountered:

4. What methods will you try in order to achieve mastery of the goals listed in #3? Per each goal describe the techniques and methods you will utilize to overcome your challenges:

VIDEO EVALUATION

NAME_____**ASSIGNMENT**_____**TOPIC**_____

Some reminders before you watch your video. Keep your viewing of your speech in perspective. Remember that this is not a professional tape. We use older equipment that provides a poorer image and less clear sound so resist the temptation to compare yourself to a professionally lit and produced performance. Additionally, the image you of see of yourself fails to capture the true dynamics of the live speaking situation. Also, keep in mind that you are not a professional speaker. You are a beginner. You should evaluate your performance against what you think is a realistic and fair standard for you, not for a professional.

Overall evaluation: Circle the one that comes closest:

> Very satisfied with my performance
> Somewhat satisfied
> Somewhat dissatisfied
> Very dissatisfied with my performance

Vocal Dimension:
After hearing the tape I decided I like the following things I did with my voice (i.e. rate, pitch, volume, etc.):

_____
_____
_____

After hearing the tape I decided I disliked the following things I did with my voice:

_____
_____
_____

Nonverbal Dimension:
After seeing the tape I decided I like the following nonverbal aspects of my delivery (i.e. stance, gestures, audience contact, etc.):

_____
_____
_____

After seeing the tape I decided I disliked the following nonverbal aspects:

_____
_____
_____

COURSE EVALUATION - Public Speaking

This feedback form is designed to provide you with an opportunity to evaluate this course as a whole. Since you're not signing your name to your paper, let yourself go! Help me be a more effective teacher!

1. Comparing the extent of your commitment with how productive this class has been for you,check which of the following statements is more appropriate:
    _____   I got more out of this class than I put into it.
    _____   I got the same amount of this class as I put into it.
    _____   I got less out of this class than I put into it.

2. Did you feel free to participate in class? Why or why not?

3. Rate the class grading system on the following scales:

    a.   0   1   2   3   4   5
            Unfair   Very fair

    b.   0   1   2   3   4   5
            Did not like   Liked very much

    Comments:

4. Rate the assignment materials value to you.

    a.   0   1   2   3   4   5
            Not Helpful   Very Helpful

    b.   0   1   2   3   4   5
            Did not like   Liked very much

    Comments:

5. What did you like or dislike about the assignments and activities used in class?

6. What single public speaking skill have you improved the most and why?

7. What single public speaking skill do you feel you want to work on and why?

8. What were your expectations of this course in the beginning? How does the course compare with your expectations?

9. What one aspect of this course seemed of most value/enjoyable to you? Why?

10. What one aspect of this course seemed of least value/enjoyable to you? Why?

11. What do you feel **I** (the instructor) should have done to help you learn more and prepare you as a teacher?

12. What do you feel **you** should have done to help yourself learn more?

13. Do you have suggestions for activities, assignments, or changes in the course (grading system, structure, etc.) that you feel would be of value? Please be specific.

14. Do you have any other comments, criticisms or suggestions?